I0223743

DON'T POKE THE BEAR

Don't Poke *the* Bear

A Memoir About Recovering From Abuse By A Narcissist

MARIA SCHMEIG

Don't Poke the Bear
Copyright © 2023 by Emerald Publishing, LLC

All rights reserved. No part of this publication may be reproduced, stored or transmitted in any form or by any means, electronic, mechanical, photocopying, recording, scanning, or otherwise without written permission from the publisher. It is illegal to copy this book, post it to a website, or distribute it by any other means without permission.

Maria Schmeig has no responsibility for the persistence or accuracy of URLs for external or third-party Internet Websites referred to in this publication and does not guarantee that any content on such Websites is, or will remain, accurate or appropriate.

Designations used by companies to distinguish their products are often claimed as trademarks. All brand names and product names used in this book and on its cover are trade names, service marks, trademarks and registered trademarks of their respective owners. The publishers and the book are not associated with any product or vendor mentioned in this book. None of the companies referenced within the book have endorsed the book.

Cover and interior design by Danna Mathias Steele

First Edition

ISBN: 979-8-218-31982-3

To Grace, Jimmy, and Matty.
You are my world and always have been.

Contents

Part 1: Love-Bombing and Devaluation   1
Chapter 1: The Plan   3
Chapter 2: Special Occasions   16
Chapter 3: A Tale of Two Dads   35
Chapter 4: Mom   47
Chapter 5: Deception Comes to Light   53
Chapter 6: Vacations   74
Chapter 7: Finances   81

Part 2: The Discard   89
Chapter 8: The Break-up   91
Chapter 9: Wedding Plans   105
Chapter 10: More of the Same   117

Part 3: The Long Road Out   127
Chapter 11: Ejected   129
Chapter 12: A New Year   150
Chapter 13: Showers of Love and Hate   160
Chapter 14: A Broken Process   169
Chapter 15: I Poked the Bear!   180
Chapter 16: More Legal Wastes of Time   199
Chapter 17: End of the Nightmare   214

Afterward   233
About the Author   237
Discussion Guide   239
Acknowledgements   241
Endnotes   243

Preface

I have never written a book before, but I feel this is a story that should be shared. Through my journey, I've encountered countless stories of others who went through a similar experience. Many were long-term relationships like mine. Some encountered much worse than I. The experience was bewildering for all. We did not understand what we were dealing with throughout much, if not all, of the relationship. When someone told me I was in an abusive relationship just before divorce proceedings started, I was shocked at the very idea. Now that I've been away from my spouse for over a year, I can see more clearly that it may very well have been abusive. The abuse was mostly emotional, although there were a few instances of physical abuse. My spouse did not beat me up, and the few times he was physical with the children, I was against it, but thought it was his way of disciplining. He told me he had been hit with a belt as a child, and I rationalized on those occasions that those scars were coming to the surface. I did not grow up with physical discipline, but I knew plenty of kids who did, and most of those parents would not have been classified as abusive. I never put those few instances together in my mind with the regularly occurring emotional abuse. And I never considered that his behavior was emotionally abusive. I just thought he had a bad temper that he couldn't control.

I know differently now. I didn't know that for just about all my marriage. While the emotional abuse made for a not-so-happy life, it was nothing like you hear in news stories or see on TV dramas.

Perhaps, it was because my spouse didn't have the control over me that an abuser hopes to gain. I, quite frankly, had too much going for me. I had a good job and a supportive family. Perhaps, it was because my spouse was moving in that direction but hadn't gotten there yet. There are signs of that. Perhaps, my spouse is just not as bad as the abusers in the stories we hear. I'll let you be the judge.

I've researched to better understand emotional abuse and anger issues. There is a distinction between someone with a bad temper and someone who is abusive. Does my spouse simply have an anger management problem, or does it rise to abuse? From what I understand, abuse stems from a need for power in the relationship and an abuser will blame others or circumstances for his behavior. Someone with anger issues accepts responsibility for the behavior. Throughout my marriage, I always assumed my spouse had an anger-management problem. It never occurred to me that he could be classified as abusive. I have a better understanding in hindsight.

Is he a narcissist? I'm not a psychologist, but I would say he definitely has strong narcissistic traits. There are various indications of that throughout these pages: exaggerated sense of self-importance, constant lying, never taking responsibility for his actions, etc. After further reading, I came across a new term: *covert narcissist*. This is someone with the traits of a narcissist who keeps them hidden from the rest of the world. There is probably a broad spectrum from the obvious ones to the hidden ones, but having learned this new term, I believe my spouse fits the bill. Most of the outside world had no idea what he truly was like, and many thought he was a great guy. Through my research I also learned that there are four main stages in a narcissistic relationship: love-bombing, devaluation, discard, and hoovering. The hoovering stage generally only takes place if the narcissist is not satisfied after the discard; then he tries to suck his victim back in like a Hoover vacuum only to begin the devaluation stage once again.

Thanks to technology (text messages, social media, etc.), sporadic journaling and memories, I was able to piece together the events contained in these pages. It is by no means the universe of events as many have been forgotten. I believe the brain allows us to forget as a way of getting us through the darkness. This book is mostly about the darkness. But light always comes, especially if we try to move toward it. Some might conclude that I should have gotten out sooner, and that is probably right. But like most victims of abuse, I didn't see myself that way, particularly since I was not physically abused. I just viewed my spouse as a difficult person with whom I had to endure life, and the alternative of breaking up my family and being alone was not desirable. And there were happy times. The problem was I could never truly relish them because the darkness would come out of nowhere, without warning, seemingly without provocation, so I always had to be somewhat on edge with my guard up. The only exception in recent memory was my son's wedding. Despite my spouse's presence, I managed to completely soak in the joy of that day. It was one of the happiest days of my life, and I am forever grateful for it.

As I said, this book is mostly about the darkness. Because I don't share the good times, it paints an unfair picture. My spouse also had good moments. For example, he watched the kids' sports, and he drove them back to college from their breaks. He was a very good provider. Financially, we were quite comfortable, and my heart goes out to those who have to endure financial strains in addition to the abuse. The random, unpredictable outbursts of rage that my children and I had to endure occurred roughly several times each year. After each outburst, I needed time to recover and typically withdrew into myself during that time and developed my mental armor for the next one. Children are more resilient, and mine bounced back more quickly than I. We'd then have a period of relative peace until the next occurrence. As a result, my children look back and see primarily a happy childhood speckled with the periodic abuse. I am grateful that they feel that way.

One of the few good things my spouse did was give me my three amazing children. I always took measures to protect my children. I always made them see that this behavior was not normal and not acceptable. My children are my finest achievement. I could not have asked for better human beings on this planet than my children. While it certainly affected them, my spouse's irrational behavior did not infect them, and they grew into outstanding adults.

However, I still grapple with how I got into a relationship that may be classified as abusive. I'm reasonably intelligent, highly educated with a good job. I'm an attorney for goodness' sake. I don't think my self-esteem is low. How did I end up here? I don't know if I'll ever find the answer to that. But it shows that these types of relationships cut across all socioeconomic classes.

I never really told anyone what I was dealing with until more recent years, and even then, I didn't say too much to most people. My work friend Ava knew bits and pieces over the years, and I confided in her when my spouse flew into the biggest rage I had ever experienced. Her first concern was for my physical safety. Around that same time, I also confided in an old friend from law school. I pretty much told her the whole story. Her response at the time was, "He needs to be medicated." Some of my extended family got glimpses of his behavior but had no idea of the extent. I guess I just didn't want to air the dirty laundry and I also thought if we were going to stay together, I didn't want people to change their opinions once they found out the truth. I would often hear the saying, "you never know what goes on behind closed doors," and I would think how true that was. As a result, all my friends and neighbors, with rare exceptions for the more astute ones, thought we had a picture-perfect family. I hated the hypocrisy of that but there didn't seem to be another way. They were in for a huge shock when the truth came out. Despite that, if I didn't know before all this, I know it now: Never underestimate your friends and family. Mine have been amazingly supportive through all of this.

I have changed the names (including my own) and places to protect the privacy of all involved. The events are all real and exactly as they occurred— at least how I, and to a large extent my children and sometimes outsiders, perceived them. The quotes are as they were written except for removing identifying information and fixing obvious typos. Truth really can be stranger than fiction. It is not my intention to use this as a vehicle to denigrate my former spouse. Rather, I hope this might help someone who is experiencing the same thing to see it for what it is and get out. The peace and clarity on the other side is worth the trouble to get there. Here is my story.

PART 1

———◆———

Love-Bombing and Devaluation

CHAPTER 1

The Plan

December 15, 2020 (present day)

This nightmare ends today.

I rub the sleep from my puffy eyes as I wistfully think of a better future. It's Tuesday, December 15, 2020. Ten days before Christmas. My stomach is in knots. I've been an emotional wreck for months. I have been powerless for so long. The legal system causes that. But now, I have a plan to change everything—to end this madness. I have discussed my plan with my youngest son, Matty. I waver between giddiness and terror. But it should go smoothly.

I'm alone on one side of my Sterns and Foster queen-size bed in the master bedroom. My husband, Nikolai and I bought the bed two years ago at Nikolai's insistence. I had slept well on the old bed. I've slept alone on this mattress for three months now, which has been a good thing. I'd like to say the master bedroom is my sanctuary, but that's a stretch. I lock my bedroom door at night, although it gives me small comfort. I know with the slightest push Nikolai could get in if he chose to.

The master bedroom is the newest room in the house. We had built the addition over the two-car garage thirteen years ago. To make it look nice on the outside, we ended up with a very large bedroom, almost cavernous, with two walk-in closets. Our ceramic-tiled, full bathroom has a jacuzzi, two sinks with granite countertop, and a completely enclosed glass shower—with four showerheads on the wall, in addition to the regular one on top, that completely engulf your body in water. For some reason Nikolai never used the shower body jets, but I loved how relaxed they made me feel. Even they don't work for me now.

The bedroom is a drab, dark beige color. I had a hard time figuring out what color to paint it, so one day Nikolai just picked out a color and painted it. I was never keen on it but learned to live with it—like so many other things. Twenty years ago, Nikolai secured a great job in sales, and by the time we decided to do the addition, we were flush with money. Normally frugal by nature, we opted to splurge on this addition, and as a result, the bedroom has a beautiful oak floor, and the bathroom tile has inlay throughout, in addition to all the other perks. I love the bedroom floor; it's so much newer than the wood floors in the rest of the house.

Nikolai has spent the last three months essentially living in the office. He has effectively made that his refuge, and he has no worries of an intrusion by me or Matty. Several years ago, he installed a new doorknob with a key lock. At the time, I thought he was quirky. Now I realize that was naive. He clearly had other reasons. He might as well have installed a dead bolt lock; it's impossible to penetrate despite my repeated attempts. The office is a small bedroom at the top of the stairs right next to the addition. When Nikolai obtained his job in sales, he needed a home office to work in, so we made that room for him. We always kept a bed in there for any overnight guests, but Nikolai laid claim to the room as his own from the beginning. He now locks the door any time he is not in the office. He started locking the door continuously a little over two months ago. He sleeps and eats most of his meals there. He uses the master bathroom to shower, and while he still has some things in his walk-in closet, over the last three months, he has gradually removed most of his clothes.

I've had my usual four hours of sleep. I haven't slept in a very long time due to the strain of living this way. I get out of bed and perform my ritual of looking into my five-times magnification makeup mirror to see what new lines have appeared on my face. My brow is now furrowed and getting deeper. There are new lines across my forehead. I must have aged five years in the last five months. At this rate, I'll look eighty in no time. My blonde highlighted hair is a mess, but surprisingly I still have no gray, despite approaching sixty. My blue eyes look weary. No one should have to live this way, but that should change today. I throw on jeans and a sweater and make my bed, a ritual I'm compelled to start each day with. My jeans are getting looser each month from the weight loss. I can't eat when I'm under stress. I have a petite frame and stand only 5'2". I'm naturally on the thin side to begin with but am now officially underweight. I open the shades, which lets in the morning sun. The room is so bright we had to install room-darkening shades on the four windows. I think back to a time before we had the addition, when we first bought the house over twenty years ago.

We didn't have much then, other than two-year old twins, Jimmy and Grace and another on the way, Matty. We ended up with more house than was in our price range because it needed significant TLC. Entering the house was like going through a time warp to 1970. The living room and dining room floors were covered with slimy gold shag carpet, the family room walls were paneled in dark brown, and the kitchen with dark brown cabinets and a green linoleum floor was not the most inviting of rooms. It didn't matter though because Nikolai was very handy. We set to work the day we moved in. We cut down massive trees and overgrown bushes, removed the paneling in the family room and painted everywhere. Once Nikolai was working in sales, we paid someone to put down wood floors in the living room and dining room, and over time, Nikolai gutted the kitchen and half-bath and installed all new cabinets, fixtures, and appliances. We cut out a section of the hill in the back yard and built a pool with a deck surrounding it, and on top of the hill we installed a large patio with pavers. We made it into a beautiful home. But it wasn't really a happy home.

———◆———

I have some hope that tomorrow will be a new beginning if I can execute the plan today. I need to get rid of Nikolai before Christmas. I hope to have a nice Christmas for once. I always had nice Christmases growing up. My dad couldn't put enough toys under the tree for us. By January, my dad couldn't stand the clutter and would start to throw out the old toys. I hated January, but I loved Christmas.

If all goes well, I will have all the kids for Christmas—Jimmy and his wife, Emily; Grace and her fiancé, Patrick; and Matty, of course. Matty's been home since he finished college last May. Age twenty-two, he's three years younger than the twins. He's the tallest of the three at 5' 11" with medium blond hair and blue eyes. He seems to have very little of Nikolai in him, in both physical attributes and personality traits. As emotionally untethered as Nikolai is, Matty is cool and objective. Matty is into health and fitness and as a result, he has grown quite muscular. He is my philosopher. He loves to talk about self-improvement, whether it's physical, mental, or spiritual and his dreams for the future. He regularly encourages me to figure out my dreams and pursue them. We can talk about life for hours, and sometimes we have. He's extremely self-disciplined, almost too regimented, often scheduling wake-up times at 5 a.m. to read and meditate followed by a workout at the gym and a green smoothie that he has concocted. He will prove to be my rock.

Jimmy moved out in July when he married Emily. They have their own home forty minutes away and the cutest dog, a Goldendoodle named Rover. I can't believe how much I love that dog. Jimmy is 5' 9" with a medium build. His light brown hair is thick, almost bushy, and he has lots of it, which will serve him well in the future. He wears it short. He's probably a mix of both Nikolai and I with hazel eyes, bushy eyebrows, and a high forehead. Jimmy and I have always been close. I describe him to my friends as "my sweetheart." He is such a loving, thoughtful person. In some ways he reminds me of his name-sake, my brother. He seems to always find the perfect gift for each person, something the recipient didn't realize he or she wanted until opening the gift. One year he gave me an indoor green house to grow plants during the winter. I love to garden in the summer but never would have thought to get a winter greenhouse. I don't remember how he figured it out, but sometime around age eight, he had decided he was going to be chivalrous. We were going to my goddaughter's baptism in the pouring rain. Nikolai wasn't terrible in that area, but he wasn't a model either. Many a time Nikolai would walk through a door ahead of me or let a door slam in my face. So, Jimmy did not get chivalry from him. Perhaps, it just came naturally, or some people more easily pick it up. On this day, my little eight-year-old insisted on meeting me at the front door with an umbrella in hand. He walked me to the car and opened the car door for me while holding the um-brella. Later, he was disappointed when I got out of the car so fast that I didn't give him a chance to go around and open the door for me. Both quiet by nature, our personalities are somewhat similar. We are both easy-going and don't get readily riled up. Jimmy has a knack for technology and fixing and creating things. I used to joke that one of his first words was *contraption*. He was always designing something with my couch cushions or string or empty boxes, which his brother and sister enjoyed playing with. I will come to rely on his mechanical abilities.

Jimmy's twin, Grace moved out in 2019 to be closer to Patrick, her now-fiancé. Grace is stunningly beautiful but doesn't know it. I believe she gets most of her features from Nikolai, although some have claimed she bears a resemblance to me. Her skin tone is like Nikolai's; they never burn like the rest of us. She has big blue eyes and long eyelashes, both of which she likely inherited from my side. She wears her luxuriant hair long and has blonde highlights put in, although

I don't think she needs to. It's a pretty brown color. When she was little, I could make banana curls by simply twirling her hair around a brush. Barely 5' 2" with not an ounce of fat, Grace is the tiniest of the five of us. When she was four, Grace woke us up at five o'clock every morning belting out "Rudolph the Red Nosed Reindeer." She "feels your pain" and has channeled that empathy into a successful career as a nurse. She feels her own pain as well. We are very similar in that regard; our tears flow easily when we are hurt. She is generous to a fault, heaping an abundance of lavish presents on us every Christmas. She has often said she enjoys being the giver much more than being the recipient. She is outgoing like Nikolai and can always think of something to say in a social setting. My mom refers to it as the "gift of the gab." I wish I had it.

I was happy and sad when Jimmy and Grace moved. I was happy for them that they got away from Nikolai and all his heartache. I was sad for me because I missed them a lot. They know about the plan, and I have their full support. They are also anxious to end this madness.

It is time to start my day. I hesitate at my bedroom door. The nightmare that is my life awaits on the other side. I take a deep breath and open the door.

———— ◆ ————

7:30 p.m. I have initiated implementing the plan. It is now time to change the locks. I had purchased the locks from Home Depot at least a month ago and have been driving around with them in my car along with all my Christmas presents for the kids. I want Nikolai to know as little as possible of my life, especially that I have new locks. I lock my car whenever I leave it, even though it's in the garage.

The most important lock is the one on the front door, so we begin there. I don't know how much time we have so we need to act fast. I am relying on Matty to get this done. I have no idea how to change a lock. Matty has never done it either, but he thinks logically and assumes he can figure it out. Living this way these last three months has been hard on Matty. Nikolai cloisters himself in the office all day and lurks around the house at night. We frequently hear him on the phone talking with other women. Each morning, Matty and I confer about the latest outrageous thing that Nikolai has done. I am in tears more often than not. At twenty-two-years-old, Matty has endured more than he should in his young life. He is angry a lot, and he has every right to be. He's not an emotional person, but the insanity we've had to deal with has caused his anger. Olivia, my neighbor across the street, has instructed me to not let Matty's anger get the better of him, and if anything should happen, I am to send him to her house at once and they will protect him. I hope it never comes to that, because I can't have Matty's life jeopardized because of this absurd life that we have been forced to live. He's been my sounding board, my support system, my shoulder to cry on, and my clear-headed thinker with sound advice. I never could have made it without him.

Matty begins by unscrewing the covering to the deadbolt. The next step is to unscrew and pull out the deadbolt. Matty successfully removes one of the screws but is having difficulty with the second screw. It seems to be stripped. My hands are shaking as Matty does this, and my stomach is queasy. No amount of strength that Matty exerts—and he has much to spare—will remove this screw.

"What are we going to do Matty? We're running out of time," I say. How can a simple screw be the roadblock to my plan?

"Just chill, Mom," he says. "I'll FaceTime Jimmy and we'll figure it out. He's really good at this stuff."

Jimmy advises Matty to drill out the screw; it's the only way. Matty raises his eyebrows, skeptical that it will work. I go into the garage to get the drill. Of course, Nikolai has taken it with so many other things that he has stealthily stolen while I slept. I call Olivia and ask if she has a drill I can borrow. Olivia and her husband moved in seven years ago when she was pregnant with their first son. They now have two boys who call me Aunt Maria. Olivia is more like a sister to me than a neighbor. I know I can depend on her. She has a drill, and I can come right away to get it. She calmly walks me through all the steps on how to use it. "These are the bits. Place one here. Turn this to tighten it. Press this to turn right. Press this to turn left…"

I anxiously listen with as placid a face as I can muster, but inside, I am frantic to get back and complete the plan before it is too late. At last, she hands me the drill with a hug, and I return home. Matty drills into the head of the screw as Jimmy advised and much to his surprise, it immediately falls out. Matty at last removes the deadbolt. Matty then proceeds to install the new one. The new one is slightly bigger than the old one and Matty cannot place it in the hole properly. Another obstacle. I don't know if my nerves can take much more. Matty finds a tool from the few that are left to shave the hole. Ultimately, he manages to get the deadbolt in, and I have a new lock on the front door. I breathe a slight sigh of relief that there is now a little sense of security, but there are still two more doors to do: the garage and the back doors. The garage lock goes smoothly, and it is nice to have a deadbolt without a key, something Nikolai should have done years ago. We now proceed to the back door. This is the final link to give me a feeling a security. I need to unlock the old deadbolt, but I have no idea where the key is. I never use this door. I frantically search for it in the laundry room, in my desk, in the kitchen drawer; finally, I find it. The space is tight to work in because the back door is in the laundry/furnace room. The width of the room is just barely more than the width of the door and the furnace is on one side and the washer and dryer on the other. Matty gets the door opened and proceeds to remove the lock. It's not as difficult as the front door but takes more manipulating than the garage door. I wait anxiously while Matty does his work. After what seems like an eternity, he finishes. All the locks are now changed. No one can get into the house. I am flooded with relief. I assume this is the beginning of a better life.

10:00 p.m. The police are ringing my doorbell. This is not part of the plan. Changing the locks was supposed to keep people out. The plan has in fact taken a turn for the worse. I answer the door, and I am forced to allow two officers inside my home. I am sick to my stomach. My year from hell has begun. How did my life get to this point? I often think in moments of bewilderment, *How did this happen to me?* But, when I step back with some clarity, I can often see that the signs were there from the very beginning.

———◆———

I met Nikolai on January 3, 1991. I was approaching thirty, and the tick-tock of my biological clock drowned out other sounds. Oh, how I wanted to be a mother! I was born for it. In the pre-internet days, the equivalent to Match.com was the personals in the newspaper. SWF seeks SWM etc. I placed a personal ad. I had been in a serious relationship for almost three years. He had his own issues. After about a year, he cut off all contact with his family. After two years, he cut off all contact with mine. I had always had a close relationship with my family, so at that point I couldn't take it anymore and got out. Was he abusive? I'll never know since I got out early enough.

I went for some counseling to recover from the breakup of the relationship. This counselor's practice was called the Center for Coping. I had found out about it in the early 1980s when I was diagnosed with Crohn's Disease at the ripe old age of twenty. There's a horrific disease to slap on a twenty-year-old. I can't say I just rolled with that one. It was hard. The main effect of the disease was that I was acutely aware of where every bathroom was at any given time. I managed to get through college, spending my last semester studying from home because I was too sick to attend class. I was in and out of the hospital with one stay lasting an entire month. I was forced to defer law school for a year. The only way to "cure" the disease at that time was through surgery. So, that same year, right after I graduated college, when I was twenty-two, I had to have two major stomach operations, each lasting around eight hours. For the first surgery, my almost twenty-six-year-old brother Jimmy took off from work, flew from Pittsburgh to be near me, and later called me every day to keep my spirits up. He was amazing. He could put a positive spin on almost any dark thing I was going through. I would tell him my weight, and he would congratulate me on gaining two pounds. I would respond that my clothes made it seem more. He would subtract a couple ounces and declare that I gained a pound and a half. He got me through a rough surgery and the ensuing summer, and I assumed he would get me through the next surgery. I was wrong. Two months before my second operation, Jimmy was killed in a car accident. I cried and cried and cried. How does one deal with that? And, to think of my poor mother who lost her son. She nearly fell apart. I couldn't fathom that type of grief until I became a parent, and even then, when the thought would enter my head, it was too horrific to dwell on and had to be immediately suppressed. But life gives you no choice. I had to push forward, and I had to take my mom—whose grief was incomprehensible—with me.

The second operation was rough without Jimmy, but I had an amazing nurse who was so caring she gave me a little knickknack that said, "Thumbs up. You did it. You're on your way!" Almost forty years later, I still think fondly of that nurse, and I still have that knickknack. After the second operation, I would never wear a bikini again, but my health ultimately improved. Never perfect, but manageable. One day, I went to an event related to the disease, and a counselor from the Center for Coping gave a talk that stuck with me. I reached out to that counselor since I didn't know of anyone else to reach out to. I was living in the city at the time, and he was not close by, but I did telephone sessions, which worked out great for me.

Eventually, the counselor suggested placing the personal ad. At first, I thought he was crazy but later warmed up to the idea. It ended up being quite the ego boost. I think one day alone, I received about thirty handwritten letters. Some included pictures. I went on several dates until I met Nikolai. His letter talked about how important friends and family were to him, but it almost seemed to be responding to another ad. We found out later he had meant to respond to the ad above mine, and we viewed it as fate bringing us together. He included a picture of himself. He was quite good looking, with dark curly hair, thin, but not too tall, around 5' 6". He was wearing jeans and a polo with a gorgeous background I later discovered was Russia. He was a little younger than I, which gave me pause. But after a lot of Amaretto and a long walk with my younger brother Jack on Christmas Eve, my brother suggested Nikolai's age was okay, but I shouldn't go any younger.

I set up the first meeting for January 3. We met at a diner. I wore the equivalent of today's black leggings and a black and white shirt with a black jacket. Nikolai had on black jeans, a polo, and deck shoes, my favorite look on a guy. Nikolai was so charming and easy to talk to. He seemed self-assured. We were supposed to meet for coffee, but he insisted on ordering a hamburger, so I ordered soup. The coffee meeting turned into dinner. We were seated right by the kitchen door and breathed in oven cleaner throughout the dinner. Nikolai spoke freely about himself and even indicated that he was a borderline atheist. That should have been a reg flag fluttering in my face, since my faith had always played a role in my life, but stupidly, I thought it didn't really matter since we connected so well. We saw each other several times each week after that, and by July, I figured he was the one. He essentially had swept me off my feet.

That July gave the first of many indications of what my future life would be like. A saner person would have run far and fast, but I assumed it was an isolated incident. Little did I know it was the first in a pattern of behavior. One Friday night, we went out with some of Nikolai's friends in New York City. Nikolai drove us home around midnight. We needed to navigate the narrow city streets, but Nikolai grew up there, so he was very skilled at this. The yellow traffic lights were very brief, because traffic gets so backed up; it's a way to keep it moving. But there was no traffic at this time of night. In fact, the streets were deserted. At one point, Nikolai ran one of those quick changing yellow lights, and immediately we heard the sirens. A police car pulled us over. I thought, *Oh well this is a bummer, but c'est la vie.*

Nikolai, however, was not happy. In fact, he was quite agitated. One officer stayed in the car, and the other came to our driver's side. Officer Favre was a short, young man of Hispanic descent. He was a bit obnoxious and asked for Nikolai's papers. Nikolai asked what he did wrong. The officer informed him that he ran a red light and started writing him out a ticket. Sitting next to Nikolai, I was thinking how annoying this was. I was tired and this was going to delay getting home. What an inconvenience. But I remained silent.

Suddenly, out of nowhere, Nikolai became enraged. His jaw tightened. He clenched his fists into balls, opened the car door, and stepped out. I didn't know what was happening. I stared wide-eyed at him. Nikolai then started screaming at the police. "You mother f***ers..." He ranted on and on with additional expletives, but I was in too much shock to remember precisely what else he said. What on earth brought this on? It was just a stupid ticket. I didn't know what to do. I pleaded with him to calm down, but there was no hope of doing so. At this point, Officer Favre got out the handcuffs. I couldn't believe this was happening. How did this happy evening devolve into this? Over a red light? The officer handcuffed him and put him into the back seat of the patrol car. The other officer told me to follow them with my car. It wasn't even my car. It was Nikolai's pride and joy, a white Sterling with gray leather interior and all the whistles and bells available back then, including a leather wrapped steering wheel and a top-of-the-line stereo. I'd never driven it before. My hands trembled as I started the car and drove to the precinct where they processed Nikolai. I waited hours in a dirty waiting room that looked like it hadn't been painted in twenty years with cracked, faded linoleum tiles. Finally, they released him with a disorderly conduct charge, and we drove home, in silence at 3 a.m.

The next day, I was celebrating my mom's birthday with my family. I had invited Nikolai to join us but was lost as to how to proceed now. Nikolai showed up to my mother's home and was contrite about what happened. He was concerned about how I would react, and the charm had returned. We talked about it, and he described how the obnoxiousness of the officer got under his skin, and he shouldn't have let it. I bought into it, outwardly at least, since the officer was unpleasant, but I was never too comfortable with it. At this point, however, I was in too deep emotionally to do anything but let it go.

Later, Nikolai appeared in court. Like an idiot, I took off work and represented him. I presented myself as his attorney but also his witness. I was uncomfortable with this and inwardly prayed it would not affect my career. I had only been a lawyer for four years at this point. Lucky for him, the paperwork wasn't properly executed by the officer, and the judge dismissed the case. Relief poured over me. As time went on, Nikolai would tell the story as if it were all the officer's fault. His voice would drip with derision and contempt whenever he said the name Favre. Seven months later, we married, and I would soon discover that neither Nikolai's behavior nor the ensuing blame game was atypical.

CHAPTER 2

Special Occasions

March 2020 (9 months earlier)

It's Saturday, March 7, 2020. Wedding plans are in full swing. We are all so excited to be going to my future daughter-in-law's shower. I'm dressed in an emerald-green sweater dress I purchased from Nordstrom. It was a splurge, but if I can't splurge for this, when can I? I've done full-blown make-up, which is unusual for me. I look pretty good, but I'm not completely happy with my make-up. I've had two bouts with skin cancer, and the second time the doctor had to scrape into several layers. It left a scar down my cheek, which I've been self-conscious about, so much so that every morning I've taken to looking in the mirror and saying out loud, "You are a beautiful child of God." If only I can truly convince myself. But my make-up will have to do.

The shower is an afternoon tea at a small shop with several tables crammed in. About thirty-five of my friends, neighbors, and family members are there. Everyone is dressed up. The room is abuzz with conversation and anticipation of Emily's arrival with Jimmy. It is a surprise. I am particularly excited because this is my first child to marry. Since I'm the mother of the groom, I don't have a lot of involvement, but I'm informed of what's going on. It's such an exciting time, having your child get married. I had made a needlepoint for them, and I can't wait to give it to her. It has a little blue house in the middle with a garden around it, and the words, "Home is where the heart is," are repeated four times as the border with a pink heart in each corner. The background is white, done in a needlepoint stitch that makes it look like lace. It's something I had started for myself thirty years ago but never finished. This event gave me the incentive to finally complete it. Nikolai expressed his displeasure that I was giving it away—it was supposed to be for us—but I didn't care. I wanted to gift it.

We hold our collective breath as Jimmy brings Emily through the door, and then we all scream, "Surprise!" Emily immediately puts both hands over her face in shock. She had no idea. Such fun! Bella—my friend from church—my neighbor Olivia, and my mom are at my table. My friends are next to us, and my sister-in-law, Grace, Mia and my two nieces are in back. I eat my little cucumber sandwiches and drink tea and play the usual shower games. Emily opens her gifts and eventually gets to my needlepoint gift. I hold my breath, watching her every move as she opens it. She holds up the needlepoint for all to see with a smile on her face. Later, I show it to all my friends, and they give me the obligatory oohs and ahhs. I am so proud. We take lots of pictures in a life-size, bridal shower-themed frame to commemorate the day. Olivia snaps a picture with her phone of Jimmy and me when he comes over to my table. It ends up being one of my favorites, and I use it as my wallpaper for my phone. The day is a smashing success. I relish it and enjoy every moment. Since Nikolai was not involved in, nor invited to, the shower, I don't need to be wary of how he might behave, a rarity for me. Holidays and special events were always dicey.

———————◆◆———————

Christmas

Christmas Day seemed to bring out the worst in Nikolai. There seemed to never be a Christmas Nikolai wouldn't ruin. When the kids were little, we always had my family over for Christmas to exchange gifts and share a Christmas meal. In 1997 I was eagerly awaiting Christmas, although I always knew there was a good chance the day would be ruined. I was six months pregnant with Matty, and the doctor was concerned that I might have pre-term labor because I had delivered the twins six weeks early. Of course, the fact that I am 5' 2", weigh 115 pounds, and was carrying twins may have had everything to do with it! The doctor insisted I use a monitor regularly to see if I had any contractions. I faithfully monitored each day, and all was quiet. I was starting to think it was a waste of time. On Christmas morning, I strapped the monitor around my belly and lay down in bed for the duration. After I transmitted the results, the service called me to monitor a second time because they were seeing a lot of contractions. You've got to be kidding me! I still have three months until the due date. So much for the small-body-with-twins argument. They told me I needed to rest. I wasn't feeling that great anyway, so I sprawled out on the recliner in the living room, trying to make the best of the holiday. Nikolai seemed put off by this inconvenience.

The twins were old enough to understand Santa, and their excitement was palpable. Santa had brought the kids silly putty in their stockings. The kids had never had silly putty before. I grew up with it and remembered it fondly. I used to take out the Sunday comics and press the silly putty to them, and the image of the comics would appear. It seemed so exciting at the time. The advent of technology killed those simple pleasures, but at that point, my kids were still sheltered from that. The kids were sitting on the living room couch near the Christmas tree with my brother Jack.

Three years younger, Jack was my first real friend. He could be exasperating when he was little, intentionally knocking over my vanity chair so all my hats and gloves went flying everywhere when he was mad at me, but he was also my confidant. We shared our dreams. When I was eleven and he was eight, I told him I wanted a bra. When I was very sick in the hospital with Crohn's, he was just seventeen but told my mom he wished he could take my place because he was stronger and could fight it better. We've had bumps in the road, but he's been there for every life event and has helped me through the darkness. The kids were proudly showing Jack their silly putty and how it worked, and he was kidding with them, tickling, and horsing around. Somehow, the silly putty got stuck to the couch. Nikolai was never the most careful person and didn't seem to care if he slobbered up or ruined things. The garage and his office were always a pigsty. I could never find a tool I needed. It could be anywhere in the garage, and most days I could barely find a path to walk in the office. But, for some reason, silly putty on the couch was offensive to Nikolai. Without warning or provocation, Nikolai's anger pulsed through his veins. As his face reddened, he screamed, "We shouldn't have any guests. You need to rest because of the contractions."

I was bulging at the stomach, dealing with two-year-old twins, and now I had to deal with this infantile behavior on Christmas Day? His words, seemingly showing concern for my well-being, masked his desire to rid my family from our home. Nikolai then stormed upstairs. My brother felt terrible and frantically tried to remove the silly putty from the couch by scrubbing as hard as he could with wet paper towels. That silly putty would not come off. In the end, I simply flipped over the cushion. My family didn't know what to do. While they had seen glimpses of Nikolai's behavior, this was the first full-throttle explosion for them. I convinced them to stay and got through the day. I hated that I had to "get through" a holiday. I should have been able to relish it, but I couldn't with Nikolai in the picture.

Most Christmas mornings were similar, whether my family was present or not. Nikolai and I were up late the night before, and the kids were up early—excited to see what Santa brought them—so, everyone was tired. At least that's how I excused Nikolai's behavior when almost every year when they were little, he made at least one of them cry.

In 2003, Nikolai's father died. Nikolai flew to Russia for the funeral and was not home for Christmas. I felt bad because I liked his father. He was a kind soul who would lie on the floor to play with the kids even when he was well into his eighties. He was the only one in Nikolai's family who ever gave me a present—a bottle of perfume from Russia. I cherished it and kept the empty, trapezoidal-shaped bottle for years afterward. The year Nikolai and I were engaged, I bought Christmas presents for everyone in his family, but no one did the same for me because they never gave gifts to anyone. When Nikolai went to Russia for his father's funeral, I had one of my best holidays. I drove the hour to my brother's home for Christmas Eve dinner. The kids and I walked in the front door and could barely get in because his Christmas tree blocked the way. His tree was already up since, unlike me, my brothers did not wait until Christmas Eve to put up the tree. Pushing open the door with all my might, I said, "Hey Jack, are you sure you got a big enough tree?"

The tree was massive, standing twelve-feet tall in his two-story foyer and was so wide it came right up to the front door. He laughed in response while giving each of us his typical bear hug. He made a feast fit for an army, which consisted of every kind of parmigiana: chicken, shrimp, eggplant, etc. After dinner, everyone, including my mom who was staying with me, posed for a picture in front of that massive tree. We left for home right after, and I immediately put the kids to bed. But I was already getting a late start. I had to set up the tree and put all the presents around it. I grew up believing that Santa brought the tree along with the presents, and I wanted to do the same for my kids. My brothers did not carry on the tradition, and in retrospect I can't blame them. It did put a lot of pressure and stress on Christmas Eve. This Christmas Eve, I had a little help from my seventy-nine-year-old mother, but it was primarily on me. I dragged the tree in from its outside hiding place. Nikolai had purchased the tree before he received the news of his father. I somehow managed to get it upright in the stand. I decorated it with lights, ornaments, the star, and, of course, lots of tinsel. Then I climbed the attic stairs and brought down all the presents I had hidden up there. That involved several up and down trips. I arranged them under the tree and finally filled the stockings, which we always hung on the stair railing because we didn't have a fireplace. I didn't get to bed until 1 a.m. The kids got up at 5 a.m., and I was exhausted. But I had no stress, no tears, just good-natured fun with my three little darlings. They bounded down the stairs, anxious with anticipation to see what Santa had brought. I relished their excitement. My mom and I sipped tea while they went through their presents. "Mommy, look at this game Santa brought me. I wanted it so much!" It was the best Christmas to date. But it was an aberration, and unfortunately, there were other holidays for Nikolai to ruin.

Birthdays

Every July my brothers and I and our families went to the house we grew up in—where my mom still lived—to celebrate her birthday. I grew up in a four-bedroom, two and one-half-bath colonial in a quiet suburban neighborhood about a half mile from the bay and a twenty-minute drive from the ocean. Near the bay, giant sand dunes sprung up, and as a child I would bicycle to them with my friends and climb all over them. Eventually, development took that pleasure away. So as a teenager, I would ride my bike the ten plus miles to the ocean.

My parents purchased the house brand new in 1963, and while my mom did many updates, some of the original style remained. The bedrooms were large, and the master had its own bathroom. That bathroom had the original pink shiny mosaic tile with little squares and rectangles in a repeating pattern. The fixtures consisted of a square pink sink attached to the wall, a pink toilet, and a small stall shower. The hallway bathroom was identical but in yellow. The master bedroom was painted a mint green and carpeted in the same color. The rest of the house had the original oak floors, although my mom had the living room and dining room floors refinished and stained a dark brown. In the 1970s, she had the kitchen cabinets refaced to a dark brown and installed new beige linoleum on the floor. The red-cedar paneled family room was separated from the kitchen by a half bath, and as children we spent most of our time there or in the basement that was finished with brown wood paneling and brown asbestos tiles. In recent years, my mom used some of the garage to add a full bathroom off the family room and installed a door in the entrance to the family room. She did that to rent out the room to supplement her income.

By her eighty-fifth birthday in 2009, our families were growing, and there were thirteen of us to sleep in the four bedrooms for the weekend. Our usual routine for the birthday weekend was this: we would all go out to dinner Friday night, we would go to the beach Saturday, we would have dinner out on my older brother Ben's treat, which was his birthday gift to my mom, and later play cards at night. We returned home late Sunday morning. Every one of us loved the beach. As time progressed, alcohol was introduced, and ultimately copious amounts of it, but in 2009, the oldest kid, my nephew, was only nineteen and the youngest, my niece was seven. So, we were relatively dry this night. I remember thinking how nicely the weekend was going. Everyone was getting along, and there were no problems. Things are never how they appear to be.

As Saturday night came, we found ourselves doing our usual activity: playing cards. Our game always was Hearts. In that game, the goal is to score as few points as possible. So, you don't really want to win the tricks; rather, you want someone else to. However, if you take all the tricks, everyone else gets twenty-six points for that round. That's called sand-bagging. The first one to reach one hundred loses, and the game is over.

My extended family is ridiculously competitive, and we take our card-playing a bit too seriously. The thirteen of us were crammed around my mom's oval, French provincial dining room table, her 1960's crystal chandelier illuminating our cards. We had taken off the tablecloth so the smooth finish of the table could facilitate our card playing. My brother Ben was at the end of the table where the dining room opens into the living room in an L-shape. He sat in his t-shirt and bathing suit with his wallet bulging in the front pocket of his bathing suit. Nikolai was across from him, and I was next to Nikolai. We were all tanned and our hair sun-kissed from the day at the beach. We were all tired. Jimmy, who was fourteen, played a card out of turn.

Suspicious that Jimmy's play was intentional, my brother Jack and my nephew both expressed loudly that Jimmy should be "fined" twenty-six points for his "error." Many others in my family nodded in agreement. I was annoyed, thinking this should just be a friendly game, especially with kids and said, "I am not going to play if you are going to play like that."

My brother Ben, who had not voiced any opinion on the matter, regrettably laughed. For some reason, that laughter set off Nikolai, and the next thing I knew, Nikolai propelled out of his chair, slamming it backwards, and screamed at my brother, "You are nothing but a f**king self-centered a**hole!"

He then moved into the living room and proceeded to scream at everyone, totally out of control, in constant motion, snarling with his jaw clenched. No one moved or said a word. Nikolai raced up the stairs, muttering curse words as he climbed. When he got to the top, with his anger induced adrenaline, he piledrove his fist into the wall, creating a hole about the size of a basketball in the Sheetrock at the top landing. He grabbed his clothes, raced back down, and demanded that we all return home, at once. It was 10 p.m. on Saturday night, and we were supposed to sleep over. The kids were crying, and my nephew begged us to stay, not wanting us to leave with emotions so raw, but I didn't seem to have much say in this. So, we all piled into the car and returned home around midnight.

The kids fell asleep, and I stared out the window for the hour and thirty-minute drive. I couldn't bear to look at Nikolai. The rest of my family was extremely upset, and I'm sure had plenty to say after we left.

Later when we were home, Jimmy started sobbing and confided in me that he intentionally played the card out of turn. That is, he had cheated. He blamed himself for the whole incident. Obviously, it was not his fault that his father couldn't behave like an adult, and I hugged him and told him exactly that. Ultimately, my brother Jack repaired the wall and the incident got swept under the rug, but it was the last time my family ever played cards together, another casualty of Nikolai's outbursts.

There were many other birthdays that Nikolai ruined, but the other one that sticks out was my fiftieth birthday celebration the following year. Five of my girlfriends took me on an afternoon cruise around New York City. It was so much fun eating, drinking, and dancing. The beef, potatoes, and vegetables were elegantly plated, and the ice cream pie for dessert had drizzles of fudge making beautiful swirls throughout. I had never done something like this, just an afternoon cruise, going nowhere. The food was delicious, and we all imbibed more margaritas than we should have, danced to 1960's and 1970's music and made great memories. We then came back to my house to celebrate more with the guys.

One of my girlfriends on the cruise was the mother of Mia, Grace's best friend. Mia's dad was with the guys while we were on the cruise, and Mia stayed to hang out with the kids. The kids were upstairs doing what young teenagers do: sharing things on their phones primarily. Jimmy and Mia always had a love/hate relationship. One minute they were great friends, and the next he was ready to kill her. This was a latter moment. The girls were acting like sixteen-year-old girls do and being a little too bold in their behavior. Mia decided to play with Jimmy's computer without asking. Jimmy, ever the perfectionist, was not happy about it, and after everyone had left, he discovered that Mia had broken a part to his computer. Jimmy was upset and came to Nikolai and me to show us. In retrospect, he wished he hadn't. I had been through enough after all these years to know that Nikolai's reaction is unpredictable. I tried to make light of it, asking if he could still use the computer.

From Jimmy's perspective, even if the computer were functioning, that it would not be perfect would drive him crazy. In any event, Nikolai was not interested in coming up with a fix; rather, his fury sprang to life. I watched as his jaw clenched and his fists balled up. He paced back and forth, screaming obscenities. He went upstairs to Grace's room and shrieked, "Mia is never allowed back here. You understand me? Do you understand me?" He then smashed a sign that Grace had hanging on her door with her name on it and pushed her door so hard, he made a hole in the wall behind it with the doorknob.

It's surprising that Nikolai would agree four short years later to allow Mia to live with us, but his acceptance of that would prove to be short-lived.

Halloween

What kid doesn't love Halloween? When my twins were eighteen months old, after trick or treating at only three houses, they caught on that all they needed to do was stick out their pumpkins and they received free candy. As they grew older, they still liked the free candy, but they enjoyed the trick part of it as well. In October 2007, the kids were old enough to fully love decorating the house and wanted ours to be the scariest on the block. We would get lots of spider webbing to drape all over the front door area and various skeletons, mummies, and scary decorations—such as the rock that moaned, "Go back."

One Saturday as Halloween was approaching, Nikolai and I went out shopping to Home Depot. Since Nikolai and I enjoyed home improvement, we frequented this store. The kids were really excited about Halloween, and Nikolai and I agreed we would set some time aside later to decorate. While we were shopping, the kids decided to get out all the decorations and set them up by the front door to "scare" us when we walked in. There they were, three kids, ages nine and twelve, all giggles and excitement and then quieting down when they heard us approach so they could give us the big scare. They had the skeletons, the "go back" rock, the bats, witches, and mummies all in a semi-circle either on the floor or in their hands by the front door. As we walked in, Grace, in her excitement, knocked down the grim reaper. Grim, as we affectionately referred to him, was one of our more expensive decorations. He was essentially a scary looking head with arms who, when activated by noise or movement, slowly came down a few feet from where he hung and moaned as he did so. Seeing Grim on the floor, Nikolai snapped and flew into his now all-too-familiar rage. He screamed and kicked one of the mummies clear across the room. Grace stood frozen, wide-eyed and tears began to fall. The boys were aghast as well. When they started to protest, Nikolai screamed at them to "suck it up" and stormed off. Grim wasn't even damaged.

I wrote in my journal that I brought this incident to confession. The priest was kind and suggested I should know by now how to handle his temper and I should pray for him. It's clear from my journal that I was grappling with how to deal with his outbursts and desperately trying to find a way to prevent them. Married fifteen years at this point with three impressionable children, it seemed more important than ever that I find a way to better deal with Nikolai. In retrospect, it's sad that I thought I could. The next entry in my journal was several days later when I described Nikolai getting annoyed because the kids and I were watching *Little House on the Prairie* together. He wasn't interested in the show, so he went upstairs and slammed doors and then punched the wicker hamper full of dirty clothes and threw it down the stairs. The hamper had a giant hole in it and no longer stood straight. It was destroyed.

Mother's Day

I came to realize that part of the motivation for Nikolai's outbursts on holidays was because they weren't about him. Mother's Day 2016 was no exception, although his behavior was mild compared to how it was on other occasions. My brother came over with my nieces, and we had my mom with us. Naturally, I had to plan everything for the meal and cook most of it, even though it was supposed to be my day. It was that way with most occasions. That's the way life usually went around here. But I didn't care if we were going to have a nice time together. Nikolai barbecued the chicken, and I made all the salads and mini strawberry shortcakes for dessert. My brother, his kids, my kids, my mom, Nikolai, and I were all seated around the dining room table eating, and we started to get into various discussions, some political, some scientific. My family loved to talk politics, as did Nikolai. The kids hated it. When they "debate," my family tends to get louder and talk over the other person—especially my brother. It's not an uncommon trait in a lot of people as well. That is exactly what happened this day. My brother was across from Nikolai at the table and talked over Nikolai while they were debating politics. Nikolai, offended by my brother's dominance, skulked away from the table without a word, went into the family room, lay down on the couch, and watched a Mets baseball game. My mom went in to ask him if he was all right, and he muttered that he was fine. He basically refused to speak to anyone the rest of the day.

———◆———

Over the years, I have come to believe that there wasn't a single holiday, birthday, or special occasion that Nikolai wouldn't ruin over some perceived slight.

Grace sends me an article, "Why Narcissistic People Love to Ruin Birthdays and Holidays."[1] In sum, these types want the attention, and the holiday takes that away. They are abusive, so they trigger easily, and the slightest provocation sets them against their usual target. According to the article, "People who compulsively spoil holidays or ruin festive moods of others have an abusive personality and are most likely targeting or scapegoating you for personal, social, or emotional extinction."[2] It all makes sense now, but since I didn't know then I was dealing with a narcissist, I was always bewildered by his behavior.

April 2020 (8 months earlier)

Life is mostly good (other than the undercurrent in the background) until suddenly it isn't. Two days after Emily's shower is the last day that I will go to work for two years because of the COVID-19 virus. But, unbeknownst to me, a much more insidious sickness is brewing in my midst, one of deception, lies, and betrayal.

By April everyone is in total lockdown. I'm working exclusively at home. Jimmy is also working at home. Nikolai has worked at home since he got the job in sales in 2001. So, the three of us are together 24/7. Every morning Jimmy and I go through a ritual where he checks how many new COVID cases there are and how many hospitalizations. He keeps an excel spreadsheet with a bell curve. He and I are anxiously waiting for the peak and then the fall off that we keep hearing about in the news. Jimmy and Emily are to be married in July. I am certain by then this will be behind us since it's still three months away. The virus has other plans.

During this COVID time, Jimmy and I grow even closer. I enjoy sitting across from him at the kitchen table every day with our laptops in front of us. When there is a lull in our workloads, we converse about everything under the sun, primarily wedding-related details. He is understandably anxious about the wedding taking place in the midst of this virus. I know in the back of my mind that this is my last time with him all to myself, so I know to relish every moment. I am lucky in that sense. We often are not aware of those opportunities until it is too late.

Nikolai's behavior is a little off. He has two cell phones now, and when he comes out of his office, he brings the two and stacks them face down one on top of each other on the table next to him. I was suspicious when he came home with the second cell phone the previous December. For nineteen years he had exclusively used his work cell phone. Suddenly, out of nowhere, he decided he needed a personal cell phone. I find it highly suspect, but my kids tell me I am overreacting and I shouldn't worry about it, so I table the thoughts. I convince myself that his placing the two phones face down is quirky, and I try not to read too much into it. Little do I know the cell phone behavior is nothing compared to the deception that awaits me. Still, I can't help but think about Nikolai's duplicity in the past.

———— ♦ ————

By 1994, Nikolai and I had been married for two years and were considering starting a family. We had bought a split-level house in a nice neighborhood and had spent the last two years scraping off old wallpaper, painting, refinishing wood floors, and upgrading the kitchen and baths. Everything seemed to be going well. Nikolai had been working as a chemist in a lab for an environmental company that closed, and he received a severance package. He needed another job and decided to go through a headhunter. The headhunter liked him and set up an interview with a major company in his field. He had a call-back, and it was looking good. I started to get excited. I began thinking that when we started a family, I could go part-time so I could be home with my (future) babies. He should make enough that we could swing that. It sounded like a great opportunity that would give us the life I had dreamt of. Then, the bomb dropped.

I came home from work one day just as the phone in the kitchen started ringing. I raced up the stairs to our small kitchen on the second level to answer it. The phone was attached to the wall in the corner near the stove. It was Nikolai's headhunter on the line. She asked for Nikolai. I told her that he wasn't home yet. She then asked, "Are you, his wife?"

A bit taken aback and wondering why she wanted to know, I said yes. Standing in the corner, I nervously started to play with the long rose-colored phone wire. I felt in my gut that something was off.

"You're an attorney, correct?" she asked.

I began to feel like I was being cross-examined. I said yes, wondering where this was going. Then she said, "And you, as an attorney, approved of his behavior?"

I closed my eyes, bent my head forward, and pinched the bridge of my nose, thinking how bizarre this was. My stomach started to churn. Since I had no idea what she was talking about, she spelled it out. "How in good conscience could you approve of him lying on his resume?"

I gasped. "What?"

She said, "You're an attorney, and you know he doesn't have a college degree, but he represents that he does?"

Now I felt like I wanted to vomit. What does this mean? What do you mean he doesn't have a college degree? How do I respond to something like that? My head was spinning. Somehow, I got through the rest of the call as gracefully as possible. I think she might actually have believed that I had no clue, not that that mattered to my life. She said something like, "Good luck, miss. You're going to need it."

Little did I know how much.

Nikolai had told me he graduated with a degree in physics from New York University. It turned out he flunked out midway through his junior year while majoring in mathematics. Now what do I do? I clearly married a liar. I've always tried to be a truthful person. I've even hated telling the proverbial white lie and sought advice from a priest on how to avoid doing so. What else has he lied to me about? I was devastated by this news, but I was in my early thirties at this point and that biological clock continued to tick. And I was just married. I got advice from Mom and my work friend, Ava, and they were consistent in their advice and insistent that I listen to it. He must go back to school and get his degree. No ifs, ands, or buts. I should move forward with starting a family. In the end, it would all work out.

So, I got past this one too. I did tell him that he absolutely must get his degree and never lie to me again (wishful thinking). He went to

Rutgers University in New Jersey to get a history degree. He was too insecure to try science or math again. I took out loans from my 401K plan to pay for his college. My twins were born in early 1995 while he was working part-time at an electronics store and going to school. This was not the life I dreamt of, but he did give me two (ultimately three) of the most beautiful babies ever created.

After he obtained his history degree with very good grades, Nikolai decided he had enough confidence to pursue a degree in chemistry, which was better suited to his career. It was a long tough road, but I supported him through it both financially and emotionally. He ultimately secured that job in scientific sales where he ended up making a lot more money than I did, which did allow me to work part-time and be with my little darlings. The life I dreamt of was just delayed by five years. Or so it seemed.

———— ♦ ————

During this same period, Nikolai received a letter from the Environmental Protection Agency, which was conducting a criminal investigation of a former environmental firm where Nikolai had worked. They wanted to interview him with respect to the investigation. Cocky as ever, Nikolai didn't think much of it. I knew better. This was serious stuff, and he could potentially face charges if he had done anything wrong. I quizzed him on what he did at the job. After multiple teeth-pulling sessions, I got out of him that he had back-dated tests that the lab was performing for other companies so they could be compliant with EPA regulations. This was bad.

At the time, I was working under a brilliant government attorney in my office who was something of a mentor to me. He was one of the best litigators our agency ever had, and I was privileged to have worked under him. I went to him with my concerns. He immediately said Nikolai needed a lawyer to represent him, and it couldn't be any of us. He needed an immunity letter. Not having dealt with criminal law, other than at law school, I had no experience with an immunity letter. I learned that while they come in all forms, essentially the letter is signed by a prosecutor who agrees that he will not charge you with any crimes that are uncovered while questioning you as long as you tell the whole truth. Fortunately, my mentor had a friend in private practice, and he called in a favor for me. His friend agreed that the EPA agents could interview Nikolai at his office, and he would serve as his pseudo attorney. My mentor and I worked on drafting the immunity letter and the EPA agreed to the terms. I sat next to Nikolai at a long conference table with the EPA agent at the head, and my mentor's friend popped in and out throughout the interview. I prayed internally that Nikolai would tell everything truthfully. Nikolai revealed the backdating, and we never heard from the EPA again. Another bullet dodged.

———————•◆•———————

May 2020 (7 months earlier)

Unknown to me, Nikolai is withdrawing large sums of cash from his bank accounts through the ATM. He has opened multiple individual bank accounts, the existence of which I am completely unaware. He makes the rounds from bank to bank on a given day and withdraws the maximum. Since it is in the height of COVID, he uses excuses like going to the store to get food. There aren't many other reasons for him to leave the house at this point. This month his ATM cash withdrawals total $16,000. The previous month was $12,000 and $9,000 the month before. As I find out later, the ATM withdrawals began in earnest in July 2019 with a withdrawal of $3,600 and the following month $9,000. He withdraws varying amounts each month for an average over twenty-two months of close to $6,000 each month, totaling over $126,000. I later discover that he has withdrawn several thousand dollars from our joint bank account this month as well. The deception is immense. Where is he putting this cash? I never find out but have my suspicions.

It is still deep into lockdown with COVID. My family celebrates Mother's Day with just our immediate family socially distanced outside. Matty finishes college this month, but there is no real graduation due to the pandemic, so we again have a small celebration outside with close family members. I make Matty dress up in his cap and gown, I put on the blue and white dress with brass buttons I had bought for his graduation, and we take pictures as if it were a typical graduation. The rest of the day we eat barbecued chicken and salads and play Cornhole. It is a nice day, just not how you would hope to celebrate such a milestone. I hope for better times ahead, but that was not to be.

July 2020 (5 months earlier)

It's wedding time! Jimmy and Emily are to be married on July 11. As I later find out, Nikolai withdraws only $5,000 cash this month. Perhaps the wedding festivities constrict his plans. Jimmy and I have discussed our concerns about Nikolai possibly making a scene and ruining the wedding. His track record for special occasions is not good, and he does not seem to possess any filter mechanism to control himself for something special, for someone else's day. Jimmy indicates that if Nikolai does anything, their relationship will be severed. But the wedding goes on. It's been a crazy up-and-down ride planning this wedding. We're in total shut-down mode, then we're open, then indoor dining is open, then indoor dining is taken away. Joys and heartaches continually. Fortunately, Emily's family booked with a phenomenal vendor. He rents out a large tent so they can have an outdoor wedding. They have invited around 180 people but only 90 people attend. The wedding is still amazing. In fact, I would argue it's more amazing because it's smaller. Somehow, I'm able to put aside all the heartache from Nikolai and just have an incredibly good time. That there are fewer people makes it nicer from my perspective. I can talk to all our guests and have a great time dancing. The party bus back to the hotel is one of my favorite memories. My extended family is all together belting out songs like "Sweet Caroline" and "Piano

Man." We have so much fun. Despite many more being invited, only two from Nikolai's side show up. That is all too typical of them. Most of them don't even respond to an invitation. His brothers rarely showed up for family events in the past, especially if costs were involved. Nikolai's sister-in-law sends Jimmy and Emily a gift, a check in a card, clearly emphasizing that it is from her alone. We don't know what to make of that. At the same time, she sends Matty a belated graduation gift, also a check, clearly only from her. Nikolai does manage to behave himself, so we get through this event unscathed.

CHAPTER 3

A Tale of Two Dads

Eleven days before my twelfth birthday, my father passed away, changing my life in an instant. He was fifty. He had been diagnosed with lung cancer two years prior. An inveterate smoker, he tried to quit and told my mom he had, but she knew he continued to sneak cigarettes. She was just shocked when he revealed to the doctor that his contraband cigarettes amounted to a pack each day. As much as we like to complain today about the state of our medical care, medicine has advanced quite a bit since 1973. The doctors decided to operate on him, which meant they broke several of his ribs and cut him open from the middle of his chest to the middle of his back. He showed me his scar one day. It looked like a long black zipper that went halfway around his torso. After opening him up, they saw that the cancer had spread to his heart and was beginning to wrap around his aorta. They took a small piece of the tumor for biopsy, closed him back up, concluded that the tumor was malignant and informed my mom that with radiation he might live two to five years, and oh, she should not ever tell him because he couldn't handle the news. He lived just barely two years. My mom spent those two years pumping him with vitamins and trying to convince him he had every virus or innocuous disease she could dream up. For Christmas he told me he wanted a bag of air. My mom told my two older brothers of my dad's diagnosis but felt my younger brother Jack and I couldn't handle it. The night before he died, as I was getting ready to go to bed, I went to his bedroom and asked for a stamp. He was standing in the doorway and pulled his wallet out of his back pocket. As I leaned in to take the stamp, I smelled his familiar Old Spice cologne, which, along with his hair gel, he continued to apply despite the ravages of cancer. I turned to leave, and he said, "Aren't you going to kiss me goodnight?"

I looked at him and said, "I'm almost twelve years old. I'm not a baby anymore, Daddy. I'm too old for that stuff."

I thought I detected sadness in his eyes as he responded, "You're too old to kiss your father goodnight?"

I replied, "Yup," pivoted, and went to bed. Those were the last words I ever spoke to him.

He died two months before his fifty-first birthday, eleven days before my twelfth birthday, on a Friday. Some of the details will forever be burned on my brain. I was in sixth grade and in the "advanced" class in public school. My parents originally had sent my older brothers and me to the local Catholic elementary school. In those days, the tuition was negligible, and since both my parents were products of Catholic schooling, it seemed the natural thing to do. We all went to public school for kindergarten because the Catholic school only started at first grade. When I was in third grade, my brother Jack was in kindergarten and the school system concluded that he had a speech problem. I, as his eight-year-old interpreter, could have diagnosed that since I was the only one who understood what he was saying. He needed speech therapy, which was only provided in the public schools, and thus, he could not attend the Catholic elementary school. My parents, having also concluded that Catholic high school was not worth the cost, had already sent my brother Ben to the public school and my brother Jimmy was to go there the next year. That left only me. They gave me the option of staying put or transferring to the public school. After a year of Sister Jean traumatizing us by beating up the boys with her ruler, I bolted, along with Kevin Armstrong who was one of her ruler victims.

Fourth grade was a joke. I couldn't believe how easy it was. I clearly was the smartest kid in the class and quickly established myself as teacher's pet. In return, my teacher recommended me for the "advanced" class for fifth grade. As soon as I stepped foot in the fifth-grade classroom, I was intimidated. These kids were products of doctors, lawyers, and school principals. Who was I? My parents were high-school graduates. My dad had dabbled in college after "the war" (WWII), going for free on the GI Bill of Rights, but his parents convinced him to drop out and get a job and earn money. He went to work for an insurance company. His entire life, he regretted listening to them. He vowed that each of his four children would graduate college, not because he had such a love of learning, not because he valued education, but because as he watched younger, less hard-working college graduates advance over him, he saw what that piece of paper could do.

After a year and a half of feeling intimidated, I found my groove. Toward the end of sixth grade, I was doing better academically and had begun to feel more comfortable with the kids in my class. As it turns out, some of those kids in fourth grade did quite well for themselves and many of the kids in fifth and sixth grade did not advance academically and professionally to my extent. All that glitters is not gold.

And so, on that fateful day, I was practically skipping the mile home from school with a smile on my face thinking about my day. Life was good. The kid who lived across the street, four years younger than I, drove up on his bike, also on his way home. I groaned inside, thinking, *What great thing is he going to tell me about himself this time?*

But he didn't. He said, "You look like you had a good day." A little taken aback, I smiled shyly and then chattered on about my day, and before I knew it, we were home. I couldn't believe how great the day was going that even this kid could be nice. Little did I know, my whole world was about to be rocked.

I walked in the door and felt like I was entering an alternate reality. My three brothers were in the living room to my right, all of them crying. I saw them, but my brain refused to register it. My Aunt Kate was straight ahead in the kitchen. She was my mom's first cousin, but they grew up like sisters. She was our closest extended family member. I gave her a warm hello, surprised to see her on a Friday afternoon. She responded by telling my mom I was home. I was confused by her lack of a greeting. I was carrying my spiral notebook with my golden-brown pocketbook on top. I went into the kitchen, and my mom immediately hugged me, something that was never done in my family. Hugs and "I love you's" were basically nonexistent. She then told me my father had died. The tumor had squeezed his aorta until the aorta burst. She found him dead in the master bathroom, blood spread out everywhere. I broke down, clutching my notebook and pocketbook, in my mom's arms. My life would never be the same.

My dad was a quiet, gentle man. He stood tall at six feet but most of his life was quite thin. His nose, crooked from being broken several times from various mishaps, such as falling off a ladder, was on the big side, and when he blew it, we thought a ship was entering port during a densely foggy night. He had two gold teeth, which I thought was pretty cool. He thought he looked better by slicking his hair back with gel, and until the undertaker prepped him, we had no idea he still had a full, thick head of hair. I inherited his blue eyes, his wavy blond hair, a lot of his personality, and his penchant for beer. My dad liked to drink one bottle of Pabst Blue Ribbon beer with dinner each night and a second beer on Saturdays when he was working around the house. One Saturday, when I was around two, my mom left me with my dad to go shopping. He plopped me down in the middle of our fenced-in yard to trim the hedge. After all, the garden didn't stop growing just because he had to babysit a two-year-old, which by the way was "women's work." While he was intently designing his hedge, I maneuvered over to where he had set his beer bottle, sat myself down and gulped what was left. My mom arrived home to a very tipsy toddler and a sheepish husband who had to deal with an irate wife. I just napped for the rest of the day.

My dad was old-fashioned, a bit introverted, and somewhat of a perfectionist. He regularly yelled, "Keep your hands off the wall!" And he went around the house once a month with a paint brush to paint over our smudges. Ever the gentleman, his standard attire was either a suit for work, or, for leisure, blue trousers accompanied by a button-down shirt. Even when he was working around the house and yard, he simply wore older versions of the same outfit. I never saw him in a pair of jeans. A curse word never passed through his lips. In fact, as a family story portrays, he had no tolerance for bad language. When my brother Jack was around two, my parents had a poorly functioning stove that continually frustrated my mom to such an extent that she would often mutter under her breath, "That damn stove." At the time, Jack had a little toy workbench where you hammer down the brightly colored pegs, flip it over, and hammer them back the other way. It was probably a hand-me-down from my older brothers because the pegs had gotten too loose for it to work properly. My father "fixed" it by tightening it up but went a little overboard. One day, Jack was playing with his toy, and he hammered and hammered but couldn't get the peg to go down. Just as my dad walked in the door from work, he heard Jack say, "That damn toy!" As the story goes, my dad went out the next day and bought my mom a new stove.

My dad could get angry like most parents. At dinner, he'd get on my brother Ben's case to get a haircut. My dad didn't tolerate hair below the top of the ear for boys. He's probably rolling over in his grave at the "man-buns" today. But he never lost control. He would yell, and we knew when daddy was yelling, we were in trouble. But it never went beyond that. And he had such a gentle side. On vacation one year I couldn't get my hands warm, and he put them in his jacket pocket and warmed them with his hands. He taught me how to ride a bike, he helped me make a bird feeder for Girl Scouts, and he always helped me with my math homework. He was a whiz at math despite his lack of education. I can only remember him through the eyes of a child, not even a teenager. But I also remember that after his death, when my mom informed the pharmacy that he no longer needed the medicine, the lady's response was, "He was such a gentleman." That was my dad.

I wished my children could have had some of what I experienced with my dad. Nikolai was vastly different. Nikolai was a good provider like my dad, and they were both handy around the home. Nikolai was a bit handier than my dad because my dad would not touch plumbing. But the commonality ended there. Expletives freely flowed from Nikolai's mouth. Nikolai never helped the kids with their schoolwork. That was always on me. When Matty was applying to college, I spent hours helping him write essays and filling out applications. We had gotten to the stage of writing essays for small scholarships, and one had us stumped. The three of us— Nikolai, Matty, and I— were at the kitchen table eating dinner one night, and I figured maybe Nikolai could give us some ideas. After bringing up the topic, Nikolai stared at us, said he didn't know, and went into the other room to watch TV. Matty was disgusted that his father refused to do even that. Nikolai's child rearing and patience with young children was vastly different from my dad's as well.

———— ◆ ————

Sometime in 1995, the twins were infants and, having been born prematurely, had trouble sleeping through the night—Jimmy in particular. He had what they call pyloric stenosis—although it was never officially diagnosed—which basically is that the stomach opening isn't wide enough, so the food doesn't go down properly. Food often comes back up, which was the case with Jimmy. I would give him his bottle and smile to myself watching him ravenously suck it down and finish it off. But then came the burping. I would rest him on my shoulder and gently pat his back with trepidation as nearly every time, at least half of the formula would burst out of his mouth and down my back. It didn't matter how soft a tap, what position I placed him, or if I tried to slow down his intake, most of it was coming back up. It's fairly common and most grow out of it, as did he. Because of this condition, I was concerned about having Jimmy sleep on his back as is recommended. Also, it was hard to fill Jimmy up, and I imagine he was often hungry, which is why he didn't sleep. We were, of course, very tired from lack of sleep, having to get up often through the night with twins. I did the lion's share since I was home on maternity leave, but I couldn't do it all with twins, and Nikolai also got up at night. Frustrated one night when Jimmy woke up in the middle of the night, Nikolai threw Jimmy's bottle across the room, picked up a lamp, and smashed it to pieces. We were only married three years at this point, and I hadn't experienced too many blow ups, so while I thought the behavior was idiotic, I was able to pass it off as the result of sleep deprivation.

I always joked that Jimmy came out of the womb whining and complaining. Since he was a twin, I also joked that he kicked out his twin sister because he wanted the space all to himself, which is why they were born six weeks early. He didn't realize that he would only have seventeen minutes in the womb all to himself! And ultimately, he would have to share his time with a third person when I gave birth to Matty in early 1998.

Jimmy was a little over three when Matty was born. My mom spent lots of time at my house helping me, as I had my hands full with three children aged three and under. On this particular day, Jimmy was in the family room playing with Grace, and my mom was watching them. I was taking care of Matty, who was an infant. Jimmy was likely being difficult as he could be. When he was little, he could try your patience. (I subsequently concluded that I didn't feed the kid enough, which is what made him cranky. Who knew?). Whatever he was doing had set off Nikolai. He flew into his rage, picked Jimmy up and violently shook him, causing his head to sway back and forth. My mom screamed so loud, I immediately ran in. Nikolai stopped when I came in. My mom was frantic with worry for Jimmy and shocked by Nikolai's behavior. How someone could do this to a small child is inconceivable to me. He could have ended up with brain damage but for my mom's screams. Thank goodness Jimmy was okay.

I was disgusted with Nikolai's behavior and worried for my son. I watched him constantly to make sure he was okay. I still didn't think of this as abuse. Maybe that was my stupidity or naivete. It simply never entered my mind that I could have married an abuser. I just felt he had a bad temper and would lose control from it. I felt it stemmed from his childhood and the way he was raised. It's not like he beat any of us up. And I think perhaps because I was so adamantly against any physical punishment, it tempered his impulses to be physical. His raging outbursts were predominantly verbal. Making physical contact with one of us during a rage only happened roughly four times during our entire marriage. However, I think this is when I began to see myself as the protector of my children from Nikolai. Even if it were just a verbal outburst, my children had to know I would keep them safe. And they had to know this behavior was not acceptable. That became my mission.

These seemingly unprovoked rages were not directed only at Jimmy. About a year later when Jimmy and Grace were around four and Matty was one, Nikolai went into a rage and smashed Matty's "busy box." I have no recollection of what prompted this rage, although there never seemed to be any real provocation. By this time, I was weary of his outbursts, and I knew it was not a good example for the children. I scooped them all up, packed them in the car and took them to the park to play. I left Nikolai to stew in his own juices. This, of course, was not to be the first time Nikolai lost it with Matty. Matty was never an emotional kid, and he is more on the tough side. These character traits proved critical in supporting me through the darkness. When Matty was around two or three, he did something that warranted a time-out. I did not believe in and never allowed corporal punishment. I used time-outs when they were little, and when they were old enough and capable enough, I made them write, sometimes twenty-five times, "I will not hit my brother," or later, a short essay on why they shouldn't hit. Jimmy ended up writing the most, but he swears it's the reason he's one of the few engineers who can write decently. When Jimmy was desperate for words, he would add lots of "verys" and would appeal to my faith by stating that God would not want him to hit his brother, for example. He told me recently that he is grateful for the discipline because he learned self-control—unlike his father. Because Matty had better control over his emotions, he rarely had a written punishment, but when he was little, sometimes he needed correcting. This instance, Nikolai put Matty in time-out, and Matty just sat on the step quietly, seemingly undisturbed by the whole thing, showing no emotion. That did not make Nikolai happy. He wanted the kid to show remorse, so much so that Nikolai screamed right in this three-year old's face with all the venom he could muster and did not stop screaming until he made Matty cry.

It broke my heart that Matty had to endure this, but I felt powerless to do anything. It never occurred to me to leave at this point. I had three small children and felt an intact family, although not ideal, was better than a broken one. Confronting Nikolai was not an option as it would only provide fuel to the fire of his rage. Walking on eggshells, constantly trying to figure out ways to prevent Nikolai from getting upset, seemed to be the only answer.

Nikolai's patience did not grow as the children grew. On January 15, 2012, the boys were seventeen and fourteen. They were fooling around during a football game, which Nikolai was watching. Just good-natured banter. During their escapades, they hit the guide button on the remote twice. Nikolai demanded that they give him the remote, which seemed perfectly reasonable to me, since they kept interrupting the game. What came next was not. Nikolai took the remote and smashed it to pieces on the floor. Naturally, destroying a remote was psychological abuse to the boys but was not an impactful punishment in any other sense —it impacted us. Now, we somehow needed to figure out how to get a new remote from the cable company. But rationality never entered the picture when Nikolai was like this. Nikolai always came up with an excuse for his behavior: he was tired, stressed from work, or the most common, he had a migraine.

Nikolai's behavior caused the kids to draw closer to me. They knew they were safe with me. They knew I would always love them no matter what. As the years progressed, it became the four of us as a unit, separate from Nikolai. When Nikolai was away on business, the four of us had a wonderful, carefree, relaxed time together. We fondly remember dinners together where we would joke and talk about whatever we wanted. We didn't have to worry about an unexpected outburst directed at one of the boys or Grace. While I remember more incidents with the boys, Grace was his primary target after me.

———◆———

When the twins were babies, I had a live-in au pair who cared for them while I worked. I called her every day from work to check in. One day, it was pouring rain when I called, and the phone rang incessantly. The au pair did not drive so I became alarmed, called the agency, and raced home, as did Nikolai. It turned out the au pair had a headache, turned off the phone, and went to bed. I arrived to screaming babies desperate to be fed. When the agency representative arrived, she asked if we were willing to give the au pair a second chance. Nikolai held Grace tightly against his chest and said, "Not with my baby." It seemed so sweet and protective. As life unfolded, I came to question the sincerity of it.

Grace was drawn to medicine in high school and volunteered for the town Rescue Squad. In college she did the same. She loved every aspect of it, even insisting on learning to drive the ambulance (which she managed to drive into a cement wall, costing the school over $10,000. Thank goodness for insurance!).

It took Grace longer than most to master the skills of driving, but she ultimately did. At seventeen, Grace was a newly minted driver.

She barely had her license when she plowed into another car. I was at our vacation home with the boys when she called. She was so hysterical that the police officer took the phone from her and spoke to me. No one was hurt and insurance covered the damage to the car, so we escaped unscathed. Around a year later, her driving still needed work. One summer day, Jimmy was working as a camp counselor, I was at the office, and Grace and Matty were home with Nikolai, who was working. Grace decided to go out and backed out of the driveway and rammed right into Nikolai's company car. This was not as easy a fix as going through our regular insurance. The honest thing would have been to tell the company what happened and take the monetary consequences, but that was not how Nikolai operated. He never wanted to pay for something if he didn't have to, but I surmised he couldn't figure out how to get around this one and that became his excuse for his behavior. He immediately became enraged, glaring eyes, clenched fists, total loss of control. He got in Grace's face, screeched at her, and took our ceramic fruit bowl, held it up high and smashed it into a thousand pieces right in front of her. He then demanded that Grace pick up all the pieces. Grace called me and was inconsolable.

Matty got on the line and said, "This is a really bad one, Mom. He's completely out of control."

There wasn't much I could do from almost two hours away. I told Matty to get Grace away from Nikolai. I suggested the two go to McDonald's because they could walk there. I told them to stay there as long as possible. I really didn't know what else to tell them as I was never sure what to do when Nikolai was in this state. Perhaps that was part of the problem. I just didn't know how to handle it. Was there a way to handle it? I've looked through my journals over the years, and there was always that underlying question. Was there something better I should have done? I had spoken several times to a priest about it. At first the priest would tell me to pray for him, but over time I think he began to see that there was something more going on, and he would just try to help me cope. I guess one can't cope indefinitely. There comes a breaking point and then it's over. Perhaps I'm too resilient as that breaking point was still years away.

Over the years, I've thought about Nikolai's behavior toward Grace. While I was his primary target, Grace was definitely his secondary go-to. It became acutely obvious when years later, Matty, a new driver, took a turn too fast and smashed into a street sign, knocking it over. Nikolai couldn't do enough for him. Nikolai did not yell or even get annoyed. Why the difference? When Jimmy found out how nice Nikolai was to Matty after the accident, he was incensed, knowing all that Grace had gone through. He is loyal to his twin sister, and it made him sick that the standard was so different. I could only conclude that Nikolai was a glorified bully. He picked on those who were weaker. Matty always received the least of Nikolai's wrath. Matty turned out to be the tallest and ultimately the strongest of the three kids. Nikolai was likely a bit intimidated by him. But Nikolai knew he could overpower Grace or me. My mom, on the other hand, was another story.

CHAPTER 4

Mom

My mom is one of the strongest people I know. She grew up during the Great Depression. She was very close to her parents and "granny," her dad's mom. When my mom was sixteen, her mom died from breast cancer, which she developed from the intensive radiation treatments she had received on her back for tuberculosis. After eight long years suffering from TB, she was almost better when she noticed the lump. She asked her doctor about it, and he told her to come back in six months. She died before her return appointment. My mom's granny died a week later, three weeks before Christmas. My grandfather asked my mom if she wanted a Christmas tree that year, and she said yes. She wanted to celebrate despite the grief. The combination of those events must have created an inner core of strength in my mom. She subsequently lost her husband and son and managed to go on from that. She is now ninety-eight and still kicking, although health problems have taken their toll. COVID has impacted her as she now takes turns living with one of my brothers and me rather than the assisted living facility where she had been. The constant change is hard for her, but caring for her while working is hard for us, which is why we opted to share the responsibilities.

Barely 5' 2" (and that's with her rounding up) she never wore anything but a dress until my dad died. After he died, she bought her first pair of pants and wore them every Saturday: red and white checked pants and a white blouse, which she paired with purple, squared-toed, velvet, lace-up shoes she found for a dollar. I hated being seen with her in public in that outfit. Her short, permed, dark brown hair, which is all white now, has always been curled in soft curls around her head and it shows off her deep blue eyes. Despite her big, crooked teeth, her smile is infectious. We came across some slides one day that my dad had taken on their honeymoon. She was quite the looker, clad in a two-piece bathing suit in a very sexy pose. A bit risqué for 1948, I would surmise.

She was a stay-at-home mom with no education past high school and no job skills until my dad died. We went from being comfortably middle class to poor in an instant. She knew nothing of the financial world when he died, and since my brother Ben was going off to college, she simply wrote out a check for his first year. She quickly realized she was in financial trouble when the bank balance showed only $40. She needed a job fast and went out looking. The job market was tough in 1973, and one potential employer told her he'd call her without ever asking for her name or number. She was near defeat when she managed to secure a job on the assembly line of a coffee filter factory making $1.85 per hour. It put food on the table, as did the hamburgers my brother Jimmy brought home for dinner a couple times each week from the local joint where he worked. Mom was frugal in every way possible, one being milk. She switched to powdered milk, which tasted like cardboard. Oh, how Jack and I hated that milk! We still get queasy when we see the blue box. We were ecstatic when she was able to get a better job and buy real milk. That's when Jack asked her if she could get him a real winter coat to replace the plastic one that he had. She even tried her hand at college and was close to getting her associate degree when she found a decent government job. She managed to hold onto the house and did as much maintenance on it as she was capable. She mowed the lawn and trimmed the trees well into her sixties. One day she went to purchase a power tree trimmer, and the salesman refused to sell it to her because he said he would never let his mother do something so risky. She fulfilled my father's dream of putting all four kids through college. Widowed at forty-eight, she never remarried. She's often said she had too much responsibility to date someone when she was young and still looked good, and by the time she was free, she was set in her ways and not interested.

My brother Jimmy's death devastated her. It was the first time she nearly broke. At his funeral, she kept lamenting that he "did not pass on his seed"; that is, he didn't have children. She was heartbroken that his wonderful qualities would not be passed on to a future generation. She took a leave of absence from her job for an entire year and went for counseling. Eventually, she picked herself up and went on with life, but there was always a hole from his death.

She and I were close when she was younger, talking on the phone almost daily. She almost always gave me sound advice. When Jimmy was ten years old, his fifth-grade teacher, who had a reputation for not liking boys, accused him of cheating on his spelling test. He told me about it when he came home, very upset and adamant that he didn't cheat. When I told my mom, she insisted I march down to the school before it opened the next morning and have it out with the teacher. I heeded her advice, and the teacher backed off and treated him fairly after that. Her advice will prove critical in the future.

———— ◆ ————

In April 2019, my mom called to tell me she had fallen and needed help. I took the day off from work and drove an hour and a half to her house. My immediate assessment was she must come home with me. She could not stay by herself. I learned that this was the second fall. The first fall was the day before, and she couldn't get up. The lady who rented a room from her helped her up and took her to an urgent-care place. They checked her heart and determined she was okay and sent her home. They suggested she consider going to the hospital. That's not a place my then ninety-five-year-old mom would ever go voluntarily, so she had her tenant drive her home. She managed to get herself up the flight of stairs for bed and back down the next morning but fell again in the kitchen. After I took her to my home, she steadily deteriorated. Her breathing became labored, and it became increasingly difficult to get her up the stairs. I took her to urgent care by me, and they determined that she had pneumonia and advised that I immediately bring her to the Emergency Room. The ER doctor concluded that she had five broken ribs and double pneumonia and admitted her into intensive care. She was there several days when they determined that she had heart failure. We figured this was the end of the line for her. It became increasingly clear that she could not return to her home.

April morphed into May, and my mom continued to stay with us and struggle. Jimmy proposed to Emily, and we had a great celebration with her parents. We went out to dinner and even managed to bring Mom with her oxygen tank to the restaurant. Mom wasn't doing well at all, and Grace didn't think she would last two weeks (my mom proved to be a tougher cookie than that). I had my brothers come to see her in case this was the end. My nephew came as well. She was declining rapidly at this point, and when we got back home from the engagement celebration, my mom asked me if I could get her a chair for her room because she couldn't sleep lying down, a typical sign of advanced congestive heart failure. Grace and Patrick went down to the family room and carried up the recliner for her. Nikolai was infuriated that we would take the recliner that he rarely used for my dying mother and offered no help in getting it up the stairs. Grace started tearing up. She loved her grandmother and couldn't understand how her father could be so uncaring. I didn't know how open to be about my feelings toward Nikolai at this point because I didn't know what Grace had told Patrick, so I didn't say too much. Later I found out he knew everything. We kept the chair in her room for the next month.

June rolled around, and then it was Father's Day. My mom was still recuperating. She was better but still had a long way to go. There is never a holiday that Nikolai can't ruin, even one that is about him. Grace and Matty came home for the day, and Jimmy was still living here. We celebrated in our usual way with Nikolai grilling meat and me making the rest of the dinner. All seemed to be going well until it wasn't. Nikolai started complaining to Matty about my mom. By the time I entered the room, Nikolai was moving in the direction of a rage and angrily stated that he would no longer help with my mom's care. All I needed from him was to help her get downstairs in the morning and give her breakfast and lunch on the two days each week I had to go into the office. He worked at home every day. But he refused to do that. His lame excuse was that if anything happened to my mother, he could be accused of doing something to her. He used that same excuse in the past in a different context. So, he effectively kicked my mom out. With a heavy heart, I reluctantly moved my mom into assisted living in July 2019.

Amid all Nikolai's screaming, Grace started crying, and she and Matty both wondered why they made the effort to come home and celebrate Father's Day with a father who acts this way. Later, Nikolai got into a screaming fit with me and told me that no one likes me, which was why I had no friends. A few days later, he appeared remorseful. He said he meant the comment about himself. Then, he contradicted himself and said he never should have said it. Then, he said he wanted to take a trip with just me. I was dizzy trying to keep up. He further indicated that he was under stress because his brother was having health problems. This was his typical modus operandi. Find a reason to excuse his bad behavior. My texts to Jimmy during that time indicated that I was seriously thinking he may have a mental health issue, and I didn't know how to deal with that since he would never admit to it. Matty at one point indicated that Nikolai was losing his perception of reality. I subsequently learned the term, "hoovering," which is what a narcissist does when he is concerned that he may be losing his "supply." The narcissist sucks his victim in like a hoover vacuum to ensure he or she won't leave. That may be what was happening to me, although it didn't appear yet that I was being discarded.

My mom's assisted living was one mile from my home. I visited her every day. It proved to be something of a haven where I could talk freely and get some of her sage advice. She will be there when the beginning of the end comes.

CHAPTER 5

Deception Comes to Light

February 2, 2020 (10 months earlier)

It's Super Bowl Sunday. In the past, my neighbors across the street would have a party. They didn't want kids at it, so Nikolai would go and eat and watch football while I stayed home with the kids. In more recent years, they stopped having the party and then moved away, so we took it over. This year we are having a big crowd: four different neighbors and their families, all of us (except Matty, who is at school), Jimmy's soon-to-be wife, Emily, Grace's fiancé, Patrick and Patrick's parents. Nineteen total. Jimmy, an avid sports fan, loves Super Bowl Sunday. The only thing he doesn't like is if the Patriots are playing and our guests talk over key plays. This year, the Patriots have managed to not make it so Jimmy can relax and enjoy the party. Since we are having so many guests, Jimmy and I decide we need to move the living room couch into the family room for more seating. First, we try taking the couch through the kitchen, but it won't fit through the hallway going into the family room. Next, we try going through the door in the garage, but it won't fit there either. Finally, we take it outside through the front door, carry it around the back and push it through the sliding glass doors. We now have crammed two couches, a love seat, a recliner, a rocking chair, and a few folding chairs into the room. The room is cramped with still-not-enough seating for nineteen, but it will have to do. We have the usual fun food: pizza, wings, buffalo chicken dip, ribs, veggie platter, an assortment of desserts, etc. Everyone gorges themselves and enjoys the game, the commercials, and the company.

The problem with Super Bowl Sunday is everyone must work the next morning, and Nikolai is leaving on a business trip. The game usually isn't over before 10 p.m., and by the time everyone leaves, and some basic cleaning is done, it's close to midnight. Nevertheless, it is a fun night until it is over. As everyone is leaving, I am in good spirits. Nikolai has managed not to offend anyone with his constant predictions, something that drives Jimmy crazy. Nikolai would constantly say things like, "They are going to score a touchdown now." In Jimmy's mind, and everyone else's, he jinxes it. Of course, Nikolai has a fifty percent chance of being correct. He's been told by us and even one of my neighbors that his predictions are not appreciated, but he continues to annoy us with them anyway. But he didn't do too much of that this time. Nikolai is stressed about packing for his trip, and suddenly we are arguing. I don't even remember what the topic is. Nikolai starts screaming at me. In that fit, he yells that he was justified in violating my trust two years prior. This violation was profound, something that would immediately break up most marriages. I am stunned. I am speechless. I never thought he would sink this low. This puts a new perspective on things. Since he will be gone for a week, I have time to think about what I want to do. Why is it so hard to make the break? This was not to be the first time he expresses that he is justified in his behavior and once again, I am the reason for his unhappiness. This has been a growing trend for many years now.

It was November 21, 2011, and we were just sitting down to dinner. The cleaning lady had just cleaned the house, an extravagance I gave up soon after. I relished having the cleaners come every two weeks and for one brief instant having an entire house clean. I'm a neat person but had learned over the years with Nikolai to just let things go. Perfection is not possible with someone who never puts anything away where it belongs. I learned to pick up after him a lot and close my eyes a lot. The cleaners were barely out the door, and the kids were in their designated seats for dinner. I grew up with assigned dinner table seats because we were three lefties and three righties, and my parents wanted to eliminate any arguments about bumping elbows while we ate. Since Jimmy and I are lefties and the others are righties, I implemented the same rule. Jimmy was in his seat on the side of the table with his back to the rest of the kitchen. My seat was next to his. Grace was in her seat across from me, and Matty was seated at the head of the table between Grace and me. Nikolai's seat was across from Jimmy, next to Grace. The foot of the table, near the sliding glass door and by Jimmy and Nikolai, was empty. Nikolai and I were putting dinner on the table when Nikolai spilled red cabbage all over the kitchen floor. I couldn't hold my tongue this time and obnoxiously complained, "I just had the house cleaned!"

This triggered Nikolai. He glared at me, bared his teeth, and screamed, "Get out of my face you nagging b**ch!"

I furrowed my brow, stunned at the reaction. He then stormed upstairs to his office, which is right over the kitchen table. I motioned to the kids that we should just eat without him, something we were used to doing. I sat down in my chair, and as we started our dinner, suddenly, we heard thunderous sounds overhead. Nikolai had taken the office chair and smashed it to pieces right over our heads. He did it with such force that he put a gouge in the hardwood floor, and we thought the light fixture over the table on the kitchen ceiling would fall on us. Jimmy started tearing up. Nikolai then bounded down the stairs and screamed, "I'm not going to spend Thanksgiving with your f***ing family!" He sneeringly followed up with, "You're a hypocrite. You read your stupid Bible, but you don't honor your husband like the Bible directs."

I was speechless as he flounced out again. Later, to justify his reaction, he claimed he had a migraine.

———◆———

I had hoped that Nikolai would mellow as he aged, but the opposite happened. His rages grew more intense and more frequent with each passing year. On New Year's Day 2015, we returned home from our yearly Christmas celebration at my brother Ben's house in Maryland. My brothers and our families got together with my mom every year for a weekend around Christmas. In past years, we had met at my house, but since my brother bought a very large house a few years prior, we started gathering at his home. This year we decided to celebrate the New Year together. It was a happy weekend. My nephews went all out, decorating with 2016 and Happy New Year signs all around. And, of course, the liquor flowed freely. We left for home the next morning in my giant SUV. I always referred to it as a boat. We had Grace, Mia, who was living with us now, and Matty in the very back and Jimmy and my mom in the middle. Nikolai was driving, and I was next to him. Nikolai did not want to get gas before we left, even though he knew we wouldn't have enough to get home. I could never understand the mentality, but it wasn't worth making an issue over. My best guess was he wanted to get gas in New Jersey where it was cheaper.

Sure enough, about a half hour from home, Nikolai pulled off the highway to a gas station. After getting gas, he couldn't figure out how to exit the gas station. Every exit said no left-turn, but we needed to go left. After circling the gas station twice, I suggested he just make the illegal left so we could get out of there. If only I had learned to keep my mouth shut. Nikolai heeded my advice and, of course, the sirens immediately wailed. Nikolai was pulled over for an illegal left, and it was all my fault. Nikolai was irate. I felt bad that I made the suggestion. I never would have expected the police to be out in this quiet area on New Year's Day. Perhaps they were looking for leftover drunks. After taking Nikolai's papers, the policeman went back to his car to write up the ticket. I did not say a word because I did not want to poke the bear. I figured the less I said, the better the chances of getting through this without too much emotional drama. Since a policeman was only a few feet away, I assumed Nikolai would behave. The monkey never learns! He didn't behave in 1991, why would he now?

Predictably, Nikolai exploded. He started screaming and cursing at me, "It's all your fault! Why do I listen to you? You don't care about me. You have no regard for my feelings." And on it went, but this time, there was a new wrinkle. "I want a divorce," he bellowed. "I want you to go file the paperwork on Monday. Do you understand me?"

This was on Thursday. Besides the ridiculousness of thinking that a divorce could be done in three days or that I would accede to his stupid demand (You want it? Go do it yourself), I was taken aback that the words were spoken. A divorce? Where did that come from? Okay, you've been a jerk for years and I've put up with it and it's not like we're super connected anymore, but what suddenly brought this on? Ah to be so naive and not know what he has been doing. By this time, I was mentally done with him. And I did what I did best: shut down and clammed up. My brain went into overdrive. I started to text the kids. I said I didn't know what the future held but we would be okay regardless. Everyone was shocked and grew silent in the car—except my mom. At ninety years old, she didn't hear well. I was quietly texting the kids that everything would be okay, they shouldn't worry, and I would figure it out. But my mom kept saying, "Why is the police officer taking so long and what's the matter with Nikolai?"

I nicely told her to zip it. Inside, I was in turmoil, frozen in fear. What did this mean? Was this the end of my family? What else would my kids have to endure? Would I be better off in the long run? I had long ago lost any feelings for him. Why couldn't I just be done with him? I don't know. Nostalgia? The appearance of a happy, intact family? The fear of the unknown? People would often tell me how strong I was but maybe I really was weak. Maybe that's why I couldn't do what needed to be done.

We drove the rest of the way in silence. When we returned home, Nikolai insisted on staying in the guest room/office where my mother would have slept. He said, "There is no way I'm sleeping in the same bed as you."

We put my mom in Jimmy's bed, and Jimmy slept on a mattress on the floor in Grace and Mia's room. My mom went immediately to bed and the rest of us whispered quietly in Grace and Mia's room. Jimmy was very upset and crying but nevertheless decided to attempt to reason with Nikolai. He went downstairs to the kitchen where Nikolai was sitting at the table alone. Nikolai told him how awful a person I am, and then he violated my trust. Nikolai knew something about a prior bad break-up that was never to be shared with our kids, but he shared it anyway. To me, it was a profound violation. I listened in horror from Grace's room. Shaking all over, I was shell-shocked by the depth of the breach of trust. Now, I had to explain everything to my kids, which I did. They assured me that they didn't think any differently about me, and we all hugged and cried. I told the kids I had no idea what the future held, but we would get through it. Soon after, I left for a seven-week trial in Chicago, and when I returned home for a quick break midway through, Nikolai expressed remorse about what he said. We moved on from it, or so I thought.

Mia commented that this was the type of dysfunction she was hoping to get away from by not living with her mother. Mia has been best friends with Grace since second grade. They are so close that Mia was Grace's maid of honor at her wedding. Mia came to live with us in July 2014. She is an only child. Her mother is a dysfunctional alcoholic and likely an overt narcissist. Her behavior is strikingly similar to Nikolai's, but she is more obvious to the outside world. She was a close friend of mine at this time and until years later when I concluded she was using me. In looking back, I wonder if I am somehow a magnet for narcissists. Mia's father was a wonderful person, but he passed away from pancreatic cancer in June 2014. I think a lot about him now and miss him tremendously. Prior to his death, he asked Nikolai and me if we would be willing to take in Mia since she would not want to be with her mother. He had separated from Mia's mother because he wanted peace. Her mother then filed for divorce and made the process as vicious as she possibly could, wiping out the bank accounts, calling him daily, and screaming about any minor thing, even though she knew the man was battling cancer. Unfortunately for Mia's financial position, he died before the divorce was finalized. I always liked to think of Mia as that second daughter that I had really wanted but didn't have. We agreed to take her in. She was mostly away at school but came to us on vacations and the summer. She paid for her school herself. We basically just gave her room and board. She became a part of our family. She was my ray of sunshine, waking up with a smile on her face no matter how bleak life might seem. The boys affectionately referred to her as their sister.

Unfortunately, for Mia and the rest of us, the dysfunction only continued to multiply.

———— ◆ ————

Six months later, on July 12, 2016, we had all sat down to dinner, including Mia. Mia sat in the chair at the foot of the table between Nikolai and Jimmy, near the sliding glass door. The dinner conversation somehow evolved into talking about Matty's friends. Nikolai started making fun of Matty's friends. Matty was eighteen now, as were his friends. One was a joke about one friend who was overweight at the time. Another was a joke about another kid who had a lot of facial hair. Matty grew increasingly upset about Nikolai's mocking and complained about Nikolai constantly making fun of his friends. Nikolai got agitated, telling him to not be so sensitive. Then Nikolai looked across the table to me for support. He attempted to include me in his joking. I tried to remain neutral and stay out of it in the hopes that I would not trigger Nikolai. I just smiled sheepishly, kept a laser focus on the dinner on my plate, stayed quiet and effectively, provided no support. I couldn't see how I could support his putting down of Matty's friends, and Matty was right: Nikolai did it regularly. Unsurprisingly, Nikolai erupted, screaming, "You never back me up! You always take the kids' side. I never have any support."

He stood up from his chair, smashing it into the wall behind it, picked up the bottle of hot sauce he had used on his dinner, and hurled it at me with such force that it put a big dent in the refrigerator. It then ricocheted off the refrigerator into the dining room about fifteen to twenty feet away. There was hot sauce everywhere in the kitchen and dining room, all over the china closet, the table, and chairs. Fortunately, he missed me. Had it hit my face, I might have had serious damage. He then continued to rant and raced upstairs. Later he stormed downstairs and with his face about two inches from mine, accused me of turning the kids against him. I cowered thinking he was going to hit me. Maybe it would have been better if he had. Maybe I would have ended things then. He blasted out the front door and left in his car. We didn't see him for three days. He claimed afterward that he had gone to a baseball game with a friend. I found his explanation wanting.

At this point, I decided I needed to take some measures to protect myself. I was a little slow to the gate but better late than never. With the demand for a divorce six months prior in the back of my mind and now his behavior getting physical, I opened a bank account in my own name and funded it with $10,000. I'm not sure why I thought that amount was enough to do much of anything. In retrospect, it would have only paid for about two months of legal bills, but at least it was a start. And it did serve me well later.

One month later, we went on a cruise to Alaska. In view of his tirade the month before, I wasn't even sure we would go on it. It was supposed to be in lieu of a twenty-fifth anniversary celebration (an endurance celebration for me). But we did go because Nikolai didn't want to lose the money for the trip. It was mostly uneventful in terms of our relationship—except for two things. We became friendly with a couple on one of the excursions and went out to dinner with them and joined them for other activities. One evening the four of us went to browse at the shops on the ship, and the man we were with bought a very expensive ring for his wife. That prompted Nikolai to want to do the same. He kept pushing me to buy a ring. First, I didn't need or want a ring. Second, I didn't want to spend that much money. Third, I didn't think the ship shops was the best place to make this kind of purchase. Fourth, I didn't want to copy this other couple or worse yet show them up. I prevailed, but in view of what was to come, I found his desire to buy me the ring odd. The only thing I can think is it was ego-driven; he didn't want to be outdone by this other man. Soon after, Nikolai became nasty to me. This was toward the end of the cruise, and I had gotten sick with a bad cold and a fever. I just went through the motions but couldn't wait to get home.

What was more intriguing about this time was what was happening at home, specifically in the office. The three kids and Mia were home for the summer. Jimmy had secured an internship, and the other three were camp counselors at the town camp. They all enjoyed the week together, being independent, cooking meals together, and just having fun. One day they had a problem with the Wi-Fi. The modem and all associated internet paraphernalia were in the office, so, they went to the office to reset everything. The door had been closed, something Nikolai was doing more often. I never understood the need but didn't question it. The kids went to open the door and had trouble getting it open. They had to use brute force to pry the door open. Once inside, they discovered that Nikolai had duct-taped the door shut from the inside. He had put duct tape all around the sides and top of the door. The only thing they could conclude was that Nikolai had taped the door and gone out the window with a ladder (the office is on the second floor). There was no other way for Nikolai to have exited the office with the door taped like it was. Why would he do this? I will get some insights in a few years. They also discovered jars of urine in the closet. They didn't tell me about this until much later. They simply fixed the Wi-Fi and closed the door. Shortly after, Nikolai installed the new doorknob with a key lock, which he would randomly lock for no reason that was apparent to me.

———— ◆ ————

By September 2017, things had deteriorated quite a bit. Matty had gotten himself into a little bit of trouble with the police right before he had to return to college for the first semester of sophomore year. The day before we were to move him back to school, he confided in me that he and his friend had driven to a parking lot nearby late at night to smoke pot. It was Matty's car but his friend's pot. The police came, and since it was Matty's car, he knew he was in trouble. He made a snap decision to save his friend and told the police it was his pot. He was arrested. I was devastated. Would his whole life be ruined? I'm one of those nerds who never even took a puff of a cigarette, let alone an illegal substance. But I decided it was best to take him back to school as planned and inform Nikolai afterward. Why poke the bear sooner than necessary? There was nothing that could be done immediately, and although I was upset and frantic, I didn't want to spoil Matty's return to school. I wanted it to be as happy a time as it could be, despite the cloud hanging over him. We later found an attorney, and he received a conditional discharge. Subsequently, our state legalized pot, and his record was expunged. So, it all worked out, but at the time, I was fraught with worry.

Jimmy and Mia went with us to Matty's school, and we had a good time getting him set up, although I had knots in my stomach about my upcoming confrontation with Nikolai. As soon as we got home, I told Nikolai what had happened. Instantaneously Hurricane Nikolai made landfall, and it was a category five. The veins in his neck popped out. His mouth was agape like a loaded gun ready to fire bullets of rage. He screamed at the top of his lungs. "How did this happen? How did you allow this? Why did you wait until now to tell me?"

I answered whatever questions he had as calmly as I could and just let him rage. And rage he did. This was the mother of all rages. Of course, it was all my fault that it happened. By this time, no matter what happened, it was my fault. I took out my phone and started texting the kids, warning them to not come downstairs. Nikolai was in constant motion, like someone high on amphetamines, but he was high on rage. He kept moving toward me and back out, coming closer each time and crossing the boundary of my personal space. Finally, nostrils flaring, he menacingly approached and smacked the phone right out of my hand. The hairs on my skin stood up. I looked at Nikolai wide-eyed. This was physical. In all the prior rages, he had never made physical contact with me, although he had with the kids to a certain extent. How physical would he get? This was one step beyond the hot sauce bottle being thrown at me. He was in my personal space. Was it really different? Or had I evolved enough to start to sense that Nikolai was abusive? He had gotten so much worse in so many ways—the rages, the disinterest in the rest of us, the sensitivity, and desire to be the center of attention. He seemed to be moving more and more in that direction as time went on. I was so tired of it all. I had hoped things would improve as he aged, but I couldn't have been more wrong in that hope. I learned in my research that physical abuse in relationships is nearly always preceded and accompanied by emotional abuse.[3] Was the physical abuse going to escalate? I didn't know, but I was apprehensive.

Nikolai was totally out of control. He went outside and screamed at Matty's friend who was involved in the incident. He came back in and screamed some more. He slammed doors. It just went on and on for hours. In his rage, he cornered me on the staircase and said, "I want to sell the house."

I said, "Why?"

"I need money."

"What do you need money for?"

He said, "I just do."

"I'm not selling the house," I said.

He then said, "I want to sell the Pocono house [our vacation home that we rented out]."

Again, I asked why.

Again, he said, "I need money."

"What do you need money for?"

"I just do."

"I'm not selling the Pocono house," I said.

Naive me didn't know then why he wanted money so desperately.

He got in his car and left, and so we had a few hours of peace. My next-door neighbors came by to see if I was all right. Their eyes were opened to him—but just a little. Nikolai went to the hospital because he worked himself up so much, he thought he would have a stroke. Whether that was legitimate or not is unknown. He was always a bit of a hypochondriac, constantly thinking he had some serious illness. I could never be sick just by myself and have my mate take care of me or at least be left in peace. Anytime I was sick with a virus of some sort, he immediately was certain he was sick also, so much so that when I was diagnosed with skin cancer, he was immediately convinced he had skin cancer too and went to the doctor for it (he didn't have it). But since he was in quite a state this time, it was possible he had elevated his blood pressure to dangerous levels. He came back later that night, complaining that no one asked about him and continued to rage.

He screamed, "I'm going to burn this f**king house down while you all sleep."

Would he? I wasn't 100 percent sure he wouldn't, so I didn't sleep the whole night. And I mean that literally. I sat up in bed the entire night. I had too much adrenaline to go to sleep. I had knots in my stomach. This was the first time I truly felt fear. My heart still wouldn't accept that he would truly do something so evil, which is why I didn't even consider calling the police. But my brain was beginning to think he might, which is why I didn't let myself go to sleep. Grace, Jimmy, and Mia were in bed. I had to be on alert to protect them if Nikolai did anything crazy. I gathered everything of importance that I could find in my bedroom. Fortunately, all the papers and my computer were there, and Nikolai didn't come in. I started researching divorce law on my computer. The rage continued all night. He smashed a picture of Matty.

I went downstairs at around 1 a.m. I don't remember why. Grace came down too. I talked to her and tried to comfort her when suddenly, we heard Nikolai coming. We were in the kitchen, and I frantically whispered, "Quick, hide in the dining room!"

She scuttled there and cowered in the corner behind the server, afraid that Nikolai might find her. The poor girl stayed there for thirty minutes while Nikolai screamed some more at me. Finally, when she figured she had an opportunity to escape undetected by Nikolai, she tiptoed back to her room. I continued to listen to more of his screaming.

The next morning, I got up early for work like usual, as did Jimmy, and I gave Jimmy all the important papers and my computer to hold in his car. The rage continued the entire next day as well. Was he having a breakdown? It honestly never occurred to me. In my head, this was another rage, just more intense. And since the trigger was more intense, it didn't seem shocking that the rage was as well. I just needed to steel myself and get through it. He would calm down eventually. Fortunately, Jimmy and I went to work, and Grace and Mia scurried out of Dodge as soon as they could and took refuge at Starbucks for the day. At lunch that day I sobbed to Ava and could barely eat. She expressed concern for my physical safety and gave me emotional support. I lost over five pounds that month.

Nikolai calmed down for about a week or two and justified his behavior as concern over Matty and stress at work. But then he became fixated on Mia. She had to go. Mia had graduated school in May 2017 and was floundering a bit on what to do next, which Nikolai found frustrating, as did I. I was working with her to figure out what she wanted to do, and she was looking for jobs. That was her status when Nikolai pulled the rug out from under her. Nikolai gave me an ultimatum. He claimed he wasn't safe in the house with just her. She might accuse him of something untoward. That excuse is eerily like the one he will make two years later with respect to my mother when he effectively kicks her out. It was Mia or him, and he had even found an apartment! If only I could go back, I would choose her. But, alas, I was still ignorant of all the facts and felt I had to choose my husband and keeping my family intact over a girl I took in. I'm broken-hearted about it to this day.

How was I to know he was living a lie? Perhaps, I should have known. He was after all an inveterate liar. Part of me suspected but didn't want to believe it. He always put on a good show when he wasn't raging. He was affectionate with all of us and readily told us how he loved us. It was confusing to try and reconcile the two sides of him. I guess he gave me enough of the positive to keep me from leaving and to keep me from believing the full truth about him. You can't judge a book by its cover I was soon to learn.

———— ◆ ————

December 27, 2017, rocked my world more than any other day. We had had a nice Christmas with no drama, no blow ups. Grace had gotten Nikolai a thoughtful gift. Since they both like to jog, she suggested they enter a race and go out to eat afterward. She included a gift card to Red Robin. It was personal and meaningful. He teared up when he opened it.

Back in 2015, when I was on the seven-week trial, I had stayed in a Marriott for the duration. I opened a membership and Nikolai subsequently used my membership, and we had a very high status as a result. We needed one more night to maintain our "platinum status." So, on this day, we booked a cheap Marriott about thirty minutes away from us with no intention of staying there. We had to check into it, however. At around 8 p.m., Nikolai was driving us to the hotel. When we were about ten minutes away, I got a notification on my phone that some unknown person had sent me a message through Facebook. I opened it up and stared in horror. This person had a friend named Bonnie who had been dating a guy, and the guy suddenly disappeared on her. The friend was suspicious that he might be married and did some digging on social media and discovered the guy was Nikolai. She messaged me to tell me about this and say that her friend never would have dated a married man. She sent me pictures of the two of them together. I stared at Bonnie with her curly blonde, obviously dyed hair and her crooked smile with Nikolai snuggled up against her with his arm around her, also smiling broadly. They were out to dinner in some pictures, what looked like a vacation in others. Nikolai continued driving while my blood ran cold. I was frozen, staring at this message as tears began to well in my eyes. What should I do? I had no idea. As bad as Nikolai's behavior had been over the years, I never expected this. In retrospect, maybe I should have, but since I never would have been unfaithful, I just assumed the same for him. Nikolai pulled up to the Marriott, and I got out to go check in while he waited in the car for me. I barely knew what I was doing, but somehow, I managed to check us in, get the room key, and get a bottle of water as a "gift." I got back in the car and said it all went smoothly. We drove back home and internally I was a mess. I opted to say nothing until I could figure out what I should do.

The next day I went for a quick visit to Olivia's house. Even though it was bitter cold, I opted to just run across the street without a coat. Just as I was leaving, my mom called. Under normal circumstances, I would have ignored her call and called her back later once I got in the warm house, but I was burdened with this nightmare and needed someone to confide in. I took my mom's call and unloaded everything while standing in the street shivering with teeth chattering. I kept saying over and over, "I don't know what to do. I don't know what to do."

She responded with very wise words: "If you don't know what to do, then you do nothing except for one thing. You must take measures to protect yourself financially."

I realized she was right on that. My $10,000 in my own account would not go very far. I thought back to September when he kept saying he needed money in his rage. What did he need money for? His paramours?

There was a lot of money in Nikolai's stock accounts. As part of his sales job, Nikolai received shares of the company stock at a discounted rate. From the outset, I encouraged him to take part in this program. I hadn't gotten into investing back in 2000 when I advised this, but I knew it was the best way to grow our money. As years went by, I became an investor. Nikolai never had any interest in it, and so he just gave me the log in information to the stock accounts. I would transfer money from our joint account into his stock accounts to invest in more stock. I enjoyed watching our money grow and developed a knack for it. By this time, Nikolai didn't even know how to access his own accounts. I was the finance person in the marriage, and I had complete control over the accounts. I had complained in the past about there being a lot of money in just his name, and his response was that I should transfer it all to me. I stupidly felt like that would show I didn't trust him, so I never did. I knew now: I needed a plan to get that money.

That night, I decided to bring Matty into my saga. For some reason, I felt he could handle it better than my other two kids, perhaps because he's not as emotionally driven. I shared the news about the affair and showed him the message and the pictures. We were both sitting on the edge of his bed, side by side. He grew quiet. I figured because the news was upsetting. After a bit, he responded in a very soft voice, "I'm not surprised."

Huh? I gave him an inquisitive, puzzled look. He then took me back to February 2015 when I had been away in Chicago for seven weeks for the trial. That was right after the January blow-up when Nikolai screamed that he wanted a divorce. I had flown home for a brief weekend in February in the hopes of catching one of Matty's basketball games. He was a junior in high school, and I knew my time was running out to enjoy his sports. Nikolai acted very remorseful about the blow-up and divorce request in January. He bought me a cheap heart necklace and told me how much he loved me. That was probably more "hoovering" on his behalf, although I didn't know it at the time. Matty told me that while I was away, when it was just Matty and Nikolai home, Matty saw Match.com notifications pop up on Nikolai's phone. Matty was not quite seventeen at the time and didn't know what to do with the information, so he kept it to himself. My eyes opened wide, and my stomach reeled. So, this was not a one-time mistake where he just happened to connect with this woman. This had been going on for almost three years, and Nikolai had set it in motion. I said to Matty, "I don't know what to do."

This nineteen-year-old didn't know either. If nothing else, this revelation steeled my resolve to protect myself financially. I told Matty not to breathe a word of this until I could figure things out. I knew I could trust him to keep quiet.

So now I had to figure out how to get that money from Nikolai's stock accounts to my name alone. After spending time searching all the settings and options on the accounts, I realized the only way was through our joint account. I had to sell the stock, transfer the proceeds from the stock trading accounts to the joint account, and transfer money from the joint account to my account. It took about three days to go from each account to the other. So, I needed about a week. I began the process and was on edge the entire time.

A few days later, I was about midway through the transfer process. I had to initiate the requests on my computer when Nikolai wasn't in eye shot. Nikolai had gone out for a run, and I was downstairs in the kitchen with Matty when Grace suddenly called for me. She sounded frantic, her voice cracking and quivering. Somehow, I immediately knew she knew. I raced upstairs and found her sitting on the hope chest in front of my bed. She simply handed me her phone and started crying hysterically. Having gotten no response from me, Bonnie's friend had messaged Grace the same message with all the pictures. I wrapped Grace in my arms and told her I already knew, and everything would be all right. I calmed her down and told her I just needed time to figure things out. I needed her to be strong and act naturally until I could take care of a few things. I worried she wouldn't be able to handle it, but she proved up to the task. At this point I decided I might as well bring Jimmy up to date. Unknown to me, he had gotten the same Facebook message from this woman but had not opened it. Upon hearing the news, he looked like he was about to retch.

Nikolai happened to leave his phone on the kitchen table when he was out running, and the kids and I went into it and looked at his pictures. There were pictures of him with Bonnie but there were also pictures of him with various other women, always with his arm around them, smiling big. These pictures, coupled with the Match.com notifications in 2015, made it a vastly different picture. Bonnie had contacted me on LinkedIn also, apologizing for dating a married man. I responded to her and asked that she remain quiet until I could get all my ducks in a row. She agreed to do so. The kids kept their cool and put on a good show, perhaps too good. Or perhaps, Bonnie alerted Nikolai. The kids decided to go skiing at our vacation home, which left just Nikolai and I at home. One day, Nikolai brought up our relationship. He indicated that he knew I knew. He could tell the kids were not right, so he assumed they knew as well. At least that's the story he gave me. He did not seem remorseful, just matter of fact. His attitude was we needed to figure out where we were going from there. I didn't say much, just agreed that we needed to do that. Inside I was thinking I needed time for these money transfers to go through.

By early January 2018 the transfers had gone through, so I was protected for the time being. I had also changed the deposit of my paycheck to my own account. Nikolai had gotten wind of everything

I did but seemed very remorseful. He literally was crying all the time, saying he didn't know why he did what he did. Regardless, I told him he had to leave, at least temporarily. In Matty's words, he had to suffer something for his actions. Nikolai looked for an apartment and even asked me to go with him to look at one, which was just a couple miles away. I went along but thought it rather odd that I should help my cheating husband find a new place to live after discovering his affairs. Nikolai said he didn't want to be far from the kids. I said I was willing to find a way forward, but Nikolai had to go for counseling. I could not live with the explosions anymore. The explosions had done so much damage to our relationship and to our family. Every time Nikolai exploded, a little bit of a protective wall went up in me and my feelings toward him hardened. I thought I could find a way forward from the affairs more easily than the explosions (not that either was easy). Once he could better manage his anger, I felt we could do some type of joint counseling. Nikolai agreed to my terms, or so it seemed.

In the end, Nikolai stayed at a Residence Inn Marriott. It helped the Marriott status and was more temporary, which better allowed for a reconciliation. He only stayed there five weeks and then went away for one week on business. He attended a total of three counseling sessions and abandoned it, later claiming the counselor told him there was nothing wrong with him.

The rest of the year was mostly uneventful with Nikolai actually being a pretty good husband. He didn't explode, he helped with dinner and the dishes, and overall, he was the best behaved of our marriage. There was only one exception: Nikolai periodically brought up the money I had transferred. He wanted it back, and he wanted us to return to jointly paying the expenses. I had continued to have my paycheck deposited into my own account, and we paid all the bills from his paycheck, which was deposited into our joint account. I had relinquished control of the stock accounts and his 401K. He viewed the money I transferred as his own money, which was ridiculous. I explained multiple times that I transferred our money into my sole control, but he refused to get it. I indicated that I was not ready to transfer any money back. In my view he had done very little to earn my trust back, and I'd be a fool to. Good move on my part as subsequent events would prove.

———— ◆ ————

February 2020

In our argument after the Super Bowl party, Nikolai screams, "I was justified in having the affairs!" It is this violation of trust that he claims is justified, and this justification claim shocks me to the core. I am not prepared for this response. Does he really think his cheating is excusable? I am stunned. So much for all the supposed remorse he had exhibited after getting caught. This is the straw that breaks the camel's back for me—for the moment anyway. The past remorse wasn't genuine. How can I stay with someone who has no respect for me?

I spend the week after the Super Bowl talking to the kids and deciding what I want. I haven't told anyone about the affairs except my mom. My mom advises me to try to hold it together for Jimmy and Grace's upcoming weddings and get through them. This has been her mantra for the last year, and I've tried to hold it together for the weddings. But I don't want to "get through" them, I want to enjoy them, and I've pretty much reached the end of my rope. How can someone say they are justified in having affairs? It's truly mind boggling. I have many conversations with the kids, and I decide he must go. I can't do this anymore. I'm too old. I need peace. I'm not looking to divorce; I just can't live like this. I will tell him when he returns.

A week later, I have the difficult conversation. I tell Nikolai he must find another place to live. I cannot go on like this. He is not surprised. In fact, he states that he expected to be served divorce papers upon his return. He agrees to look for a place. I call the kids and tell them exactly what transpired. They are completely supportive.

Three weeks later, Nikolai is still here. He's doing the model husband thing again, painting the staircase risers, which I had indicated I wanted done for Jimmy's wedding, fixing the toilet in our bathroom, and doing other odd jobs. He's quiet and meek. One day, I come home with the needlepoint I made for Emily and Jimmy, which had been recently framed, and I'm not happy with the results. The framer put on an old-fashioned wood with gold speckles frame. It's not the look I wanted. Nikolai offers to go back with me to have it changed. Since the framer is in a secluded, somewhat run-down place, I agree. After we return, Nikolai begs me to let him stay. He states that he will not see the children much if he leaves. He starts to cry. Once again, I relent. Bad habits are hard to break.

CHAPTER 6

Vacations

August 30 – September 5, 2020 (3 months earlier)

As I find out later, Nikolai's ATM withdrawals total $12,000 in August.

Nikolai has been pushing for a while for us to take a vacation, which means he wants me to plan something. Since COVID lockdowns are still all around, I am happy to get away somewhere that is more open. I suggest Acadia National Park with a plan to stop at Newport, Rhode Island, on the way back. In retrospect, I can't figure out why Nikolai wanted this vacation. Matty says the only logical conclusion is that I'm just a tool for Nikolai to get what he wants. He doesn't care about going with me in particular. He wants to go and the only real way to do so at this point is with me. The vacation is okay. The park boasts Cadillac Mountain, the highest point on the eastern seaboard; Thunder Hole, where the coastal rocks and waves meet to create the sound of thunder; Sand Beach; and 120 miles of hiking trails. After a few days, I feel like I did most of the 120 miles, moderate and strenuous ones. One trail called Beehive makes me tense the entire time with steep cliffs to climb with precipitous drops from which to fall. Other than the hiking, there isn't much else. We go to Bar Harbor for meals, but I don't find the food that spectacular. Everyone is mask crazy. They wear masks while hiking alone in the woods where there are very few people. Nikolai seems to enjoy himself. He likes the challenging hikes. I'm leery on some of them. During each hike, I can't help but think that he could easily push me over and say I slipped. Am I crazy to feel this way? I just don't trust him anymore. I don't really believe he will do it, but I'm not completely certain. It's an uncomfortable feeling. At one point, in the middle of the woods, he gets amorous. I'm open to something with him to move our relationship in a positive direction, but I'm too old to consider anything in the middle of the woods. Also, while I'm open to it, I'm not necessarily dying for it either. To be completely transparent, I haven't been interested in it in a very long time, and we haven't been together in years. Perhaps, that's my failing. Nikolai seems disappointed. I don't know if that ruins the vacation for him, but I don't really care. There are countless vacations that he ruined over the years.

———— ◆ ————

One of our earliest vacations was a trip to Niagara Falls in 2001. The kids were three and six and very excited to embark on this adventure. We drove six hours and stayed in a budget hotel near the falls on the American side. At the kids' ages, staying in any hotel was exciting. We viewed all three falls and were partial to the Horseshoe falls on the Canadian side, although all the falls were magnificent. The force of the falls truly is spectacular, the sound deafening. We went on the boat tours, got soaked, and took lots of pictures. One day we decided it would be fun to play miniature golf, and we found a place nearby. As we were putting at each hole, Jimmy grew increasingly whiny. He may have just been hungry but was still too young to articulate it. He started complaining and getting into arguments with his siblings— nothing too significant, just an annoyance. But not to Nikolai. After one brief spat among the kids, Nikolai went over and walloped Jimmy right across the face. Naturally, he started to cry, and Grace and Matty were flabbergasted. I was angry. I have never hit my children. I made my position clear to Nikolai, and overall, our children were very well behaved. They just weren't perfect. In my view there was absolutely no justification (and never would be) for Nikolai to smack Jimmy like he did. I hugged Jimmy, glared at Nikolai, and said, "What's wrong with you?" We went home soon thereafter, but what would have been a happy memory was now tarnished. But it would not be the first.

In 2002, we decided to take the kids on a little trip to Washington DC. The twins had been learning about the government in school, and I thought it would help them to experience the three branches and visit the monuments and museums. We stayed with my brother Ben, who lived nearby, and we walked miles every day touring the city. We went up to the top of the Washington Monument and visited the Lincoln and Jefferson Memorials, the White House, the Capitol, and many of the Smithsonian museums. Not surprisingly, the Air and Space Museum was the favorite. The kids dipped their toes in the water at the World War II Memorial, and we were overwhelmed by the breadth of the Vietnam Memorial. On our last day, we traipsed through Arlington National Cemetery, visiting Kennedy's gravesite and listening to "Taps" played by the buglers. Overall, we had a great time—with one significant exception.

One day we parked the car in a parking garage and prepaid our fee. It was the end of a long day touring the monuments, and we were tired and wanted to get back to my brother's house. We dragged ourselves and the kids—half carrying some of them—to the car, got in, and wound around and around the parking garage to where the booth and gate were. We tried to leave but the gate wouldn't go up. The attendant demanded payment. Nikolai explained that we had prepaid, but the attendant refused to raise the gate, saying he had no record of us paying. I thought this was ridiculous. We definitely paid, and I was really annoyed. But what could we do? I figured we would just have to fork over more money so we could get out of there. Nikolai, however, had other ideas. He started screaming every obscenity in the book, pressed down hard on the accelerator, and drove the car straight through the gate. The gate smashed into pieces. I was wide-eyed in shock. I related it later to my brother Ben, and he thought it was funny. Maybe in isolation and after the fact I might see it as funny but not when this was how I regularly lived. I was worried too. Would they call the police? Would Nikolai get arrested for destroying the gate? For the next few miles, I kept peeking behind us to see if a police car was following us, and for weeks, I expected a summons or warrant for his arrest in the mail. Nikolai felt completely justified in his actions. We managed to get by without any ramifications.

In the summer of 2004 when the twins were nine and Matty six, we took a trip to Williamsburg, Virginia, another semi-educational vacation. I guess I was one of those crazy parents who wanted to raise brainiacs. They had their own ideas about what fun on a vacation should be, however. The kids enjoyed learning how to make bricks by stomping in the mud but hated the displays with plaques that described every historical detail. I planned the last day to be at Busch Gardens, ending the trip on a purely fun day with amusement rides and fun food, which would leave us with a happy memory. We lined up at the gate to purchase our tickets, the kids in constant motion with anticipation of the fun that awaited us. We could hear the whir of the rides in front of us and smell cotton candy and popcorn. We paid our entry fee and found our first ride. Escape from Pompeii was a water ride that went through what appeared to be an active volcano with sparks, fire, and heat all around. After going through the volcano, the boat went into a dark area and then down a steep slide. We all thought it was fun, but the boys were a little overwhelmed by it. We then went to our next ride. It was a mild, roller coaster-like ride. Grace, pure daredevil, and big risk taker, immediately charged toward this ride. The boys dawdled, cautious and reluctant. We lined up and started winding our way through the queue. As we got closer to the ride entrance, the boys started grabbing my arm and quietly begging me not to go.

"It's not that bad," I said. "Give it a try. Be brave."

They grew increasingly agitated, however, and since I didn't see any reason to force a child to go on a scary ride, particularly when I've never been a roller coaster fan myself, I agreed that we could skip this ride. I figured Nikolai could go with Grace, and the boys and I would sit it out. I didn't care one way or another if I went on a ride. This was supposed to be fun for everyone. Nikolai really wanted to go on this ride, and before I even had a chance to suggest that he and Grace go, his jaw stiffened, and his hands balled. He screamed, "All you do is coddle them. I'm sick of this bulls**t!"

Before I could respond, he stormed off without us. He left me in the middle of an amusement park in Virginia hundreds of miles from home with three small children. This was in pre-cell-phone days. Once again, I was stupefied. I stood there frozen in line for a few seconds, then shook myself to get it together for the kids' sake and took them over to a bench where we could sit and I could think of what to do. I sat staring into nothing. Would Nikolai come back, or did I need to find an alternate means to get home? I didn't know the answer to that. I reassured the kids that I'd figure something out, but clearly, they were worried. After about thirty minutes, I was about to contact a security person to explain my problem when Nikolai returned. The day was now ruined, and Nikolai insisted that we leave for home at that instant. We paid for an amusement park and only went on a single ride. Nikolai was miserable the entire trip home.

In August 2008, I asked my brother Ben if we could stay for a week at his condo in Ocean City, Maryland, right near the ocean. He agreed. He never said, but presumably he lost out on the rental income for that week since he usually rented it out. We took the several hour drive there, and just as we were arriving Nikolai informed me that he had a headache. This had been an ongoing thing for years. He claimed to suffer from migraines but never actively sought out medical help. His headache became an excuse for his bad behavior. Anytime, he lashed out or erupted, he claimed it was because he had a headache.

I figured this headache would improve over time, so it shouldn't be a big deal. Usually after a few hours of sleep, he felt better. He could just deal with it until he did.

I wasn't even sure if some of his headaches were real or as bad as he claimed. Rather, I suspected he used it as an excuse to not do what was expected of him. He was very unreliable in that way. I would plan outings and never know if he would back out at the last minute, and he often did. After many years, I learned to only plan something if I was willing to go alone. Having a headache wasn't his only excuse. I always claimed that I would have been a better cook but for Nikolai (that's only partially true). I would cook a meal, and he would arrive home from work and say he wasn't hungry. He wouldn't eat but would make himself a sandwich later. Or worse, he would say he wasn't in the mood for what I cooked, even if it was a meal he liked. My only real motivation for cooking was to put a nutritious meal on the table for my kids.

The condo was perfect for us: three bedrooms, two baths, and two blocks from the ocean. The weather was perfect too: bright, sunny, and warm. Upon arrival, Nikolai went to bed, and the kids and I explored the beach. We dipped our toes in the water and collected some shells. This was going to be a fun week. Nikolai had other ideas. The next morning, Nikolai demanded we go home because of his headache. I was incredulous. A free week at the beach going up in smoke because of him. We had some friends there with whom we were going to meet up, and I had to contact them to tell them we needed to go home. I called the husband who said, "Can't he just suck it up? You've got to be kidding!"

But no. I never kidded about this stuff, and Nikolai would never "suck it up." The vacation was ruined, and we had to return home. Of course, the following day, Nikolai was fine. He felt completely justified in ruining our vacation and never expressed any remorse for it. I embarrassingly disclosed to my brother we had to cut the vacation short because Nikolai was not feeling well.

Should I have stood up to him more than I did over these things? I don't know. Had I done so, it likely would have accelerated our separation. I was concerned about antagonizing him further, of poking the bear. I didn't know if the behavior would then become more violent. Over time, it did become more violent without my changing anything.

CHAPTER 7

Finances

June 2020 (6 months earlier)

As I find out later, Nikolai withdraws $17,000 in cash this month.

Fixated on retiring as soon as possible, I attend a retirement workshop. After thirty-three years at the same job, I can't wait for retirement. I'm looking forward to doing something different or nothing at all. The workshop offers a free consultation with a financial advisor, and the advisor recommends that a spouse attend to get a complete picture. I stupidly convince Nikolai to do so. The financial advisor asks for basic financial records, which I provide, and I ask Nikolai to do so as well. Nikolai acts very strangely about providing his 401K statement and other data. He only agrees to provide a screenshot of the total dollar amount in his 401K account. He refuses to provide any other information, including his stock accounts and, of course, his unknown bank accounts. I am suspicious, but I haven't had any input on his 401K or what's left in his stock accounts for quite some time. We meet with the advisor with the limited information Nikolai provides, and the financial advisor presents us with an analysis of our financial position. It looks wonderful. All these years of being frugal and squirreling away our money will pay off. The advisor informs us that if we continue at our present standard of living, we will have accumulated a significant amount of assets. Therefore, we should consider gifts to our children over the years to avoid a lot of estate taxes. Who would have thought? It feels so great to hear this. Retirement is just around the corner and will be a blast—or not. I don't know what will happen in two short months, and I don't know that Nikolai is clandestinely taking money and stashing it somewhere, but I do know we've had financial disputes in the recent past.

———◆———

By the end of 2018, Nikolai could no longer tolerate that I still had control over the funds from the stock account. We would take long walks together in the neighborhood, which would start out nicely until he brought up the money. He did this multiple times throughout the year, asking me to transfer it back, and I had responded that I was not ready to do so. He indicated that the past year was the hardest in his life. I found that puzzling because for me it was one of the better years since he behaved like a decent husband, but he had not done enough to earn back my trust. In our conversations, he seemed exasperated that he could not get his way. In my view, if he had no intention of going anywhere, it shouldn't matter who had control over the money. If he intended to take up with another woman, then he would want the money for that, and I'd be a fool to transfer it. I was not willing to take the chance. I stayed firm that I would not change anything financially at this junction.

In January 2019, I was at my friend Bella's house for a church meeting with a group of six ladies. Suddenly I heard the ping, ping, ping of my phone, indicating multiple text messages coming in. At first, I ignored them, but then I pulled out my phone to see they were coming from the bank where we had our joint account. I immediately knew what was going on. Nikolai was trying to take control of the joint account. He actually thought he could pull a fast one on me, but I knew exactly what he was doing. He was trying to change the password and needed the double authentication from my phone to do so. I thought about it for a brief second and concluded that since I had taken control of a large part of the money from the stock accounts, I would let him take the joint account. This was probably a stupid move on my part, but I was trying to balance protecting myself and not agitating Nikolai. One of my failings was I was not a confrontational person, particularly when it came to Nikolai. I knew if I hadn't let him have the account, I would be facing a very angry bear when I returned home. So, I authenticated it, and within minutes, he completely wiped out the account. Since it was a joint account and I authenticated it, he had no problem taking it over. He also changed his paycheck deposits to his own account. I didn't know it yet, but he had multiple bank accounts, and he spread out his paycheck and his work expense reimbursement check between the different accounts.

There were a lot of joint expenses to pay, and by March, I quickly realized that we couldn't continue this way. Either we were going our separate ways, or we had to make a change. I proposed that he keep what he took from the joint account, and I argued that the money he took plus his IRAs made us fairly equal in terms of the amount each of us controlled. I suggested that we both go back to putting our paychecks in the joint account and leave everything else as is. Nikolai agreed but took more than a month to finally put his paycheck back into the joint account. Unknown to me, he never put his expense reimbursement checks back into the joint account. So, we were jointly paying for his business expenses while he got them reimbursed into his own account.

Later, that summer, I suggested we give Jimmy money for his and Emily's upcoming wedding. He adamantly refused. He said if you want to give them money, do it from your own account. So, I did. I wrote out a check and pretended it was from both of us. Nikolai reaped the benefit of that as Jimmy had no idea until much later.

On October 18, 2019, Nikolai and I drove to our vacation home to take the boats off the dock and put them away. It was late Friday afternoon when we left, the sun was low in the sky, and the leaves were in full fall color. The plan was to return late Saturday or early Sunday because Jimmy had asked us to go to his home inspection, which he had scheduled for 2 p.m. on Sunday. He and Emily had been searching for a home and found one they liked, which was only around thirty-five minutes from me. They hoped to have everything settled and move-in ready by the time they married the following July. Since Nikolai is so handy, they wanted him to accompany them to the inspection and perhaps see things that the engineer missed.

We were around thirty minutes into our two-hour drive when Nikolai received a call to tell him he could have the football tickets he wanted. It was a Sunday afternoon Giants game. He excitedly told me about the tickets in the car. This was the first time I was hearing about the game, and so I reminded him that we promised to go with Jimmy for his home inspection. He dismissed me, clearly feeling that the football tickets should take priority. He called Jimmy and asked him if he wanted to go to the game. Jimmy, rather annoyed, said no. His home inspection was more important. In an effort to placate Nikolai, I asked Jimmy if it were possible to change the inspection date. Jimmy did not want to do so. Nikolai hung up and erupted, yelling, "I'm sick of this f**king s**t! I never get to do what I want. No one needs me. No one includes me. I'm going to just leave and get my own place and live a happy life."

He abruptly turned the car around and said we were going home. I texted Jimmy to tell him what was going on. I was annoyed because the association for the house required that we remove the boats by the end of the month. Jimmy texted to ask if it would help if he called Nikolai back and apologized. I said it couldn't hurt, so Jimmy did so. It placated Nikolai enough that he returned to driving to the vacation home, but he was miserable. He simply hurled the kayak and canoe into the car and then tossed them into the shed. He drove like a maniac. Then we went out to dinner. The vacation home is in a secluded area, and the restaurant was not close. As we drove down these dark, winding, secluded, country roads, I couldn't help but think that he could do me in and easily dump my body there. I just didn't know anymore what he would do, how far he would go. It was awful to feel that way. He flipped between being okay and being miserable. He stupidly had his work colleague, a high-level manager, give him the tickets and he couldn't find anyone to take them. We returned to the house after dinner, and he lay on the couch and sulked.

Jimmy felt terrible, as though he were responsible for the misery I had to endure, and he texted me asking whether I thought going to the game was a good idea. I responded as follows: "I had no interest in going under the circumstances. We said we were doing the inspection. Case closed in my book. I asked about moving the inspection to try and make him happy. I couldn't care less."

Jimmy responded that he wouldn't have wanted to go even it had been his own team playing. Since it was a team that he didn't even care about, he saw no point. I related to him the details of Nikolai's rant. Jimmy texted: "Wow that's so annoying over stupid football tickets. I really can't understand why he would think I'd want to go. I'm getting an inspection on my future house and I'm not even a fan! He's so dramatic. Yeah, no one loves him because I don't want to go to the game. Give me a break! Sorry you have to deal with all this by yourself."

I convinced Nikolai to give his colleague the tickets back, a simple solution. His colleague was completely fine about it. The next morning, Nikolai woke up happy again. I was happy that Nikolai was no longer in a snit, but this erratic behavior was getting tiresome.

November 2019 brought some happy news. Grace and Patrick got engaged! Patrick's parents came over, and we did a repeat of Jimmy and Emily's engagement celebration. We gathered in the living room and gave them gifts and went out to dinner afterward. While it should have been on Patrick's turf, he was gracious enough to do it by us so my mom could join in the festivities. We had a fun night at the restaurant. All of us were there. Patrick was assigned the task of popping the champagne but couldn't get the bottle open. Poor Patrick. Of course, the kids recorded his every move in his failed attempts.

December brought more erratic behavior from Nikolai. In the early part of the month, he acted remorseful, apologizing. His apologies, however, were always laden with excuses and blame. He stated that I didn't seem happy. I responded that I was content, but he told me every other month I wasn't good enough. Nikolai said no one forgave him for what he did, and he was alone all the time. It was getting wearisome.

I shared this all with Jimmy and said that Nikolai was fine now. But in January something else would bother him. Jimmy said, "He's alone all the time by choice. He isolates himself in the office, and when he's downstairs he sits in the dark watching Fox News. No one is going to join him in the pitch-dark family room with the news on."

I suggested that one might think he'd try to spend the rest of his life making up for what he did, but he was too self-centered for that. I was overly optimistic, thinking he'd be fine until January. On December 29, 2019, Nikolai started screaming about money. He wanted the money I transferred to be transferred back to him in a week. He stated I do nothing to improve the relationship.

———— ◆ ————

September 2020 (3 months earlier)

As I find out later, Nikolai's ATM cash withdrawals total $7,000 this month. This will be the last month of the large withdrawals because once Nikolai sets things in motion, there is no reason to continue withdrawing the cash. The withdrawals drop off precipitously. For the next eight months, his ATM withdrawals range from a low of $300 per month to a high of $1,600.

On September 4, 2020, we are driving from Maine to Newport, Rhode Island. It is the last two days of our vacation. Nikolai is driving, and out of the blue, he decides to pick a fight about money once again. From my perspective, the trip has been reasonably pleasant until this moment. I can't say I had a great time, but it had enjoyable moments.

It's the same old mantra: "Why won't you transfer back the money?"

"If you plan on this as a forever arrangement," I say, "why do you care where the money is?"

He replies, "Because it's my money."

I explain once again that I have taken control over *our* money, a fact he doesn't want to accept. Until he's given me a reason to place complete trust in him, I won't transfer the money. He gets more and more heated and says, "You're the reason for my unhappiness. You do nothing to improve this relationship."

Now, I'm holding tightly to the door handle, getting more and more nervous with him driving, worried about what he might do. He then says his proverbial, "I was justified in having the affairs!"

I shouldn't be shocked at this point since I've heard this several times now, but I still am. I can't believe someone would believe, let alone say, this. I clam up for the rest of the drive. This day and the next are now soured for me. I just "get through" the remainder of the vacation. He also casually mentions that his sister-in-law has recently served his brother Boris with divorce papers. I'm curious as to why he brings this up now. He uses the unexpectedness of his brother's problems as an excuse for why he picked a fight, i.e., he was so upset about his brother, he was justified in his anger toward me.

The next day we drive home from Newport. I'm driving the last leg as we enter New York City. Nikolai suggests he take over because he is better at driving in New York City. I agree, but then he misses the turn and delays us thirty minutes. I just want to go home. I can't wait to get away from him and out of a car where he is in control, so the extra time is hell. Why did I agree to let him drive?

Nikolai informs me that his brother Boris is arriving from California in a few hours and will be staying over that night. I groan inside. Just what I need, another freeloader from his family and when things are less than ideal. We arrive home and immediately go our separate ways in the house. I wait up for Matty to come home so we can talk. He had just started dating Sarah, and I want to hear all about it plus share my stuff. He is very happy with Sarah and is planning to see her again. I am thrilled for him. I express to Matty that I was uncomfortable on the hikes with Nikolai, that I thought he might do harm to me, maybe push me over one of the cliffs. Matty is at a loss for words, staring at me for a few seconds. Then he suggests I talk to someone. He says he is happy to listen, but he doesn't have the training. He is concerned about my mental state. I realize I sound a bit crazy, but as things would later bear out, it was not my mental state that was the concern.

PART 2

---◆---

The Discard

CHAPTER 8

The Break-up

Early September 2020 (3 months earlier)

The day after we returned from Maine, we all have dinner together. Summer is coming to an end, but the weather is still warm. All the kids come. The only one missing is Sarah because it's too new for Matty to spring the entire family on her. Nikolai grills the chicken. We eat in the kitchen after playing Cornhole. Later, we decide to have a fire in the fire pit. Sarah joins us for the fire. This is the first time we really get to know Sarah. With everything going on, I decide to let loose and drink. Fortunately, Sarah has a great sense of humor. I drink too much wine and later find myself standing on the kitchen island trying to kill bugs on the ceiling. The night is a well-needed release. Nikolai's brother Boris comes back from wherever he was and whatever he was doing and sits with us around the fire.

It is strange having Nikolai's brother with us. He keeps coming in to talk to me while I'm working in the dining room. Once Jimmy moved out, I set up shop there since COVID is still ongoing. I don't have a designated office like Nikolai, and I have been home exclusively for work for six months now. Nikolai's brother seems to feel the need to justify the split with his wife. From what I can see, it's the straw that broke the camel's back, not the cause. Nikolai's brother is not unlike him, with unpredictable outbursts of anger. I guess his wife had enough too. In an effort to convince me how ridiculous his wife is, he tells me that when he couldn't get into the DMV in California because he needed an appointment, he screamed at the guard, "Get out of my way, you f**king Mexican." Another day, he and his wife were going to Home Depot, and a guy in a van was going slowly and delaying his entrance to park his car. That horrible sin caused him to say, "This f***ing n***er needs to move faster." He chuckles while he says it, indicating how absurd his wife is for using this against him. Somehow, Nikolai's brother thinks these revelations will convince me to take his side. I roll my eyes when he leaves.

Regarding Nikolai's behavior, I text Grace: "In his mind everything is hunky dory until a few months pass and he flips again. But that's been my life for twenty-eight years. Whatever." Little do I know, that is coming to an end.

There seems to be no end in sight to Nikolai's brother's stay with us. He attempts to get his old job back without success, which means he will likely mooch off us for the foreseeable future. Just like old times. When Nikolai and I bought our first house, I discovered that Nikolai owed Ford Motor Company $5,000 for a repossessed truck that he had guaranteed for Boris. We could not get a mortgage until Nikolai paid Ford. Years later, Boris decided to fix up their house in Russia and suddenly, Nikolai had to "donate" $8,000 to the cause. It's the way his entire family operates. When we were first married, his brother Igor asked Nikolai if he could co-sign his mortgage with him. I adamantly said no, and Nikolai acceded to my demands. Five years later, Igor had his house foreclosed. I shudder to think how that would have ended had Nikolai agreed to co-sign. Hopefully, the current mooching will only be room and board.

I had scheduled the following week as a working vacation at our rental house with Nikolai. It is clear that Nikolai has no intention of going to the vacation house. I have already put in for the time off at work, and there have been complaints from renters so there are some things that need immediate attention. I decide I must go regardless of Nikolai. Matty graciously agrees to accompany me. We stay there from Sunday through Thursday. I use the days away at the vacation home to think and discuss things with Matty, Jimmy, and Grace. I've decided to take Matty's earlier advice and talk to someone. I can't continue the way it is with Nikolai. I just don't know what to do.

As we arrive back home, Nikolai and his brother are coming out of the front door. His brother has his suitcase with him. Nikolai is taking him to the airport to return to California. Good riddance.

September 18, 2020

It is Friday, and with butterflies in my stomach, I resolve to reach out to my pastor. I've known him for over ten years now. He's a jovial man who, even when under stress, manages to laugh. He adores Grace. They both went to the same college, Villanova University. He wrote a letter of recommendation for her. I belong to a church group, but it does not involve the pastor, so I generally have little contact with him other than Sunday Mass and the occasional brief conversation afterward. At 7:40 a.m., I email him and express that I am at a crossroads, in a difficult situation, and need his advice. I assure him that I have no known exposure to COVID in hopes that he will agree to meet with me. He responds immediately and suggests we meet at 10 a.m. that day. I am stunned that he accommodates me so quickly, especially during the pandemic. The butterflies start doing somersaults. I have no idea what he will say. I am Catholic and divorce is not generally the prescribed course. I figure he will likely recommend a marriage counselor, and I'm open to that. I'm open to any suggestion.

I was raised Catholic, but it was during that crazy time in the Church: post Vatican II with all the experimentation. I was not properly catechized as a kid. My parents were bewildered by all the changes in the Church and didn't know what to do. Some parents stuck to the traditions; others did nothing. My parents were the latter. My mom insisted that I join the youth group when I was in high school. I grudgingly complied. It turned out to be a positive experience as I made a lot of good friends, and although they were caught up in the experimentation, I did grow closer to my faith. I'm grateful that my parents planted the seed of faith in me. As an adult, I found my way home to the Church and taught myself. My faith has gotten me through the thirty years with Nikolai and particularly the year from hell, which is soon to begin.

I park in the small parking lot outside the rectory, slowly force each foot to climb the stairs—getting more nauseous with each step—and gingerly ring the bell. A kind lady lets me in and ushers me to my pastor's office. My pastor gets up from behind a beautiful wood desk and gestures with his hand for me to sit in the chair across from him. He has exquisite taste, and the light oak floor practically glistens. I ask if I can take my mask off, and he nods. I begin by thanking him for seeing me during these trying times and so quickly. He responds that since I never ask for anything and I'm the type who just figures things out on my own, he knew I needed him. I tell him everything, the good the bad and the ugly—my past, the money transfers, Nikolai's affairs, Nikolai's comments about being justified in them, the breach of trust in other areas—everything. I want him to see it in as unbiased a light as I can give. I want him to see me warts and all. He incredulously asks if I went through COVID like this. I nod. He states that I must be a really strong person to have withstood this all this time. He asks, "What do you think God wants you to do?"

I'm thinking, *If I knew, I wouldn't be here,* but simply state that I have no idea. After asking a few questions, he says, "I think you know what you need to do."

I really don't. I need him to tell me. He finally says, "You are in an abusive relationship. I think you need to take a break from it, clear your head, be independent for a while, and then you will know better what to do."

What? I'm in an abusive relationship? How can that be? I'm a highly educated, intelligent person. I'm not like those stories you see on TV. Nikolai clearly has anger issues but abusive? My mind starts to spin. He recommends I tell Nikolai to leave for a period of at least three months. Despite being in the height of COVID, he hugs me. I am forever grateful for that hug. I need it.

I share everything with the kids. They agree with his advice. There's no hope for repair. So, now I am ready. The decision is made. I just need the right opportunity to convey it to Nikolai. No "backsies" this time. I'm so nauseous. Little do I know what is still in store for me.

The kids have been planning a get-together for dinner that night. Sarah will join us so there will be eight of us. We go on with the plans as is my want. Matty cooks. He has been getting into cooking, looking for ways to eat healthy. At around 7:30 p.m., Nikolai goes into another room to have a private conversation on his phone. How mysterious. A new woman? After dinner, we all play Cranium. Grace falls on her sword and agrees to partner with Nikolai. He's the last person I want to be matched up with. It is the last time all eight of us are together. The kids jokingly refer to it as the Last Supper.

September 19, 2020

It's Saturday morning, and Nikolai informs me that he will be gone for the day to visit his family. I am skeptical about the family part but glad to be rid of him. Matty goes to spend the day studying with Sarah, which leaves me alone to my own devices. My mind turns to the meeting with the financial advisor we had in June and the papers he had drafted for us for retirement. Nikolai had taken them from me and never gave them back, so now I want them, particularly since I am about to drop a bomb on him about moving out (or so I think). I decide to look for the papers in his office. Nikolai is a pack rat and a messy one at that, so finding these papers may be quite challenging. I open the door and a sock ball lands at my feet. I ignore it. Nikolai has not yet started regularly locking the office.

Upon entering the office, the first sight is baseball caps hung on nails all around the walls where the wall meets the ceiling. They have been up there for years, and I doubt Nikolai ever dusts them. I long ago refused to clean in here as there is too much clutter. The room is the smallest of the bedrooms with barely space for a twin bed and a dresser. With Nikolai's oversized computer desk and the twin bed, it is already cramped. He had bought one of those put-together computer desks long ago. It was the biggest one they made with a top piece the length of the desk that has shelves and cubbies. Nikolai manages to add two bookcases and an old living room end table into the overcrowded room. There is little room to walk. Nikolai has papers everywhere. Every crevice of every bookcase, closet and the cubbies of the desk are crammed with paper. A lit match in here would be a dangerous thing. I start to scour the office, wondering where he might have put the retirement folder. I come across the 2018 tax returns in the folder I had put them in. That is odd as I am the keeper of the tax returns. I have them all in a filing cabinet next to my desk in our bedroom. Or so I thought. Why would he have these returns? He knows nothing of taxes. Why wouldn't he have asked me for them? With a nagging feeling in my head and still not having found my retirement papers, I decide to look through the papers crammed in the cubbies on the desk. I see lots of work-related papers and some bank statements, which I glance through, not thinking much about them. The desk is stuffed with papers. I still haven't found the retirement folder when I come upon a strange paper. It is entitled "Confidential Information Litigation Sheet." It lists Nikolai as the plaintiff and me as the defendant. Nikolai signed it on September 9, 2020, ten days ago. What the heck is this? Is he suing me for something? Then I find another odd paper entitled, "Certification of Insurance Coverage." I examine it closely and light bulbs begin to go off. It says on top, Superior Court, Chancery Division, Family Part. The "Family Part" clues me in that this must be some kind of divorce paper. It is signed by Nikolai on September 10, 2020, nine days ago, right after we returned from our Maine vacation. My stomach starts to churn while I stare at this document. He is suing me for divorce? He has a lawyer? I'm a lawyer. Wait, I need a lawyer. When did he plan to tell me? I'm behind the eight ball now. I need a lawyer. Will he move out? Who will get the house? I need a lawyer. What will happen financially? I need to tell the kids. I need a lawyer!

I take a picture of both papers with my phone and carefully put them back precisely in the cubby where I found them. I walk downstairs in a trance. I text the pictures to the kids.

Matty responds, "What is this?"

"Some kind of divorce paper, I think."

"I'll be right home." Three weeks into his relationship with Sarah, he packs up his books and abruptly leaves the coffee shop with barely an explanation. I sit at the kitchen table staring at nothing. I'm shattered. My family is now broken. I will be alone for the rest of my life. What a loser I am. I can't even hold onto an abuser like Nikolai. Matty arrives and halts my spiraling into the chasm of despair.

"You need a plan, Mom. You need to strategize your next move. You need a lawyer. Do you want to stay in the house?"

"I – I think so. My friends are all here. Grandma will be back at Assisted Living after COVID is over. I have great neighbors."

"Okay, then. You need to slyly find out his intentions with respect to the house."

We decide that I will have the conversation with Nikolai the next morning and ask him to move out. I will not reveal that I know anything and see what I can find out from Nikolai, especially about the house. Matty thinks it is to my advantage to keep things friendly, that I will have the upper hand that way. I'm not sure I can do that for an extended time but agree to try. The friendliness will last a nanosecond. I begin searching the internet for a lawyer. I surely won't sleep tonight!

September 20, 2020

Nikolai deactivates his Facebook account again. This has been an ongoing thing over the past five years, one that was a red flag for Olivia.

I was too naive to appreciate the significance. The first time he deactivated and reactivated it, all my Facebook friends got a notification that I got married. People started congratulating me. The next time he deactivated it, I deleted the relationship status so the marriage notification wouldn't happen again. I just attributed all this behavior to his weirdness. Subsequently, he changed his name on Facebook to his Russian name with English letters. He was born in Russia and Americanized his name when he became a citizen at age eighteen. I assumed he was just getting back to his roots. Then he changed his name to his Russian name with Russian letters. A little more bizarre, but I still didn't think much of it. In retrospect, I guess he was trying to hide his identity from other women so he wouldn't get caught like in 2017. But the Facebook account is minor compared to what I learn on this day.

I see Nikolai in the morning. I am sitting at the kitchen island drinking my morning tea. Nikolai is seated at the kitchen table in his usual chair by the sliding glass door, drinking coffee. I execute the plan as discussed with Matty. Feeling like I am on pins and needles, I broach the subject with Nikolai: "I've given this a lot of thought, and I feel this isn't working anymore. So, I would like you to leave and find another place to live."

He looks at me calmly and says, "I've been meaning to talk to you for a while now. I went to a lawyer and filed for divorce. My lawyer said I do not have to leave and so I am not going anywhere."

I am aware that the law allows him to stay but had hoped he'd do the honorable thing. I've never been adept at pretending, so I don't attempt to feign shock but rather, I study the tea in my mug, saying nothing.

Nikolai says, "My lawyer said since it will be uncontested, it should be finalized in six to eight weeks."

I'm thinking, *Boy, did he give you a snow job.* Under normal circumstances, I would have burst out laughing, but I am far too distressed to fully appreciate the absurdity of the statement. He adds, "I still love you, Maria, and I will always love you, but I just can't continue this way." I start to gag on my tea but remain silent. He says, "I feel if I can get away from you, I will have a better relationship with the kids."

I have no response for that. In the meantime, Matty comes downstairs. He had been listening, waiting for the right time. Nikolai tells him the news. Matty shows little reaction but asks him about the house. Nikolai says, "That is just a material thing; we don't need to be concerned about it."

"It's the home I grew up in," Matty says, "so I have concerns about it." Matty is only trying to get information out of Nikolai. Nikolai indicates that he is not really interested in the house.

Nikolai states that he is going to spend the day with his family again. Out of the blue, he's spending a lot of time with his family (or so he wants us to believe). Matty and I leave like we're going to church as we usually do but go to Perkins instead. I'm too much of an emotional wreck to sit through Mass. We hang out there for a couple hours eating breakfast and consulting with Jimmy and Grace. Our plan is to return after we know Nikolai has left and raid the office and see what else is there. Little do we know what a treasure trove there will be.

Matty and I return to the house, and Nikolai has left for the day. How long will he be gone? When will he return? With anxiety about a sudden return, we enter the office. As we open the door, the sock ball appears again. I mention to Matty that the same thing happened yesterday. He immediately surmises that Nikolai is putting it on the handle of the door so he will know if anyone has entered the office. Sneaky. For some reason, he has not locked the door. Perhaps, he wants to see if I go into the office. We go piece by piece, very carefully and methodically so we can abandon ship at any time should Nikolai return. First, we go through the enormous desk. I see the various bank statements and figure I should start to take pictures of anything that potentially could be helpful later in the divorce proceeding. I notice that the 2018 tax return has been moved from the bookshelf to the closet. I'm not sure, why but I take pictures of that as well. There doesn't seem to be too much of note so far. I open the desk drawer and find my work bus tickets in there. With clipped words I rant to Matty about the nerve of Nikolai. I had kept the bus tickets in a small interior drawer of my desk downstairs in the living room. My employment provides me with a monthly allotment to purchase tickets on public transportation to discourage using personal cars for commuting. I use that allotment to purchase bus tickets to get to and from the office. Naturally, I haven't used them in quite some time since we've been shut down since April because of COVID, but what is he doing with my work bus tickets? Obviously, he has gone through my desk.

We find some receipts in the drawer that I take pictures of. Dinner for two in a place about an hour away. Lunch in the city. Ah, that might explain the theft of my bus tickets. He goes on dates in the city on my dime. That one seems particularly strange since COVID is still rampart. The dinner for two is $200. How nice for her. We find three ATM slips showing withdrawals of $2,500 each. Two are from early May, and one is recent. I surmise that the recent one may be to pay for his lawyer, but why the two in May? What would he need that much cash for? Later our Discover bill shows that he did not pay for the lawyer with cash. I can't fathom what he needs cash for other than dates with women. I take pictures of the slips figuring I can argue $7,500 should be partly mine. I find out later that the $7,500 is really $126,000 of cash that he was squirreling away. I take lots of pictures and feel the stuff is helpful but then we move to the closet.

The closet is where the treasure lies. I find bank statements from multiple banks accounts I didn't know he had. I take pictures. He has backpacks hanging in the closet. At first, we ignore them, then we decide to look inside. We find journal books inside the pockets of each backpack. Obviously, he felt the need to hide them. As I start to go through them, I wonder why he didn't keep this information in his car. I guess he was so cocky he never thought I'd go looking plus he didn't want to risk it in his car. On one page he has an account number with some Russian words next to it. I think at the time it's a foreign bank account. Later, I Google the routing number and discover it's Chase Bank. What is the significance of the Russian word? I ask Grace who has a little flare for the language. She responds it means "secret." Ah, so it's a secret bank account. I discover other accounts as well, sometimes account numbers, sometimes just usernames and passwords. I take pictures of everything. I have information on a total of nine possible accounts. Then, much to my horror, I discover he has written down the log-in information for my mother's bank account. My mother at this time is ninety-six years old and was in Assisted Living until I pulled her out because of COVID. She is now staying with my brother. Just prior to the COVID outbreak, my brothers and I had determined my mom no longer had the wherewithal to take care of her finances. Ever the fighter, she had lived independently until age ninety-five. My brothers and I decided I should convert her account to a joint account with me so I could pay her bills for her. I managed to drag my elderly mom, with her walker, to the bank two months before COVID hit to change the account. This is the account that Nikolai has written down. He has the user ID and the password noted in his journal. He knows well this is my mom's account. I had informed him of everything at the time when I was making the change to the account. What does he plan to do with this information? Why did he write it down in his hidden journal? The log-in information was in the side pocket of my mother's checkbook, which was in the little inside drawer of my desk. This was in a different drawer from my bus tickets. Now, I'm shaking. What kind of monster am I dealing with? Would he try to steal a ninety-six-year-old woman's life savings? I take pictures of everything I think will help and we put everything away and go downstairs.

Matty suggests that I immediately bring my computer and start changing passwords, beginning with my mom's account. I'm at the kitchen table with Matty, and we come up with a password that for the time being will serve as a password for everything. We change the log-in to my computer, then immediately to my mother's bank account. Then I start working through my accounts. I'm plugging along with Matty's help when Nikolai walks in the door. I freeze. I stare at Matty. Matty immediately closes my laptop. Thank goodness I have him. Nikolai makes small talk and goes upstairs. I am in knots.

———◆———

The next day I call an attorney and schedule an appointment for the end of the week. That evening, Nikolai asks me if I want to go get pizza together. The bile comes up in my throat, but I politely say no thinking, *Not if you were the last man on earth.*

I tell Matty if I ever waver, to remind me that Nikolai stole Grandma's bank account log-in information. That should keep me strong. The following day, Nikolai asks me if I took his wedding ring because he cannot find it. I stare at him in disbelief and say no with gritted teeth. That evening Nikolai converses with someone on the phone, showers, dresses up in nice jeans and a button-down shirt, puts on cologne and leaves. I assume it's a date. At the end of the week, I FaceTime with the attorney. She seems nice enough and knowledge-able. She indicates that it doesn't matter that I took out loans from my 401K to educate him, but she feels I will be entitled to substantial alimony. I am feeling more optimistic about the finances. She offers to write Nikolai a letter suggesting we reach an amicable settlement. She later does so, and upon receipt, Nikolai comes downstairs to the din-ing room where I am working and talking to Matty and tells me he re-ceived my attorney's letter. I just stare at him. He then says, "*Amicable,* that's what I want. A quick, amicable settlement." I just nod, thinking he wants an amicable settlement that does not consider all his hidden bank accounts.

By the end of September, a pattern of life emerges, which seems to be a never-ending loop. I get up in the morning and talk quietly with Matty over coffee and tea. Various household items and tools have started to disappear, and I take inventory with Matty. I go through the motions of the day. I don't speak to Nikolai. He stays in his office and generally does not appear where I am. He goes out most evenings and often overnight. On the weekend, he typically does not return before noon the next day. He racks up $375 in EZ pass tolls for the month. This is during a pandemic when his job does not want him traveling. He has the gall to leave two doggy bags in the refrigerator from his evenings out. He helps himself to whatever food I prepare. Matty and I continually warn each other when Nikolai is home or has gone out. Jimmy texts first when he wants to chat and if Nikolai is not home, I call him. If Nikolai is home and we really need to speak, I drive around the block and park somewhere and chat in the car.

Jimmy finally tells Emily everything that has happened. He had given her a few details but had been holding back a lot. He has been so upset that she might think he could be anything like Nikolai, which is why he is so reluctant to tell her. Emily gets teary because it is such a shock, but everything makes more sense now. She says I must be a strong person to have withstood it for so long. I spend every Sunday at Jimmy and Emily's watching football and working on my latest needlepoint. The needlepoint for Jimmy and Emily renewed my interest in the craft. I searched high and low for a similar needlepoint kit to give to Grace at her shower but could fine none. The one I gave them I had purchased over thirty years ago. So, I decided to give Grace and Patrick needlepoint Christmas stockings. Grace's is Santa carrying a bunch of toys, and Patrick's is two snowmen. They are the most challenging needlepoints I've ever done. Patrick's has lots of extras like pom poms on the hats, fringe on the scarf and French knots for polka dots. The colors on Grace's are vibrant and varied. A teddy bear, which is about two inches by two inches, has eight different brown colors, and Santa's beard has six different shades of white and gray. The end result makes it worth the effort. Doing the needlepoint also fills my days during a particularly dark period. But for the stockings, I don't have much else in my life. I'm so grateful Jimmy and Emily are willing to have me. Emily tells me to think of their home as my safe space. I am touched. I don't want to be around Nikolai. Part of me is afraid of him. On multiple occasions, I will leave Jimmy and Emily's house after dinner and go straight to Olivia's. She has set up an outdoor entertainment area equipped with a large screen TV and heaters. This way we can gather without the risks of COVID. I join Olivia and her family for movies and popcorn, and some other neighbors join as well. It is my first introduction to *Frozen*, and I love it, particularly the music. The song "Let It Go" seems especially apt for me. I enjoy the company, and it limits the time I must be in Nikolai's presence.

Periodically Nikolai calls Grace and Jimmy and asks them to call him. Jimmy calls him; Grace does not. At first, Nikolai and Jimmy just catch up, then Nikolai starts bashing me and then cries. Jimmy finds it frustrating. The conversation repeats itself in a vicious cycle. The kids conclude he's worried about them staying in his life.

CHAPTER 9

Wedding Plans

October 2020

Nikolai deactivates his Facebook page again. Grace comes home for a weekend so we can shop for mother-of-the-bride dresses. It's hard to plan a wedding for my only daughter under these circumstances. I am an emotional basket case, crying at any given moment, throughout this period, but wedding details will not wait. We shop at a few different shops, and I try on what feels like a hundred dresses. Nothing is truly hitting the mark for me. But I get to spend the day with my girl, a rare treat, and we grab dinner together. We are sitting at a high-top table with our short legs dangling as I start to cry about my life. Grace, ever the empath, starts to cry with me. Two grown women in a restaurant bawling. Does it get any better than that? We return home to an empty house. Fortunately for Grace, Nikolai is likely with one of his paramours, and she does not have to interact with him. While she is trying to remain somewhat neutral, she really isn't. There is just too long of a history with Nikolai's rages for her to have any desire to see him. We hug goodbye and she goes on her way, leaving me to face my nightmarish life once again.

Through text, Grace and I start to discuss her shower and whom to invite. I plan on having a men's table because I know Grace's brothers will enjoy being there, but I'm not thrilled about having Nikolai. I talk to Ava, and she incredulously asks me why I would consider having Nikolai. I explain about the men's table. She dismisses the notion, states it's my party and I can invite or exclude whomever I wish. I'm not sure what I will do, but I like her advice. Grace asks for advice on the wording of the wedding invitations. My heart hurts that she must consider things that normally would be standard. I suggest she go with the traditional Mr. and Mrs. request the honor of your presence.

We all get invited to a friend's wedding on Halloween in North Carolina. It's in our friend's backyard, and everyone is coming in costume. Grace agrees to attend with me. My sister-in-law is dressing up as Snow White and my brother as one of the Seven Dwarfs. They suggest Grace and I can also go as Dwarfs, but we decline. We go as ourselves. We book our flights and a hotel room and set up a brunch with my nephew who lives nearby. The weekend is an emotional roller coaster for me. My emotions are raw. Grace and I go out to brunch with my nephew and his girlfriend. They've been together for a couple years now, and we fully expect an engagement in the future. They are the consummate hosts, giving us a tour of their place and the city of Charlotte. We laugh and joke at brunch until I break down at one point. I just can't seem to hold it together. Later that day, during dinner at the wedding, we sit with my brother Jack and his wife and laugh and joke until again I break down. My sister-in-law offers to have me stay anytime I need to get away. I am touched by the gesture. Despite my emotions, overall, it's been a pleasant weekend.

Grace and I fly back home on Sunday, November 1st. I am in the aisle seat, and Grace is next to me in the middle. Masks at our chin, we are sipping coffee and tea, and we start talking about her wedding. Grace starts to cry. She doesn't know what to do relative to Nikolai. She says it's all so phony having him play a role at the wedding when she does not feel that way about him. I get her to talk more about his role to better understand what bothers her. The key responsibilities for Nikolai as father of the bride will be walking her down the aisle, doing a speech, and the father-daughter dance. Grace is particularly upset about the father-daughter dance. She says it would just be a sham for her, pretending that there are these feelings when there aren't. I suggest she not do it, but she is concerned it will look strange, particularly since Patrick wants to dance with his mom. I then suggest she dance with Jimmy. Everyone will think that is sweet, and since he's her twin, it won't look as obvious. Suddenly, a weight is lifted from her shoulders. Her face immediately brightens, and her shoulders are no longer slumped. She has hope for a nice wedding that she can be happy with. She decides she is going to write Jimmy a nice letter asking him to do the dance with her. She is excited at the prospect. I'm so happy my kids are close friends. I hope they always remain so. We land, and Matty and Sarah pick us up. After a quick dinner out, we drive Grace to her car. She has parked her car at Bella's house so Nikolai will not know she is with me.

———— ◆ ————

Nikolai attempts to reach out to the kids. He seems to be getting increasingly concerned about his lack of a relationship with them. Nikolai texts Grace asking how she is. She seeks my advice on how to answer. I suggest being generic, stating she is fine and that Patrick is studying, which she does. Nikolai responds that they should get together soon. He can drive to them, and they can get a bite somewhere. He ends the text, "Love ya." After speaking with her brothers, Grace responds to Nikolai that maybe they can see when Jimmy and Matty are free and do something together. They have all agreed that they probably can't put Nikolai off too much longer. Nikolai responds with a thumbs up to Grace. Grace is pleasantly surprised at such a short response. I know he's on a date presently and tell her that's probably the reason for the short response. He had left the house at 5 p.m. drowning in cologne and had come home at 8 a.m. that morning from the previous night's date. Nikolai is regularly gone for twenty-four hours at a time, particularly on a weekend night. It is apparent, he is sleeping with a woman or multiple different women. Sometimes I just feel "whatever," and sometimes I'm really offended. It's so in my face. That he thinks no one would have a problem with his behavior is just incredible.

On October 19, 2020, Nikolai asks me if I intend to buy him out of the house. When I indicate yes, he says he is looking to buy a place, but it's hard to find one. I say it's not practical to think he can go from living here to buying a place. He responds his niece told him he can stay with her. He then says, "It's good you're buying the home for Matty. He is broken hearted."

"For Matty's sake," I say, "the sooner you move out the better."

"For his sake?" Nikolai says.

"We both know what you're doing every night," I say. "It doesn't sit well with your son."

"I'm not doing anything," he says and walks away.

I tell the kids, "He dyes his hair, changes his Facebook name multiple times, and is gone overnight several times a week, but he's not doing anything?" The hair-dying goes back to at least 2018 when he started using Sun-In Hair Lightener. Grace had just started dating Patrick, and Patrick commented that Nikolai's hair was orange. Now, he seems to be using some kind of Grecian formula for men. I see black dye periodically in his bathroom sink and in the garbage pail.

On October 24, 2020, I decide to spend the day shopping at the outlets, engaging in some retail therapy. Anything to be away from Nikolai on a Saturday. While I am shopping, Nikolai approaches Matty who is in his bedroom and asks, "Do you know what Jimmy and Grace are up to?"

Matty says no.

Nikolai turns and leaves and then immediately walks back down the hall and says, "We need to talk soon so I can give you my side of the story."

Matty says, "Whatever."

Matty goes downstairs to the kitchen to make lunch and Nikolai follows him and says, "You know that woman drove me crazy."

"I'm not going to listen to this," Matty says.

Nikolai goes back upstairs and comes back down to the kitchen and says, "I don't know why you would be mad at me; I never did anything to you. You know I'm not doing anything."

"Yea, you're not doing anything. Where do you go every single night and don't come back?"

"A friend's house," Nikolai says.

"What friend?" Matty asks. We all know Nikolai doesn't have any friends.

"My niece's house."

"Liar!"

"I'm not lying," Nikolai says.

"Yes, you are."

"No, I'm not lying to you. I would never lie to you."

"You lied to me for three straight years during the first affair."

"Is that what your mother told you—that I'm sleeping with other women?"

"No," Matty says. "That's what I concluded off my own observations."

"I'm not doing anything. What women would sleep with me during COVID?"

Matty does not respond. Nikolai goes back upstairs but returns again and says, "If I was sleeping with women, why wouldn't I have gotten an apartment? Why would I still be living here?"

Matty still does not respond, and Nikolai wants to know where I am. While I am in Talbots looking at sweaters, my mom calls me. I exit the store to sit on a bench and talk. She calls me every day as she is lonely at my brother's home in Maryland. The sun is bright and warm while I talk with her. Suddenly, Grace texts me and Jimmy calls me. This is too coincidental, so I end the call with my mom and see what's going on. They tell me Matty had a big fight with Nikolai before he left for his weekend in Ocean City. It was ugly and Matty called Nikolai a liar. The butterflies start somersaulting in my stomach. I am terrified to go home now and deal with Nikolai alone. I text Olivia to ask if he is there, and she says yes. I talk to the kids and relay my fears of being alone with Nikolai without Matty. Jimmy tells me to come to his house and stay there overnight. I am grateful, but I still need to go home to pick up things for the night. I drive home from the outlets, shaking the whole way. Thankfully,

Nikolai is not there when I arrive, but there's no way of knowing if he is out for the night or just a quick errand. I race through the house, grabbing pajamas, toiletries, and a change of clothes and quickly pack it in the car. I then go to Olivia's. A while ago, I had brought over all my jewelry and anything else of value and asked her to hold onto it for me. I totally trust Olivia but hate to involve her in this mess. I figure it's better if I can bring it to Jimmy, who is holding a lot of my other stuff like all the photo albums. I get my stuff, thank her profusely, jump in the car and drive the forty minutes to Jimmy's. Jimmy concludes that both Emily and I need wine and pours us each a glass. We both go for a second glass and end up getting silly and having a fun dinner. Emily is very upset that Nikolai cornered Matty like he did. She now says she's in Patrick's camp. Patrick has never been neutral with respect to Nikolai's behavior. Grace had told Patrick a long time ago about Nikolai's affairs, so Patrick had a lot of time to digest it. Although he has put on a good show for a long time—so good that I never realized he knew—Patrick naturally finds Nikolai's behavior abhorrent. Emily had taken a more neutral stance since the time Nikolai filed for divorce, even asking Jimmy if he wanted to have Nikolai over for dinner. Because Jimmy confided in Emily more recently about Nikolai's behavior, it took her longer to come into Patrick's camp.

I go to sleep in the guest room. The next day is Sunday, my usual day to stay with Jimmy and Emily and watch football, which I do. Nikolai has returned home from his overnight date and sees I am not home. He calls Grace and asks where I am. Grace says she doesn't know, and he responds that he doesn't know where Matty is either. Grace says he's in Ocean City. Nikolai says he called Jimmy, but he's not answering. Nikolai says he is worried that I'm talking to Jimmy about stuff. Grace responds that Jimmy is probably busy with Emily. He then tells Grace the same thing he told Matty: "Why would I be sleeping around with other women during COVID?" He states that he's staying with his niece and spending a lot of time with his brother, Boris. He blames me for making the kids think he is sleeping around. Grace responds that Matty spoke to her and Jimmy about it and expressed his concerns, so she doesn't think it's coming from me. He tells her how terrible home is, and Grace says, "It must be hard on Mom."

Nikolai says, "It's hard on everyone." He indicates that I likely stayed over at my brother's.

Nikolai's birthday is toward the end of November, and Grace tells me that she ordered a science t-shirt for him. She figures the three of them will give it to him around Thanksgiving. She says they went with something cheap and not sentimental, and they are not getting a card as any sentiment in a card would not express their true feelings. She is not sure Matty will join them at this point, but she figures they will get the obligation out of the way and won't have to see him anytime soon after that. I tell her I think it is a good plan, that it leaves the door open if they want something more.

Nikolai tries calling Jimmy. Jimmy does not pick up. He says he has no desire to talk to him. Grace says she feels the same. Between the history of Nikolai's rages and the obvious lies he keeps telling them, the kids are finding it harder and harder to remain neutral. Matty has witnessed firsthand Nikolai making dates, taking things from the house, and lying right to his face. At this point, Matty has lost any possibility of remaining neutral.

———◆———

It's past time to close the pool. I have worked on cleaning the debris out and winterizing it with chemicals. Matty thinks Nikolai might have put a hole in the pool. His behavior relative to the pool is strange. He is anxious to get the winter cover on. He keeps commenting to Matty about the water level. I call in a leak detection specialist, and he finds nine holes in the pool. He advises that the holes are likely either from scrubbing algae too hard or from termites eating the liner. We are still suspicious of Nikolai but the following spring when we replace the liner, we conclude it was termites eating the lining. That just shows how paranoid and suspicious both Matty and I had become.

Matty tells Jimmy and Grace, "He [Nikolai] is literally lurking around the downstairs every night doing shady a** s**t, leaving constantly. He was gone for an hour without his car from seven to eight last night." Matty follows up with, "He's been hoarding cash. I don't know if you know that. He takes out 2K of cash." Matty states that everything should be settled by the spring. "If it's not, I'm moving."

Not realizing that it's nearly impossible to negotiate a divorce with such a manipulative person, Matty thinks spring of 2021 as opposed to spring of 2022!

Matty and I go to the vacation home to winterize things. Nikolai and I had purchased the home in 2009, more as an investment, but also as a fun place to get away. It's in a quiet development in the Poconos. I became the de facto head of the rental business (like most things in the household). It's very rewarding when I please a guest and they write a good review, but demoralizing when I have a guest who either destroys the place or complains incessantly. I've considered buying Nikolai out of the house. I've talked to the kids about it, and they are onboard to help. I figure we can create a partnership among the four of us. I've been working the business for ten years now, and Nikolai has no clue about any of it. He doesn't even know the access codes to the business bank account on which he is co-owner or the access code to the house. Matty and I just go for the day, primarily to take the boats off the dock. Thank goodness I have him to help me with this. Running the business sometimes feels overwhelming.

A couple days later, Nikolai asks me for the access code to the vacation house. He says he wants to "pick up a few things." I question what things, and he then he says he wants to "stay there a while." I respond it's rented out and refuse to give him the code. I say let the lawyers handle it. He then asks my property manager for it. Fortunately, I had filled her in when Matty and I were at the house. She was very sympathetic, having gone through some difficult relationships herself. She immediately texts me about Nikolai's request and ignores him at my request. While I recognize that he has a right to the house and the business, I can only assume he is up to no good. He likely plans to raid the house of anything that looks desirable, which I can't have if I'm to continue renting it out.

Nikolai's lawyer contacts my lawyer asking for access to the vacation home. My lawyer responds that it is rented, and he can't have access to it. His lawyer responds that it's not rented for November, and he wants to utilize it. I provide my lawyer a calendar of bookings, which shows it's rented every weekend, sometimes for long weekends in November. My lawyer responds to his lawyer with the calendar and states we rely on the income to pay the expenses so he can't have access.

That night, Nikolai leaves around 5 p.m. for a date, and Matty decides he's going to try and get into the office from the window. He gets the extension ladder to do so. I am the look-out, and I am nauseous from the stress. I don't know what he will do if Nikolai comes home to find him on the ladder outside the office window. Matty climbs up the ladder and attempts to open the window from the outside. He is unsuccessful. The window is locked, and the blinds are closed. He then decides to try getting in through the locked door. This is all driven by Matty. I am not altogether comfortable with it. He tries to manipulate the lock with a wire. He tries putting a credit card through the door jam. No dice. He then suggests he kick the door down. He knows he can easily open it that way. I tell him no. I don't want the confrontation with Nikolai and whatever retaliation will ensue. Matty's mad about Nikolai wanting to access the vacation home. I am concerned about Matty. I text Jimmy, "He's losing it. He's so angry. He said he's going to spit in his face when he leaves. He wants him punished. I said he will be. What kind of relationship will he have with his kids. Matty said nonexistent as far as he's concerned."

———— ♦ ————

I'm in constant communication with the kids, and I come across an article titled, "11 signs You're Dating a Narcissist,"[4] which I send to them. Matty concludes that Nikolai exhibits ten out of eleven of the traits. Jimmy states that some of them "really hit the nail on the head."

A few of the narcissistic traits stand out for me: Nikolai can be charming and then turn into a raging grizzly; Nikolai loves to talk about himself and has often attributed to himself ideas that I am certain were mine; Nikolai is easily offended; Nikolai has no real friends; Nikolai lies so much I don't know whether I'm coming or going; Nikolai always thinks he's right, everything is my fault and he never apologizes; and finally, whether it was my weakness or Nikolai's narcissism, Nikolai managed to keep us together longer than we should have. But I will soon discover how Nikolai fully exhibits trait number eleven, which is, when you show them you're really done, they lash out. According to the article, "Their ego is so severely bruised that it causes them to feel rage and hatred for anyone who 'wronged' them. That's because everything is everyone else's fault. Including the breakup."[5] They might bad-mouth you to save face. Or they might start immediately dating someone else to make you feel jealous and help heal their ego. Or they'll try to steal your friends.

To further cement my conclusions that Nikolai is indeed a narcissist, an article from my lawyer's firm lands in my inbox, "20 Signs You're Married To A Narcissist."[6] Here are the key points:

1. They gaslight. Your spouse denies your reality. They're clearly keeping secrets, you don't trust your own opinions anymore, and sometimes you feel like you're going crazy. **Triple Check.**

2. They can't empathize. You've quit going to them for comfort because they can't offer any. **Check.**

3. They're grandiose. A narcissist thinks they're the biggest rooster in the barn. Anything they do is the most fabulous, amazing achievement ever. **Double Check.**

4. They're aggressive. The narcissist has no compunction bulldozing over people to get their way. They yell, belittle, threaten, and perhaps, physically abuse. **Check.**

5. They're victimizers but act like victims. They love to dish it out but can't take it. They exploit others, and then are

easily wounded when someone disagrees with them or does something they don't like. **Double Check.**

6. They're charmers—until they're not. They turn on the charm in public, then instantly revert to their difficult self when the "important people" aren't around. You used to find their sparkly demeanor alluring, but now you find it disingenuous. **Check.**

7. They objectify the kids. The narcissist needs to see the children as exceptional beings that reflect their greatness. He loves the kids very conditionally and demands reverence from them. **Not as much.**

8. They can't apologize. Nothing is ever their fault, even when it is. They refuse to say they're sorry but expect you to grovel for forgiveness. **Double Check.**

9. They fault-find. No one lives up to the narcissist's standards, especially you. Once upon a time, you felt pretty good about yourself, but marriage to your narcissist has squashed your self-esteem. **Check.**

10. They're chronic cheaters. You were devastated to learn of their infidelity, but you also weren't surprised. Worse yet, they deflect responsibility for their actions by blaming you for the fact that they were unfaithful. **Triple Check.**

11. They lack accountability. Even when they're clearly in the wrong, they won't take responsibility for their behavior. When you call them out on their failure to honor their commitments, they complain that you're hen-pecking. **Double Check.**

12. They're attention-seeking. It doesn't matter if it's positive or negative attention; they're not happy unless they're in the spotlight. **Double Check.**

13. They treat you better in public. **Check.**

14. They treat you like The Help. You may be the narcissist's spouse, but you feel more like their personal assistant. **Not as much.**

15. They lack remorse. The narcissist does things that hurt people and doesn't feel guilty. **Check.**

16. They're entitled. The narcissist acts like a diva: demanding, arrogant, privileged. **Check.**

17. They create drama. The narcissist stirs up chaos and drama with their outsized ego and extreme behaviors. When you first met, being around them was exciting; now, it's exhausting, and often embarrassing. **Double Check.**

18. They're black-and-white thinkers. The narcissist doesn't see shades of gray. People are either all good (the ones on their side) or all bad (the ones not on their side). **Check.**

19. They're not interested in your needs and feelings. When you tell the narcissist how you feel, they explain to you why you're wrong. When you express basic needs, they tell you you're too demanding. **Not as much.**

20. They lie. Whether the narcissist is embellishing or downright lying, they just can't stick to facts. You're not sure if your spouse is aware they're messing with the truth, or if they believe their own lies. **Triple check.**

From my perspective, score: 17/20 with nine traits very strong. I send it to the kids. Matty responds, "That's scary."

Jimmy writes, "Definitely at least 18 out of 20. And number 20 is the one I think about a lot. Does he know how much he lies, or does he actually believe what he's saying?"

Matty replies, "I think both Jimmy."

Jimmy says, "Yeah, a lot of them are pretty spot on. And a lot of them we've mentioned to each other over the years."

CHAPTER 10

More of the Same

November 2020

Thanksgiving is just around the corner, and the air is now brisk. We continue to go round and round with respect to the vacation home. Nikolai's lawyer says Nikolai wants to go to the vacation home during the week. My lawyer informs me that we have no legal basis to deny him. I respond that it is fraught with problems as I often get last-minute bookings, the house must be clean for them, and why aren't I entitled to access the office that he keeps continually locked?

My lawyer emails Nikolai's lawyer that the property, historically, has been rented on short notice as Nikolai is fully aware and asks for the exact dates Nikolai intends to go. She also asks for confirmation that Nikolai will not remove anything from the property and will leave the home clean and with clean linens for the next renter. She notes that he will also need to be prepared to vacate on a moment's notice if a rental request is received. Additionally, she demands that Nikolai unlock the bedroom, or she states, I will have a locksmith come to do it.

His lawyer responds that Nikolai fully understands how the rental works and will use the rental on any days that are not currently rented. He notes that it appears that I booked the rental for a weekend in November, and thus, there is no reason Nikolai cannot also have access. With respect to the locked bedroom, he states that Nikolai is residing in that bedroom and is entitled to lock the door should he so choose.

I question my lawyer on the definition of residing and ask, "Can I argue I reside in the master bedroom and put a lock on that and remove all his things?"

My lawyer says, "Under their logic, yes. Go for it."

The weekend I have booked is for Jimmy and Emily. They have been going there every year around the eleventh to celebrate their first date. This year when Jimmy goes, he will put up security cameras for me. We have concluded that is the only way to see if Nikolai steals anything from the house as I know it's just a matter of time when I will have to cede to his demands on access to the house. I had also bought all new smart TVs with the idea of switching to Hulu from cable, but I tell Jimmy to hold off on replacing the TVs. I am not sure now if I want to keep the house. I'm beginning to think I need to simplify my life since I will be on my own. The TVs had been ordered and paid for through the business account but shipped to Jimmy's home.

Nikolai's lawyer emails that it is "absolutely absurd" that we continue to go around in circles with respect to the rental property. He states it is a simple request. He accuses me of intending to circumvent the issue, cause unnecessary delay, and frustrate Nikolai. He adds that it is time to stop playing these foolish games or else he will file a motion. He demands that I provide the lockbox code immediately.

My lawyer responds, agreeing 100 percent that it is absurd and states that if Nikolai provides the dates, I will advise him of any requests for bookings that I receive.

Nikolai never provides the dates, but eventually, I cave and provide the code because I know I have no choice. In the meantime, we have gotten many more bookings filling up most of the mid weeks. I can't be certain, but it doesn't seem like Nikolai ever goes there. Perhaps my stalling went to my advantage. I am not trying to be a total uncooperative jerk. I am just trying to protect the rental business from whatever damage Nikolai might do.

———————◆———————

We are having problems with the cable service. It is nearing election day, and I want to be able to watch the returns. I know Nikolai feels the same. Politics was an interest we both shared, although in recent years, he became a little too obsessed for me, watching the news all day long. I know this year I will watch alone. But I need cable, so I call the cable company and a technician comes to repair it. He wants to go into the office to see the connections there. Nikolai is not pleased but realizes he must let him in if he is to have a working TV. The technician must think this is a screwed-up situation. This is my first peek at the office in over a month. All of Nikolai's hats are gone, and Home Depot moving boxes are strewn all over on every inch of available floor space. I had noticed earlier that his clothes were all gone from his dresser in the master bedroom. Could he be leaving soon? Please, please, please.

What decent man would refuse to move out and then flaunt his dating life before his wife and son? One Tuesday evening I am downstairs in the family room watching TV and furiously working on Grace and Patrick's needlepoint stockings for the shower. The shower will be at the end of March, but two stockings is a lot to accomplish. Fortunately (or unfortunately), I have no life and can spend almost every waking minute doing needlepoint. Matty is in his bedroom in a remote class as part of his master's degree in taxation he is pursuing. Nikolai, regrettably, is home, holed up in his office. Matty steps out of his bedroom on a break and hears Nikolai setting up what seems to be a first date for Friday. Matty immediately whips out his phone and records the entire conversation. He then comes downstairs and plays it for me in the family room. It's not the best quality but the absurdity of everything hits us both at once, and we start hysterically laughing.

The next day, Matty relays the recording of Nikolai's date request to Jimmy and Grace with the message that in case they had any doubts, here's the proof. Jimmy responds that he hates to admit it, but he did have doubts. Although Nikolai's a proven liar, when Jimmy spoke to him on the phone recently, Nikolai started crying about how he wasn't doing that stuff. Jimmy adds that it's amazing how much Nikolai lies and just doesn't care. Jimmy also notes that it is clear from social media that Nikolai's brother is in California despite Nikolai saying he is spending all his free time with him and not seeing other women.

During this time, we also overhear Nikolai having multiple conversations with someone he calls "sweetie." The first time I hear it, I text Grace to ask if she is speaking with him, knowing that he uses that term of endearment for her. He is not, so only one conclusion can be made. One day, I hear him talking to "sweetie" in a long conversation, and he mentions his wife and kids. He tells her he's renting a townhouse with a loft and garage, and he says he ordered furniture. December 4 and December 11 are mentioned. Could the end be in sight? He also mentions that he wants to get a Christmas tree for his new place, that he always liked having a tree. I find that ironic since he would never participate in any tree decorating in at least the last ten years. When the kids were home, they would help me. When they went away to college, I did it by myself.

———— • ————

Jimmy and I next discuss how to put a lock on the master bedroom. He has me send him pictures so he can figure out the best way to make it secure. Jimmy is on his way to the vacation home. I ask him to take inventory, so we know what Nikolai steals. A few days later, I ask Jimmy if he's heard from Nikolai. He has not. I tell him Grace has. Jimmy responds, "It's ironic that Grace is the only one he has a relationship with right now.

I reply, "Yea the one he terrorized the most."

I'm furious because Nikolai has eaten the leftover pizza that I had hidden in the garage refrigerator. He should get his own food.

It is November 18, 2020, and I text the following updates to the kids:

> *Yesterday I cancelled our joint Discover card and our joint EZ pass account. I emailed your father, and he got all hot about the Discover card. He said he doesn't have another credit card, which we know is a lie and makes me think more strongly he will lie on the financial reporting for the divorce. I went into our joint bank account today and discovered he transferred all the money in the savings account to the checking account. Matty figures he plans to take it all. I went in to Discover online to see what the balance due is, and it is $4,500. I tried to pay it with our joint account but the bank won't pay until the 20th so he may beat me, and I'll be stuck with a $4,500 bill, which apparently includes a new $1,800 bed for him. At least the last part is promising. Maybe he will be out of here soon.*

I subsequently try several things like scheduling the payment of the credit card from the bank and scheduling the payment directly from the credit card, but I know none of them will beat Nikolai's theft and then the payments will bounce. Then, I get a brilliant idea. I can go to the bank and get bank checks to pay the credit card bills and just mail them the payment. With a bank check, the money will be withdrawn right away, and it's as good as cash. Feeling a bit like a criminal, I show up to the bank the next morning before it opens and wait. As soon as the doors are opened, I enter and get on the line. I can't seem to stop tapping my foot. Will they ask any questions? Can I pull this off? Can I beat Nikolai to the money? I hand the teller my request and she has me sign a few papers. I hold my breath, and the teller hands me the bank checks. I leave and sit in the car and immediately check the bank balance. The $4,500 is no longer in the account. I did it. I drive to the post office and mail the payments. Later that day, Nikolai wipes out the account. He only gets $3,000 so I feel pretty good that I outsmarted him. Sometimes, he is quite predictable.

Nikolai is up to his usual tricks. It is Friday, November 19, 2020. Matty and I discuss having a tree-trimming party if we can manage a date when Nikolai is off with one of his women. We figured it would be nice to have music for it, so we go into the living room where the stereo is located to see if we remember how to get it working. Jimmy is my tech guy, and he had hooked up the stereo to Alexa so we can just tell Alexa to play music through the speakers that Nikolai put into the walls years ago. Matty tries to get Alexa to play music when we discover there is no Alexa. As we look further, we see that the receiver that was connected to the speakers is also missing. Chalk another theft up to Nikolai. And he didn't just take the receiver. Nikolai has cut all the wires to the receiver right up to the wall to make it very difficult to splice it back. He could have easily disconnected the wires from the receiver and not cut them, but clearly, he intentionally chose to cut them. What a nice guy. I immediately call my tech guy, and Jimmy orders me a new system and new wires and sets it up even better than before.

The kids all go to Jimmy's house to have a fun weekend of drinking together. I busy myself on Saturday with some shopping errands, so I won't be home with Nikolai if he is around. He hasn't come home from the night before, but I have no way of knowing when he might. I back my car out of the garage and feel a strange sensation and hear a loud sound. I immediately get out and look at the back tire from where I heard and felt everything, but I don't see anything, so I go on my way, shopping most of the day. We all agree that I will come to Jimmy's on Sunday morning for breakfast with everyone.

I get up early, planning on going to 8 a.m. Mass and then going to get bagels and donuts to bring to Jimmy's house. I back out of the driveway and start down the street, but my car does not seem right. It's tilting to the right and making an odd sound. I get out and discover that the one tire is completely flat. That must have been the noise I heard and the sensation I felt the day before. I must have ridden over something in the garage. But what? We had only cleaned out the garage three months ago, and it was still tidy. Plus, it was growing emptier each day with Nikolai taking things at night. I get the car back home and ask Olivia's husband to help me. He's not that mechanically inclined, although he tries. We put air in the tire, and I call Jimmy and describe it to him. He tells me I should be okay to get to him, and he will take care of it. He advises local roads in case there's a problem so I can easily pull over and he can get to me. Of course, I'm bawling through all this. I really don't need this extra stress. I get there with no problems, and Jimmy and Matty manage to get the tire off and find a nail has punctured it. A very odd nail with a square-shaped head. And the puncture is in an odd position. The nail had to have been positioned in just the right way for it to puncture the tire at the angle it did. We all immediately assume that Nikolai has done this but, of course, I have no proof.

For the last few weeks and continuing until December 15, I wake up every morning to discover what is currently missing. Nikolai prowls the house late at night after Matty and I have gone to bed and helps himself to whatever he feels like. If there are two of something, he always takes the better one. My pizza cutter goes missing, as do the better strainer, the better measuring cup, a set of measuring spoons, the TV in the guest room… The list goes on and on. He had my mother's step stool hidden in his closet, which I'm sure he planned to take. I intercept it and have Jimmy hold it for me. I'm so uncomfortable in my own home. Months and months later, I will still discover new things that are missing. Things like my zip drives, which had documents and pictures on them—including one from work, which was protected, and he could not access. The following summer when we are preparing for our annual party and I get out the floats for the pool, I discover

Nikolai has taken the pump to fill them. This pump was lent to me by my neighbor down the street years ago and she told me to hold on to it. Arguably, we don't even own it. He also took the bicycle pump so there's no means of blowing up the pool toys. Fortunately, my neighbor comes through again. The following fall, months and months after Nikolai has moved out, I discover a doozy. We always buy a large box of kitchen garbage bags from BJ's, a club store for which you pay a yearly membership and buy in bulk at lower prices. One day, I go to take a bag and there aren't any left. There should be half a box. I discover that Nikolai has stuffed all my brown paper lunch bags at the bottom of the box and taken the roll of kitchen bags. I knew the paper bags had gone missing and had thought he had taken them, which I couldn't understand. I had used them to bring breakfast to work when I went into the office pre-COVID. But no. He used the bags to hide his theft of the kitchen garbage bags. Ingenious. This is a man who makes over $200,000 each year. He should be able to afford garbage bags.

During this time, we finally receive Nikolai's financial statement for the divorce, a month past the due date. It's a piece of garbage. My lawyer says it more diplomatically. She describes it as "woefully incomplete." It is missing virtually all attachments. She states that our discovery requests will be based on this. He is moving to his own apartment and has not disclosed a single penny of his future expenses, nor did he provide any information about the bank accounts that I discovered. He has also underestimated his IRAs by half and claims they are exempt, omitted his stock accounts in which he had almost $200,000 and made numerous other inaccuracies.

Nikolai goes out one day jogging, and his behavior as he is leaving seems odd. He goes to the mailbox and then to the backyard before leaving to jog. Ever suspicious, I investigate after he is far enough away. It takes me some time, but I finally figure out that he has taken the bank statements for the vacation rental business that had just come in the mail and put them under rocks on the side of the house.

I take note of what is there and a few days later some of them turn up in the mailbox, obviously resealed.

It is December 11, and we get to have that tree-trimming dinner party. A glimmer of happiness in an otherwise dark life. Matty asks Nikolai if he will be home that evening. Nikolai says he will be back late, around eleven. We immediately send out texts to everyone to come as early as they can as they need to be gone by 10:30 to be assured of not running into Nikolai. Matty cooks ratatouille, and Sarah makes her famous charcuterie board. Grace and Patrick and Jimmy and Emily come, as does our precious Rover (Jimmy and Emily's Goldendoodle puppy). It is so nice for all of us to be together. We eat and drink and take pictures by the tree and enjoy the puppy. Everyone manages to leave just before Nikolai returns.

The next day, Nikolai tells me that he needs a Certificate of Occupancy (CO) for his new place and will have it on Tuesday, the fifteenth. First, he says he can move nothing in except his bed without the CO, which he moves today. Then he says he can move everything but himself without the CO. He acts nice and says he will help me out with the house (while he tries to screw me out of every dollar). My mom advises me not to talk to him, so I don't get sucked into his web. Very astute advice but hard to follow, after almost twenty-nine years of living together. On this same day, I receive an email from the cable company saying my order is confirmed. Nikolai had put himself as an authorized user on the cable account and then added services to it for his new place. Jimmy advises that I should call the cable company after Nikolai moves out and cancel the entire account or get his new services removed. I tell Jimmy that I'm feeling overwhelmed. So many details to think about. Jimmy tells me not to worry. We'll figure out the cable, and I won't be paying for Nikolai's internet. Little do I know what's in store for me with respect to the cable service.

The legal system is so broken. I was always the health insurance provider with a family plan that costs $300 per pay period. Since I work for the government, my insurance has always been better than what Nikolai could get. My lawyer advises me that I cannot remove Nikolai from the insurance until the divorce is finalized. I ask if I can have him contribute $150 per pay period for it. She responds that it doesn't work that way. I then get a bill from a doctor for a procedure Nikolai had done and ask them to bill my soon-to-be ex. They respond by saying it's my insurance, so I am the responsible party. What a mess.

Nikolai fills up his car once again. Matty and I had gone to the store together, and as we drive up on the driveway, I see that Nikolai has my dead brother's plant in his car. My ears start to burn with my anger, and I tell Matty this is not acceptable. I've sat back and let Nikolai just take and take and take whatever he wants. I draw the line here. Matty groans, figuring there will be a confrontation. I speak up and tell Nikolai he cannot have the plant. He appears taken aback and says he thought it was his. He thought we took it from my mother's because no one else wanted it. That is true but that happened long before I knew all that I know now. That he doesn't have any kind of sense to think I wouldn't care under these circumstances is amazing. He hands over the plant without protest. Nikolai then asks me if I want to see the layout of his place. He takes out the floor plan. I nicely decline. He must be kidding if he thinks I have an ounce of interest in his new pad where he can entertain all his women.

On Sunday the thirteenth, I go to Jimmy and Emily's for my usual Sunday football and needlepoint. I come home to discover that Nikolai has eaten all my oatmeal raisin cookies. Even though he has essentially lived in the locked office for the last three months and we have barely spoken, he never has a problem taking my food. He has helped himself to soup I've made for Matty and me and whatever else strikes his fancy. I guess all the take-out and restaurant food with his various dates gets tiresome. The end will be in sight soon. I hope!

PART 3

The Long Road Out

CHAPTER 11

Ejected

Tuesday, December 15, 2020 (present day)

Arguably my year from hell began on September 18, 2020, when I discovered the divorce papers and some of the financial deception. It has been hell these past two months, a hell that crept up like the frog who's put in the pot of water and then boiled. Nikolai was always up to something, but over time his shenanigans increased, and life became more and more hellish. But I chose this day as the beginning of my year from hell because this is when I thought I was zapping the cancer in my midst with a strong dose of radiation and thus removing it from my life. But cancer cells left behind come back to haunt you until you eradicate every last one. I would soon find out that it would take much more than another year to be completely done with Nikolai. And the bear would roar periodically.

———— ◆ ————

Early morning. I walk out my bedroom door. Nothing. Silence. Could it be true? Nikolai has not come home from last night. Now it looks more likely that I can end this madness. I go downstairs and make my morning tea. Matty joins me later for his coffee. We are happy to have the time without Nikolai in earshot and speak freely of the next move.

I email my lawyer the following:

Nikolai spent the last 4 days filling his car with stuff and moving it into his new place. He told me he could not officially move in until a CO was obtained, which he expected today. He left yesterday with a carload of stuff at around 11:30 a.m. and has not been back since. He posted a picture of himself today at the company office, which is walking distance from his new place. He still has some stuff here that presumably he wants, and the office is still locked. I figured I'd change the locks tonight (which gives him today to come get any stuff) and send him the following email if you agree:

> *Since you apparently have obtained your CO and are now residing at your townhouse, I have changed the locks at the marital home. If you wish to take any additional stuff, let me know when you wish to come and precisely what stuff you want, and I will leave it outside for you to pick up.*

> *Let me know if you agree with this approach. Thanks.*

She responds that my email is perfect, and I should go ahead and send it. She asks if I know what he took. I respond:

I have a pretty good idea of what he took. His record collection, which I would estimate to be valued anywhere from $10-50k. Most was purchased pre-marriage, but he did add to it. Most of the tools in the garage. Some minor pieces of furniture, some household things, and his personal stuff. I would guess that monetarily he probably wins as I'm left with furniture that is between 12 and 27 years old and minor household stuff (pots, dishes etc.). I'm

fine with that as long as that part is done and settled, i.e.,
he can't come back for much more and no money will be
exchanged with respect to personal property. A new desk
was just now delivered to him here, so I imagine he will
be coming by to get it today.

I get through the day with a constant pit in my stomach. I must at least give him the day to return before I proceed with my plan.

After Matty finishes changing the last lock, at around 8 p.m., I email Nikolai exactly what my lawyer approved.

———— ◆ ————

8:30 p.m. Matty and I head up to the office. Matty looks at me and says, "Should we do this?"

I nod. We've been staring at this closed locked door for months now. It's a symbol of the insanity of how we live. We are both ready to remove some darkness. Matty tries to force open the office door. It does not come easily. First, he tries to jimmy the lock with no success. Matty then looks at me with a glint in his eye and says he can just smash in the door, something he's been itching to do these many months. I give him the okay, and he kicks in the door. We do not realize that there is a mirror on the back of the door. That comes crashing down and makes a huge scratch in the wood floor as we open the door. Surprisingly, the door itself is not damaged that badly. We can repair it with wood glue and paint. We enter the office and find boxes scattered all over. Those big Home Depot boxes are now filled with stuff. And some unused Home Depot boxes are ready for more stuff. How much stuff can he fit in his townhouse? We look through some papers on his desk. I find a birthday card for Nikolai from "Teena," which states how much she loves him. I wonder if she is "sweetie."

At this point, Matty decides his work for the day is over. Mission accomplished; locks changed; office open. We can sort things out tomorrow. He figures it's safe enough to have Sarah over. They hang out in the family room, and I go through more stuff. I see Nikolai has signed up for his own health insurance. I find some other financial papers. But, like Matty, I'm tired, and tomorrow is another day to sort through it all. I start to get ready for bed.

10 p.m. Suddenly, Nikolai arrives. He backs the car into the driveway, almost on the porch on an angle half on the grass, nearly in my rose bushes. Nikolai's whole demeanor is wild. He wants to come in the house. He comes to the door. Matty answers but won't let him in. Matty calls to me. I open my bedroom window, which faces the driveway and tell Nikolai to leave.

Nikolai says, "I need my work laptop."

I respond, "I'll go get it and bring it to you."

"No, I need the charger for it," he says.

I say, "I'll find that too." I go into the office, and there is no laptop or charger there. I return and tell him that.

He says, "I'm going to get fired from my job. I need other stuff, important papers."

"Tell me what you need, and I'll get them from the office."

"You went into the office? Oh, God," he says.

"Yes, I saw a card from Teena who apparently loves you very much."

That sends him into a full-blown panic. What treasure there must be in in the office! If only…

I refuse to let him in, so he calls the police. I'm guessing he tries his lawyer first and either can't get him or is advised to call the police. The police come and ring the bell. I talk to the officer and explain that I am afraid of him. The officer indicates that he has a right to get stuff that he needs, and I need to let him in. He also says he can't keep Nikolai from staying here, but he advised him not to. How crazy is that? The officer says he will be here the whole time. I agree to it because I have no other choice. Nikolai goes up into the office escorted by the police officer and carries boxes and boxes down. We don't know this until later, but he also pulls off the heating vent which is behind the giant desk. He had to have pulled out the heavy desk to do so. He apparently was hiding stuff in the vent. He must have been desperate to get what was in there to do it in front of a police officer. We speculate later as to what was in the vent. Drugs? That might explain the need for the urine. Cash? Likely, the latter, but presumably he had a safety deposit box somewhere to store over $100,000 in ATM withdrawals.

He's packed his car to the brim at this point, and the policeman tells him he's done. He was only supposed to take enough to survive. He clearly surpassed that. Matty is very upset that this all happened with Sarah here. He had taken her into his bedroom to be away from it all. They are only dating a couple months. It is just an awful night all around. But finally, it is over. Nikolai and the police leave. Matty goes in the office after Sarah leaves and says it has bad vibes in it. I say it needs some kind of exorcism.

11:30 p.m. I send the following email to my lawyer:

I did as discussed and sent the email to Nikolai around 7 tonight. He arrived at the house begging to be let in at 10 p.m. Had multiple reasons: I need my stuff. I need my charger. I need my computers. I need important papers for work. I have nowhere to stay. He asked me if I went in the office (my son kicked in the door for me), and I said yes which seemed to make him more frantic. I offered multiple times to bring out what he needed and that he could come in the morning, and I would leave his stuff out. Nothing satisfied him. He ended up calling the police. The one officer was a bit lame in that he kept saying this is his residence so he has a right to take his stuff, and we can't even stop him from staying here. I said I was afraid. They strongly suggested that Nikolai get his stuff and not stay here. I asked them to stay and monitor Nikolai, which they did. Nikolai mostly cleaned out the office. I found a bank statement with $40K in it, which I took a

picture of. I'll send it later to you. I imagine it was stuff
like that that made him so frantic. (Not to mention love
cards from women.) Unfortunately, I couldn't get more
of it. He still has some more stuff here. Hopefully he'll be
saner about getting it. I just wanted to let you know all
this in case you hear something from his attorney.

It is now time to end this day. Matty is angry that Nikolai put us through all this, especially with Sarah here. We talk for a bit but then both go to bed. I lie in bed thinking about the madness of it all.

Wednesday, December 16, 2020

My lawyer responds to last night's email saying she is sorry I had to deal with all of that and that the police were not more helpful. She assures me that while he technically still owns the home with me, since he has obtained a new residence, I have every right to limit his free access to the home. She tells me she will send over a letter to his attorney about scheduling a time to retrieve any other stuff.

She writes Nikolai's lawyer that since Nikolai has obtained a new residence and removed virtually all his belongings from the home, I have changed the locks on the doors to the former marital home. She says that I told Nikolai of this directly, and Nikolai demanded to be let into the home last night, and even called the police to the home. She adds that the police accompanied Nikolai to remove several additional items and that moving forward, if there are any additional belongings that Nikolai wants, we ask that he make arrangements with me directly for a date and time for him to do so. She tells him to advise Nikolai that he will not be given "unfettered access" to the home.

Matty composes the following text to Nikolai, but I convince him not to send it: "You really are a self-absorbed piece of s**t. Countless lies over countless years. And to call the police and throw a tantrum while my girlfriend is over. You really have no regard for my future or my happiness."

Matty later writes the following to Jimmy and Grace:

I've come to the conclusion that he's actually not that smart... I mean leaving all that s**t for 2 days was a dumb move like really dumb. I think most of his life he's been an egotistical maniac and wanted to appear smart, so we got this illusion our whole lives that he understands somewhat complex scientific ideas and what not. But at the end of the day, he just learned what he learned—that and a bunch of useless trivia knowledge to appear intelligent to feed his ego's need to appear smart while he really isn't.

I would never have made that mistake.

His brothers are also dumb.

Jimmy replies:

I think it comes down to his ego and being cocky. He was so confident in how he'd been hiding everything that he got too relaxed and didn't even consider you guys would break in. I also agree he's probably not as smart as the image he projects. Because when it comes down to it, that was so incredibly dumb to do. That stuff is the first thing you move to the storage unit/apartment or at least the car because it guarantees no one will find it. Mom has been driving around with all her Xmas presents in the trunk of her car and that's not something that will impact the divorce lol. A secret bank statement will haha.

Grace adds:

I agree. I could run with your argument about him not being smart and he may not be as smart as he comes off, but I don't think he's dumb. I think the lack of moving the

important stuff was like Jimmy said, an act of overconfi-
dence rather than being dumb. Granted, overconfidence
can cause people to act dumb.

Later in the day, my lawyer forwards me a very long email from
Nikolai's lawyer. He states that my lawyer has misinterpreted what
happened the previous night. He says that it was my request that
Nikolai leave the home as soon as he filed for divorce. It was not
a decision made by him, and to meet my demands, Nikolai found
alternate housing, which was supposed to be available on December
16. He claims Nikolai advised me that he would be moving out approximately on that date, but once again, I jumped the gun, as I did
with the vacation home, by changing the locks to the marital home
on December 15. He adds that because Nikolai had not yet obtained
furniture, he could not move in until at least December 18. As a result, Nikolai returned home only to find that once again I took matters into my own hands and wrongfully changed the locks in order to
exclude Nikolai. He claims Nikolai had no alternative but to involve
the police and the police were able to convince me to allow Nikolai in
since there was no reason why he should be denied access.

He states that Nikolai discovered that his bedroom door was
kicked in and showed that to the police officers. He argues that I
had no right to enter Nikolai's room and violate his privacy rights,
and he demands that any items wrongfully removed from Nikolai's
room be immediately returned to him. He further says that Nikolai
was only able to retrieve his work computer and a few other items,
that the police would return with him on another day to get the rest
of his things, but that will not happen until this weekend. He says
I cannot deny Nikolai access, and Nikolai will reach out to me to
let me know the date he will come. He concludes that Nikolai does
not waive any rights to the home by leaving, which was done solely
upon my insistence, and he retains the right to return to the home
if he needs to.

I show the kids the email, and they uniformly respond that it's a pack of lies. His lawyer seems to be at the same level as Nikolai.

Thursday, December 17, 2020

Matty and I go through what's left in office. There are still several boxes. I open them up and find all kinds of household goods (measuring cup, paper towels, kitchen garbage bags, light bulbs that I had just purchased…). I find Bop It in there! Bop It was one of the kids' favorite toys when they were younger. It is like a modern-day, handheld, Simon Says. It requires quick thinking and mental and physical coordination to follow voice commands to bop it, twist it, pull it, or shout it! This must be done before the buzzer sounds. Multiple people can play, and the game tells the player to pass it to the next. Like Hot Potato, you don't want to be left holding Bop It when the buzzer goes off.[7] Why would he take this game? The kids are incensed. It is their game, and they have such fond memories of it. The only thing we can speculate is he figures this is a way to lure them to come and see him. But who knows how this crazy man thinks?

I also find the paprika. We had gone to Jimmy's for Thanksgiving. Matty and I went early to help cook. Matty texted Grace who was coming later to bring the paprika. In the meantime, Emily went out and bought some. Grace arrived without the paprika, but we no longer needed it, so we didn't even mention it. A week later, we went looking for the paprika, and it was not in the cabinet. Matty was convinced that Grace brought it to Jimmy's and forgot to bring it back home. Grace insisted she forgot to bring it. We figured Grace was tired that day from working long hours and just didn't remember. But Grace was right! She hadn't left the paprika at Jimmy's; she left it at home. Nikolai took it and packed it in one of his boxes. I don't know whether to laugh or cry at this point. This individual thing may sound very silly, but I am in quite a state. Everyday Matty and I awakened to find something new that was missing. Nikolai was constantly spinning

137

tales, telling lies. I don't know if up is down or down is up. The paprika just shows us the craziness of it all.

I also find a nail identical to the one that was in my tire three weeks ago on the shelf in Nikolai's office. It's that unusual nail with a flat rectangular head so this can't be a coincidence. I tape it on the top of one of Nikolai's boxes.

Friday, December 18, 2020

Nikolai texts that he is coming tomorrow at 10 a.m. to pick up the rest of his stuff. So much for coordinating with me. I respond, "Okay, I have put the marital property in the garage that you can take. I add if you are willing to stay in the garage with Jimmy, we can forgo the police. Otherwise, they must be here."

I decide I need to tell the neighbors since the police will be here tomorrow. I'm not sure who saw what from the last fiasco. Bella was the first person I confided in and that was back in September. We were out to dinner and with many tears, I confessed that Nikolai is not the nice guy that she has believed. She was, of course, shocked like everyone else, but as I shared more and more details, Nikolai went from being a great guy to a "s**thead" very quickly. Soon after Bella, I confided in Ava (my work friend), Lily (who used to live across the street in Olivia's house), and Olivia. I drove to Target and sat in the parking lot as I told Ava over the phone. She's known bits and pieces of my life with Nikolai over the years, so she was not as shocked as the others. She remembers well how he lied about having a college degree and questions whether our entire marriage was a lie. I met Lily for lunch one day to share the news with her. I've known Lily for over twenty years before she sold her house to Olivia. That house must only attract nice people. Lily has been like a sister to me for many years. She is of course fully supportive. Other than Bella, Olivia has known the longest. I went over to her house one day to share the news. She didn't know any of the background but is astute enough that she had her suspicions from observing Nikolai and I together and particularly from seeing his constant name changes on Facebook.

Now, I have three others to tell. Matty tells me he will have my next-door neighbor's son, who is close friends with Matty, tell his parents. That relieves me of one burden. I text my one neighbor and ask if she's available to talk. She will be home later. Before then, I call my other neighbor. She is shocked, and we basically have a crying fest on the phone. It is very sweet. She feels bad for me. I go visit my other neighbor. We have a long talk. She is great. She makes me feel better about a lot of things. She installed a dishwasher herself using YouTube videos because she couldn't afford to have someone do it. It makes me feel empowered. I can do this. I can take care of myself and this house and all the things that keep going wrong. She's much braver than I am. She tells me how before they knew her husband's personality changes were caused by a physical disease, they would get in fights, and she had no qualms about pushing him— yes physically pushing him—when they were fighting. She is my hero. I only wish I had that much courage! My next-door neighbor calls me a few days later. I am in the car coming back from purchasing something to replace the large wedding picture that hangs in my living room. She is very kind. We also have a crying fest. She feels bad. She tells me the words her son said that stick with me and help me on some bad days: "Maria is better off without him." Later on, she tells me that she considered calling Nikolai to see what was wrong with him, but her husband advised her not to. He said, "The kids are all with Maria. That speaks volumes, and you need to listen to that." So, she does not call Nikolai.

Saturday, December 19, 2020

Nikolai texts me that he never received my message informing him about changing the outside door lock prior to his arrival at home.

I respond with a screen shot of my email to him. He claims he never received it. His actions that night belie that claim.

I once again say that if he is willing to stay in the garage with Jimmy, we can forego the police. If not, they must be here.

He asks what my reason is for not allowing him in the house.

"I'm not preventing you from going in the house," I write.

He answers that he doesn't need the police.

That is too vague for me, so I call the police and ask if they can come. I explain that he has a tendency to be violent, and I am not comfortable having him in the home. They agree to come, and this time they are great.

Nikolai arrives with a pickup truck. He pretty much cleans out the garage of all the tools, gifts two table saws to Jimmy, takes everything from the office, including furniture and various wall hangings, memorabilia, etc. He tells the police his lawyer said he was entitled to go in the house and take 50 percent of the property. The police say that is incorrect, that he is entitled to take what he needs to survive and maybe some sentimental things. The officer allows Nikolai inside to look and see if there is anything else he "needs." Nikolai takes pictures of the empty office, the empty master closet, the empty walls where his wall hangings were (all of which were put in the garage), the broken office door and the new security camera system I had installed. Nikolai states to the officer that his desk is gone. (He had emptied it out when he came on Tuesday and it was clear he no longer wanted it since he bought a new one, so Matty chopped it up for the garbage.). Nikolai says he had a watch collection, and there may have been watches left in the desk. This is a total lie. First, Nikolai never had a watch collection. He had maybe three watches, two not worth much and one Movado given by work as a gift. Second, Nikolai had completely emptied the desk on Tuesday. Nikolai admitted to the police officer that he had already taken multiple carloads of stuff (I estimate around ten, plus he had a truck this day that was filled to the brim, plus he filled Jimmy's car), that he had established another residence, and that he clearly had enough to survive. The police officer then tells him he is done. Anything further would be decided in family court. The officer tells me that he is not entitled to enter the home anymore, and if he comes, I should call them, and they will make him leave. Nikolai asks the officer about obtaining the police report from Tuesday night.

I relay all this to my lawyer:

> *At this juncture, I believe Nikolai has taken more than 50% by value of the marital property. I am left primarily with furniture that is between 12 and 27 years old and some household goods. I don't want to incur a lot of expenses to divide up my junk (and it's really not much better than junk), but I also don't want to get bullied by Nikolai into giving him more than he deserves (which has probably already happened).*

Sunday, December 20, 2020

Nikolai individually texts all the kids defending himself and bashing me. He tells Matty that he should get away from me ASAP because I just "instill and transfer hatred" to everyone around me. The kids see through him, and Matty's response is the best:

> *You're delusional and need help. Mom didn't poison me. You have constantly lied to me over the past 6 years and especially the past 3 months. I have overheard calls you've had with your women. I follow Uncle Boris on Instagram. He's been in California this whole time. I've seen you steal things around the house that weren't yours. You've been everything but a good person through this and have acted unbelievably dishonorably. Everything a father shouldn't be. Someone who lies, cheats and steals is not an influence I want in my life. I don't need that toxicity in my life. I owe that to myself. My mother is a good person, and if anything, I'm the one who has advised her of all the*

horrible things you've done because she is too innocent and innately good to realize any of it. If you want any relationship with me, if you have any ounce of love left, you will stop being a coward and come clean to your 3 children and admit what you have been doing...

Nikolai responds to Matty that he was a devoted father, he didn't want it to happen this way, and he wants to work on their relationship. He says Uncle Boris was here but is back now in California but will permanently move back here. Matty responds with a picture from Instagram showing Nikolai's brother in California and states:

Looks like he was there every week since the beginning of October. You want a relationship with me? Stop lying to me. Aside from the proof I can present about specific lies, you've lied so many times to me I can tell when you're bulls**ting me. If you want a relationship with any of your children going forward, you have to fix what's going on with yourself first. Take responsibility for your actions. You're the one that blew up and yelled at all your family members. You're the one that broke your marriage vows. You're the one that filed for divorce and then went about that process in an unsavory way. And the fact of the matter is you never tried to make amends and give your wife time to heal. In order to heal and repair the amount of trust you broke in the first place takes 100x more effort than what you put forth. You took the easy way out. And until you come to terms with that and stop bulls**ting your way through the relationships that should matter most to you... I'm done."

Nikolai then texts Grace and asks if she is mad at him. Then he asks Jimmy if Grace is mad at him. He says he doesn't understand why "your mom is trying to turn you guys against me. I would never turn you guys against your mom. That's not me." He asks that they all meet. He texts Grace and defends himself, saying he hadn't lied, had no affairs other than the one, that I refused to go to therapy with him, that I show him no affection, and that I throw him out of the house whenever I please. He indicates that he is handling the divorce no differently than 50 percent of other folks and is being very fair, more so than most people. Later that night, he texts Grace with a picture of his thumb and says he can't stop the bleeding. He cut part of his fingertip off. He asks if she has any suggestions before he goes to the ER.

Grace comments to us that she is "actually afraid for how mentally unstable he is...this is actually insane.... I'm shaking right now. This is psycho s**t you see in the movies."

Monday, December 21, 2020

I wake up in the morning to multiple screen shots of texts between Nikolai and the kids from the night before. I respond to the kids the following:

> *Lovely to wake up to this. This man never stops invading my peace. My suggestion for a response: 'I had gone to bed. I hope your finger is okay. I have no desire to hear you bash my mother. Like I said before I need a break.' I defer to your bothers on this since I spew all these lies about him (sarcasm). I will say there are two truths to what he said: lack of intimacy for 6 years—note the timing as we know the affairs went back at least that far not 3 years as he tries to portray—and I've valued Matty's (and all of your) opinions more than his for a very long time. In Uncle Jack's words, 'once a cheater, always a cheater.'*

I then go down to the kitchen to make my tea and hear a vibration in the island of the kitchen. It sounds almost like a phone when it's on vibrate. It is very odd. I subsequently hear it several more times and Matty hears it also, but we can never find anything despite extensive searching. Perhaps, it's acute paranoia after all we have been through.

Later that day, my lawyer forwards an email from his lawyer complaining that because I packed some of his belongings and stored them in the garage for when he came to pick up the rest of his stuff, I damaged several items including picture frames and a bookcase. He also argues that these were the only items Nikolai was allowed to remove and that his office desk and bed were missing. He says Nikolai is not giving up any claim to the furnishings and other property left behind. He also says that Nikolai must return the modem and all the TV cable boxes to the cable company since the account was in his name and needs to be closed. Therefore, Nikolai must again enter the home to get the cable equipment. He adds that if any of the equipment is damaged, I will be held responsible for the cost. Additionally, he says there are also other items belonging to Nikolai that he may need, and after he has the ability to fully inspect all the boxes I "threw" into the garage, he will advise to other items that may be missing.

I respond to my lawyer as follows:

> *Absolutely nothing was damaged. It's all a pack of lies. The bed was my daughter's when she was a kid. He has no particular right to it. As I said to you, he already has more than 50% by value of the marital property. He's done. Please convey that to him. I planned on cancelling the cable account. I will do so as soon as I can after Christmas. He came into the house, but there was nothing he wanted. I did not limit him to the garage.*
>
> *Also, my son helped him move and said he will testify that the bookcase was in perfect condition when they moved it into Nikolai's place. Is there no way to stop this constant bullying?*

Wednesday, December 22, 2020

Nikolai texts me that he needs to return the cable boxes and modem and needs a few more things from the house. He also requests that I change the gas and electric account from his name. He states he will be there after 5 p.m. that day.

I respond, "That is not acceptable. Do not come. I will take care of cable and the gas company."

He responds that he needs other stuff: Barbell weight, plant, and some other tools from garage.

I reply, "Not acceptable. You do not need these to survive. If you come here, I will call the police."

He then responds that there are a lot of tools missing, that in all fairness the bookcase was probably damaged in the move.

I write: "In all fairness you took 95% of the tools, 45% of those are mine. That being said, we can discuss what a fair distribution of all the tools are through the divorce process. Don't contact me again."

He follows up complaining that I didn't pack his stuff right, so some things broke. He mentions glass from picture frames. He states that he didn't take 95 percent, and we will discuss a fair distribution of all the property. Finally, he writes, "Do not use Jimmy or anyone else as your messenger. Cut out the 'I am the victim crap.'"

I do not respond.

Jimmy then texts Nikolai and says, "Mom asked me if the bookcase we moved was broken because you're claiming it is. Come on, Dad. It was perfectly fine. This is the kind of crap that needs to stop."

Nikolai responds that he's right. It might have been damaged in the move.

Jimmy replies, "But it doesn't stop. I was there when the cops told you that you have enough stuff and you're not allowed back. Now you want to take her internet and TV right before Christmas? You cried and told me you wanted this to be civil. Cut the bull s**t and back off. How are any of us supposed to get through this if it never ends?"

Nikolai then calls Jimmy. He tells Jimmy he's not going to come. He's doing what his lawyer is telling him to do and getting rid of the accounts in his name. Jimmy tells him, "That's fine, but you need to let Mom figure out the internet and gas accounts before you close them and leave the house unlivable. Give her a little more notice and time since she needs to work and Matty has school."

Nikolai says he wants his tools. Jimmy tells him the cops said he was done; he has enough tools. Nikolai asks Jimmy how he would feel if Emily told Jimmy he wasn't allowed to come to the house. Jimmy responds that he and Emily are not getting a divorce.

My lawyer sends an email to Nikolai's lawyer stating that Nikolai was given access to the home (not just the garage), and he wanted nothing from the house. Nothing was damaged. Jimmy assisted Nikolai in moving and confirmed to Nikolai that nothing was damaged. Nikolai left the bed, which was their daughter's, not his and left the desk because he just purchased a new one for his new residence. He has removed more than his fair share of the marital furnishings and furniture by value. She adds that I informed Nikolai that I will close the cable account and will transfer the gas and electric account into my name right after the Christmas holiday. She says that Nikolai must stop texting me and threatening me and that if he continues to show up at my home uninvited, I will call the police to have him removed. He has moved out of the home and obtained a new residence. He cannot come and go from the former marital home at his whim.

Nikolai's lawyer responds that Nikolai never stated that he didn't want the desk or the bed from the bedroom. He is not waiving claim to that property. He only took essentials with him at this time. The rest of the property in the home still needs to be discussed and divided. He also says that Nikolai never threatened me, that he has only communicated via text, and he has all the text messages saved to prove no threats were ever directed toward me. Finally, he once again says that Nikolai only moved out of the home at my request, that I changed the locks without notifying Nikolai, and therefore, he does not give up any rights to the property including access to the home upon reasonable notification.

Thursday, December 23, 2020

Two days before Christmas. I wake up to find out that Nikolai has shut off my internet and cable after Jimmy explicitly asked him not to do it and Nikolai agreed he wouldn't. In the height of a pandemic, right before a holiday, when I work exclusively at home, Nikolai shuts off the internet without notice. Fortunately, Jimmy is off, and he comes to help. We go to XFinity, and it takes a few hours, but he has me all set up again. I also open a new account with the gas and electric company since I figure I likely will wake up Christmas morning with no heat. Emily tells me later that this was the final straw for Jimmy. Nikolai lied to his face, assuring him he would not cancel the cable and turned around an hour later and cancelled it. Jimmy was done with him from that point forward. He tried very hard to remain neutral even though he was scarred like everyone else from all the violent outbursts. Being blatantly lied to ended that neutrality.

My lawyer emails Nikolai's lawyer that it is a waste of time to keep going on about this. Nikolai moved out. He took more than just necessary items. He has a new place of residence, and therefore I am entitled to my own residence as well. She says that if Nikolai wishes to have "unfettered access" to the home, then he must provide me with keys to his home, so I have the same unfettered access to his residence. She adds that Nikolai was notified before the locks on the home were changed, and they were done so based upon Nikolai's representation that his new residence was ready and his failure to return home to sleep. She further writes that Nikolai cancelled the cable and internet last night, in the middle of a pandemic when I am working from home. She says that Nikolai will be held responsible and be required to compensate me if there are any negative consequences from my employer.

All the kids come for Christmas. I am fortunate. We open oodles of presents under the tree wrapped in beautiful foil colors with Grace's famous curly ribbon bows. Despite my constant statements of cutting back, I have once again gone overboard with presents. But if not this year, when? The kids have done the same, giving me far more expensive presents than they should have. Among my gifts, I receive an Apple Watch and an Alexa with a screen. Sarah comes later, and we exchange gifts with her too. Jimmy and Emily also got stockings for everyone and filled them. It was a surprise and they creatively put things in the stockings like small airline size bottles of liquor or wine.

Nikolai wishes all the kids a "Kerry" (rather than "Merry") Christmas by text. He does not send anyone a card or a gift. Since his family was weird about gifts, I guess it's not surprising. I would have thought under the circumstances with his obvious concerns about his relationship with them, he would have made more of an effort.

The day after Christmas, Jimmy and Emily (and Rover) return home and the rest of us eat dinner and essentially go our separate ways. I am in my bedroom watching Netflix on TV and Sarah and Matty are watching Netflix in the family room. Many years ago, I had opened a Netflix account, just the standard plan at $13.99 per month for two devices. My original intention was to have it for the vacation rental but never implemented it there. I grew to like a lot of shows on it and so just kept it home for us. During the pandemic, Nikolai and I watched shows like *The Americans* and *Madmen*. While I am watching, I get a notification on my phone that Netflix has upgraded my plan to allow for more devices which will of course result in additional charges of $4.00 (total $17.99) per month. This is odd. I didn't order this. Would one of the kids have done this? I am annoyed. I don't need the extra expenses at this point, and we really don't need extra devices. I then receive a notification of a new sign-in precisely in the town where Nikolai has his apartment. This cannot be a coincidence.

I go downstairs and tell the kids what's going on. No one can believe the gall. Nikolai must have upgraded my account—and this account is in my name with my credit card—so he could watch a show since we had already reached the limit of two viewers. The kids walk me through how to change my password, and I immediately downgrade the account. Nikolai's greed comes to bite him in the end. He could have gotten away with mooching off my Netflix for a long time if he hadn't upgraded the account.

A couple days later, Sarah comes to visit, and on her way, she is certain that she sees Nikolai driving slowly down our street. This will be the first of many sightings.

I am happy to see this year close. The new year has to be much better than 2020, which brought a pandemic, lockdowns, and untold heartache from Nikolai. Sadly, I am wrong and much more heartache awaits me.

CHAPTER 12

A New Year

On New Year's Day, I post the following on Facebook:

While 2020 was less than ideal I would be remiss if I left the impression that there weren't good things about it:

1. *2020 and the advent of the pandemic brought Jimmy and I home for work and gave us three months to bond over our laptops at the kitchen table before he left the nest for his beloved.*

2. *2020 and the pandemic brought Grace and her beloved Patrick home to live with us for three months. It gave me a great opportunity to really get to know what a wonderful person Patrick is and spend time with my baby girl.*

3. *2020 brought the marriage of Emily and Jimmy. I couldn't be happier to have her join our clan.*

4. *2020 brought Matty home with online classes at graduate school. We went through some tough times together, but we came out stronger. I am forever grateful for his invaluable support and advice.*

5. *2020 showed me that I have amazing friends and family who are there for me when I need them. I hope I can be half what they've been to me.*
6. *2020 brought cute little Rover to our lives. I never thought I could love a dog so much!*
  So, I'm happy to see 2020 go but grateful for all the good it brought. I know everything impacts who you are. Here's to a happy, peaceful, healthy, safe 2021!

I'm proud of myself that I can find the good and hopeful for a better year ahead. I think back to a New Year's Eve ten years ago spent with Nikolai, two other couples from church and some other people. At the stroke of midnight, every couple immediately went to their mate and hugged and kissed. But not Nikolai. He went to someone else. I was a bit embarrassed at the time. In retrospect, it was symbolic of our relationship.

Meanwhile, Nikolai texts me asking if I cancelled the cable and returned the equipment, and if I took care of the gas company.

I respond, "You cancelled the cable service, and I took care of everything."

He replies that he thought I reinstated the cable service after he cancelled it to make it through the holidays. I share it with the kids and Jimmy responds, "That doesn't even make sense." Does he think I'm that stupid to buy this nonsense?

A few days later, Nikolai changes his name on Facebook once again. He texts asking if he can come later and pick up the mail. We agree on the next day. The next day, I text Nikolai that I am not feeling well so I left his mail in the mailbox and that I left a box of odds and ends outside the front door that he can have. I am not feeling 100 percent, but the reality is I don't want to deal with him. Nikolai comes around 9 p.m.

For Christmas this year, I have added some new decorations in addition to my wreath, outdoor lights, and welcome signs. I purchased two red banners, one that says "Merry" and the other, "Christmas." I hung them outside in front of the sidelights to the front door. We have an old door, and the sidelights each have three see-through, thin glass panes. With the banners hung, it's impossible to see out and someone can only see in if they push the banner aside. I have a security camera right at the front door that records anyone who comes. Since Nikolai and I agreed to sell the vacation home without involving the lawyers, I removed the cameras from the Pocono house and brought them home. I figure with Nikolai's erratic behavior, I need them. The camera does its job and records Nikolai's every move. He comes up, takes the mail, pulls back one of the banners and looks inside the house. He then grabs the box and puts it all in the car. He returns to the front door and again looks in the windows of the sidelights by pushing the banner aside. He spends a long time first looking right, then looking left, then straight ahead. Then he moves to the other sidelight and looks in all directions through that one. Finally, he leaves. I show others the video that the camera recorded and each respond, "He is creepy."

———————◆———————

Grace and I start to discuss the wedding plans in earnest. How to deal with Nikolai is always on Grace's mind. I have said from the outset that I am too biased, and she must make this decision without me. I will cope with whatever she decides. My only request is that I not have to walk in with Nikolai into the reception. Patrick has already said that Nikolai cannot give a speech at the wedding. He will not listen to Nikolai give marital advice. That only leaves walking Grace down the aisle. We have all expressed concerns that the diminished role will bruise Nikolai's ego and may cause him to react in his usual way. Grace is considering simply inviting Nikolai as a guest with no role to play. That seems fraught with similar concerns.

On January 10, 2021, I write to Father Dan, the priest who is to marry Grace and Patrick. He is a lovely priest. We met him a few years ago at a wine tasting at church that my group had sponsored to raise money. He was new to our parish then and decided to join us as we made the rounds tasting different wine, beer, and alcohol. We all became fast friends and had him over for dinner, invited him to our annual pool party, and Jimmy and Emily had him officiate at their wedding. He ended up getting transferred just before Jimmy and Emily's wedding, but he is not too far away. That transfer caused many tears from me. Since he will marry Grace and Patrick, I feel he needs to know some of what is going on. At this point, he still thinks we are this happy family, and because of COVID, we have not seen him. I email him the following:

> *Dear Father,*
>
> *It is with a heavy heart that I write this to tell you of my sad family news. I had thought many times of contacting you to get together, but with the virus I didn't know what to do. Last September, Nikolai filed for a divorce. This March, we would have been married 29 years. This has been a very painful time for me. Nikolai has had a violent temper our whole marriage, something very few people know. It has affected me in many ways, particularly in my relationship with Nikolai, but I've just dealt with it all these years. But at least 6 years ago (that I know of), he started seeing other women. Matty found out at the time but didn't tell me (I guess to protect me). I found out 3 years ago when one woman contacted me. I tried to find a way forward after this, but Nikolai wasn't really looking for that. He told me several times this past year that he was justified in having affairs. I really didn't know what to do at that point, and fortunately my pastor agreed to meet with me in September. He told me he thought the relationship was abusive, and I should take a break for a few months to get clarity and tell Nikolai to leave. I did*

that but Nikolai had already filed for divorce and refused to leave the home until right before Christmas. Last fall was an extremely painful time for me and my children. Fortunately, I have my beautiful children who have been incredibly supportive of me during this time.

I just wanted you to be aware of the situation, especially with Grace's wedding coming up. Please pray for me and my children, Father. We can really use the prayers right now.

All the best,
Maria

He responds:

Sorry I opened my emails just now. I'm speechless and was tearing up while reading your email. You have a beautiful family. And I am so honored to be part of it. But it's not okay if you are dying inside and losing yourself in the process, while trying your best to stay intact. This is very hard. Be strong and have faith. You have your great loving children to rely on. Always remember everything happens for a reason. Please contact me anytime you want someone to talk to. I will be praying for you and Nikolai and for your children.

I reply:

Thank you for your kind words, Father. I shared them with the kids, and they were all touched. I have been through a few hardships in my life (my father died when I was 11, my brother was killed in a car accident when I was 22, and that was in between two major stomach operations—I have suffered from Crohn's disease my whole life). So, I

know I will be okay eventually. It's not how I envisioned spending my older years, but I will figure out a new life for myself. I just need to determine what God's plan is for me. I very much appreciate your support and prayers.
Warmest Regards,
Maria

He answers:

Thank God, Maria, that you became wiser and not bitter from your sad experience. That was a lot. But your situation right now is still very hard. In the midst of your storm, FOCUS on JESUS and not the storm, for you not to be afraid. It's hard to understand fully well why it happens. But surely God will let you in His time know why. Regards to the kids. Please let them know that I am one email or phone call away if they need to talk to or hang out with me. My prayers for everybody. Please do pray for Nikolai too, for his enlightenment and conversion. He too is also fighting a battle. He needs all our prayers very much.
God bless,
Fr. Dan

I am fortunate that my parents planted the seed of faith in me as a child. My faith has gotten me through many a dark day. Like most, my faith has ebbed and flowed over my lifetime, but it has always been there. When I was very sick with Crohn's disease, I bargained with God to heal me. He didn't accept. I guess God had other plans for me. During difficult times with Nikolai, I often went to God, seeking His guidance and sometimes a priest as well. Throughout this current nightmare, I looked to God every day to get me through. Sometimes, I just needed the strength to make it through the day. Other times, I needed hope. He usually answered my prayers. The wonderful people in my life would suddenly appear with a shoulder to lean on or a pep talk. Olivia would give me a random hug. Matty would come up with some suggestion for what I could do in the future, like learning French or writing this book. My kids called or texted me constantly and friends and family called me regularly to check up on me. I know that God was answering my prayers through those people. And so many people told me they were praying for me: Patrick's mom, Bella and her husband, Father Dan, my pastor. I don't know how I would have made it through without my faith to lean on.

———— ◆ ————

Toward the end of January, Grace and Patrick ask for a group telephone call with Matty, Jimmy, Emily, and me. Matty and I sit together in what is now my office. I have completely renovated the room, painted it yellow and kept the furniture simple. My nephew's fiancée remarks how much bigger the room now looks. Grace gets us all on the phone; she is in the car with Patrick. She tells us that she and Patrick have discussed it at length and prayed about it and concluded that they will not have Nikolai at the wedding. No one speaks for a long time. We are stunned. We never expected this outcome. They had talked of diminishing his role, of obtaining security in case he "loses it," but we never expected she would disinvite him. She starts to cry and explains their position. They hate the idea of security at the wedding. They feel Nikolai's presence, even if he behaves, will make many people uncomfortable, and they don't feel they will be able to enjoy their own wedding if he is there.

We all fully understand their position and are supportive, but none of us is all too comfortable with it. Part of me is relieved that I will not have to deal with Nikolai, but much of me is uncertain this is the right thing to do. After all, he is her father. It seems so strange to not have him there. I had been steeling myself for his presence these past few months.

Grace will relay the decision to Nikolai at a later date, which predictably does not go well.

———————— ◆ ————————

It is February 4, 2021, and Nikolai texts me, asking for the umpteenth time if I want to buy the house. I'm unsure if I am making the right financial decision, but I feel that I've had too many changes and emotional upheaval to add moving to a new location on top of it. Where would I go? I would like to have a place for the kids to visit. I've been living here for over twenty years. I have friends here, great neighbors, and my church. I have indicated multiple times to Nikolai that I would like to buy him out, depending on how the financial situation plays out. I can't fathom why he keeps asking. After discussing with the kids, I decide to simply ignore his text. As Grace says, I can't trust that he doesn't have an ulterior motive so it's best to not respond. We have successfully put up the vacation home for sale and it is to close on March 1. We sold it for $20,000 over the asking price and $90,000 over what we had listed it three years prior and had five offers in less than a week. COVID does crazy things to people. That will be Nikolai's argument for the value of our home.

A few days later, I find out from my lawyer that Nikolai is entitled to my pension. I feel like I've been kicked in the gut. I've put in almost thirty-five years for that pension and now he's entitled to half. That I took out loans from my 401K to put him through college has no relevance, however. The argument is that I benefited from Nikolai's education, so I don't get compensated for the sacrifice to get him there. I'm not sure what sacrifice Nikolai made to deserve my pension. Nikolai and his lawyer do nothing to move the process forward. In fact, it's quite the opposite. In my state, divorces on average take six months to conclude. We are at the six-month mark with still a long way to go. Nikolai's financials were not worth the paper they were printed on. My lawyer has instituted discovery, which is where questions and requests for documents are asked of the opposing party. My lawyer must arrange for an appraisal of the house, despite requesting that Nikolai's attorney handle it, and, at my request, an appraisal of my pension so I can buy Nikolai out. I can't emotionally deal with having him take payments from my pension each month for the rest of my life. It may make more financial sense to do it that way, but I want to be done with him. I'm devastated by the pension news, but the kids are supportive of me as always. It's what keeps me going. My lawyer contacts Nikolai's lawyer about getting started on the appraisal. Nikolai's lawyer suggests some unknown guy to do the appraisal. My lawyer refuses and suggests a reputable firm. His lawyer refuses. They go back and forth until they finally agree on one.

On Valentine's Day, I come downstairs in the morning to find a beautiful bouquet of flowers on the kitchen island. A gift from the kids. I didn't expect anything. But they were not going to leave me without on this day. They figured my first Valentine's Day alone would be tough. In the past Nikolai would get me a dozen roses or a Dove chocolate heart. I often told him not to get me roses because they were so much more expensive on Valentine's Day, but he never listened to me. Despite that, he made a point of saying more than once that the only reason he got me anything for Valentine's Day was because society pressured him to do it. He really knew how to make a girl feel special! I practically begged him to get me flowers for no reason at all—nothing fancy—a cheap bunch from the supermarket. He never did.

In March, we go to battle over the tax returns. We are still married so we only have two choices to file: married filing jointly or married filing separately. I am a tax attorney with the government. I fully understand the ramifications of each. If we file jointly, I am jointly and severally liable for what's on the return. That means the government can go after me for any amount that the government thinks is still owed. So, if Nikolai fails to include interest from bank accounts that he is hiding, for example, and the government determines we owe taxes for that, the government can collect just from me. Naturally, I want to file separately, which will mean I am only liable for what is on my own separate return (and Nikolai is only liable for his). But under this crazy divorce legal system, Nikolai can make me file jointly because the taxes will be lower and so he does. My lawyer states that if I refuse to file jointly, a judge will make me do so and make me pay the extra taxes. No one seems to care that I will be equally responsible for any false representations he makes. After much back and forth with both Nikolai and my lawyer, I say I will only file jointly with him if he signs a certification that he is providing all necessary information and if the returns are done by an accountant. After much pushback from his lawyer, Nikolai ultimately agrees to my terms.

I start to see multiple items that Nikolai lists on Facebook marketplace. Some are from the vacation house, and some are rightfully mine. Others are things he took or new items that I don't recognize. Either he did go to the vacation house last fall, or he took these items without my knowledge when we went in June, in furtherance of his master plan of divorce. The latter seems more likely as it's mostly junk like used life vests that he could have hidden in the car from me in June rather than more valuable stuff that he could have taken in the fall. I do notice when I go to the vacation home in January with respect to selling the house that someone tried to get into the shed. The lock is damaged, and I must have it cut off. Nikolai lists a vase filled with used corks for five dollars on Facebook. I scratch my head. This begs the questions: Who would want it? How is it worth his time? He makes over $200,000 per year. Why is he selling junk like this?

CHAPTER 13

Showers of Love and Hate

I am eagerly planning Grace's bridal shower. By this time, with all that has transpired, I have concluded that Nikolai will not be included. It is going to be a surprise. Most showers today are not surprises, but I want to surprise Grace. This will be a challenge as she always knows what's going on. I decide the best way to surprise her is to have the shower on Matty's birthday on March 27. The story we give her is we are all going to have lunch at one of our favorite Italian restaurants to celebrate Matty. Meanwhile, I have forty-five guests, mostly women except for my brother, Grace's brothers and Patrick's dad, brother-in-law, and nephew anticipating her arrival. Patrick brings her in, and she stops dead in her tracks, her mouth drops open, and her eyes grow wide. Immediately, she realizes this is not Matty's birthday celebration. She sees Matty and hugs him and with gratitude feels bad that he gave up his birthday for her. I'm thrilled we pulled off the surprise. Many of my friends and neighbors are there, including Nancy, a friend from church. I met Nancy through her son, who was good friends with Jimmy in second through sixth grade. Over time, Nikolai and I grew to enjoy Nancy and her husband Victor's company, and even after the boys grew apart, we remained friends and the four of us would go out together. I never had an opportunity to talk to Nancy about what happened with Nikolai. The day after I changed the locks and Nikolai moved out, Victor called me. At first, I thought he knew what happened and wanted to ask about it, although I would have expected Nancy to call me. As the conversation proceeded without him mentioning anything about my situation, but rather asking me for tax advice, I concluded his calling was just a crazy coincidence. In retrospect, it likely was not. Soon after that phone call, Nikolai began to post on Facebook that he was out to dinner with Victor. Since no one in his Facebook group knew Victor and Victor didn't have a Facebook page himself, I assumed his posts were for my benefit, essentially to say, "I've got Victor on my side." The kids and I went to Church on Christmas Day and ran into Victor and Nancy. Victor offered to take our picture for us, but Nancy seemed like she couldn't get away fast enough. When I invited her to the shower, I had hoped she would call me to RSVP, which would give me the opportunity to explain things to her. But she didn't; she just texted me she was coming. All seemed fine at the shower until Nikolai's affairs came up in conversation at the table. Nancy acted very strangely from that point forward and said an abrupt goodbye as soon as it was over. I found the situation with Nancy and Victor frustrating, and they ultimately declined the invitation to Grace's wedding.

When I expressed my frustration to Matty, his response was, "F**k them. They take up too much rent-free space in your brain." I knew he was right. It was unlikely I would ever have a relationship with them in the future since we only ever went out as couples. It was just my competitive nature at play that didn't want to lose anyone to Nikolai. Plus, I felt strongly that they were duped by Nikolai as to the reality of the situation. It really wasn't much of a loss, however, and the fact that Nancy never reached out to see what I was going through spoke volumes. She wasn't a true friend.

Despite the disappointment with Nancy, the day is wonderful. Grace is showered with much love and presents. The girls decorate the restaurant with banners and signs with the theme, "Traveling from

Miss to Mrs." The favors are little airplane bottle openers. The chicken parmigiana—the meal I selected—is excellent, and the service could not be better. Everyone seems to enjoy themselves. After we return home, the kids, my mom, and I sit around the fire pit outside and eat wings and fries from a local restaurant and have some drinks. It's a great ending to a fabulous day, but Nikolai will soon dampen that joy.

———— ♦ ————

Three days before the shower, Grace texted all of us that Nikolai had left her a voicemail asking her to call him. Jimmy responded that he received a similar message three days before her and that Nikolai sounded angry, and thus, there was no way Jimmy was going to return the call. Grace replied that she guesses she'll have to move up the "you can't come to the wedding" conversation. She followed up with, "I hate this. Just leave me alone and let me live my life without you, at least for now." Jimmy agreed.

In the meantime, a neighbor from down the street texts me that she has heard from Nikolai. He sent her a message saying he wanted her to know that it was not his choice to not be invited to Grace's shower, that I am very vindictive and am turning the kids against him. He just wanted to end his marriage, and he filed for divorce. He wanted it to be amicable, but I don't want it that way. He said she really doesn't know his wife, or maybe she does after years of interaction. She thinks she's got the support of everyone, but they are really criticizing her. He ended by saying he just wanted to let her know because she is great, and he misses her friendship. If she wants to get together, he's always available.

I apologize to my neighbor, and she asks if I want her to respond in any way. She indicates that Nikolai's request is bizarre considering they are not close, and he has moved away. She can't fathom why she would want to be friends with him. My neighbor next to Olivia gets the identical message. She gags when she reads it, wondering, *Why would I want to contact him?* My next-door neighbor gets the same message, again verbatim. She asks me what she should do. She tells me she thought of telling him what she thinks but her husband advises her not to. I tell her to ignore it. Patrick's parents get the identical message also. I am horrified at that. At least my friends have known me for twenty-plus years. Patrick's parents are new to our family dynamics, and their son is about to marry the daughter of this man. Fortunately, they are good-natured enough to tell Patrick that they will do whatever Grace wants, which is nothing. I guess this was Nikolai's attempt to steal my friends. He likely would have sent the same message to Emily's parents but didn't know how to contact them.

After seeing this, Jimmy says, "All I can say is he is digging his own grave. I don't think he can go any deeper. I hope it's comfortable down there. If that really is his reality, then I don't want anything to do with him."

My friend Lily says that the people who know and love you will not respond to his manipulations, so he is providing entertainment and wasting his time. It turns out she is right.

It is now March 30, 2021, and Grace sends us the following draft of what will be her conversation with Nikolai:

> *Patrick and I have had a lot of time to think and reflect. What you've done to Mom is completely unacceptable— and I do want to point out that all of us are making our own opinions. We are grown adults, and Mom is not brainwashing us into thinking a certain way. We've seen enough ourselves in order to figure out where we stand. Everyone was able to get past everything from 4 years ago, but what's recently happened is not acceptable. Not only have you had other affairs while still married (in the divorce process or not is still unacceptable), but you've also stolen things from the house, you've been stealing a lot of money from mom for years, and you've manipulated*

everyone around you. Patrick and I discussed the wedding A LOT. We thought of every route our wedding day would take, having or not having you there. We came to the conclusion that there's no way that everyone (including myself and Patrick) would be care-free, happy, and stress-free if you were there. So unfortunately, we don't want you at our wedding. It wasn't an easy decision but was one that is best for everyone. I want our wedding to be the best day of our lives and everyone else's lives and having you there would cause people to walk on eggshells trying to avoid you. We're truly just not in a place right now to have you there, especially considering all of this could have been delayed 8 months. Forgiveness takes time and healing takes time. We're all working on it but there's so much hurt that you've caused everyone that no one has any desire to have you at our wedding.

I tell Grace that Matty and I had discussed this previously and believe she should lead with her two strongest points, which is that he couldn't wait a lousy eight months knowing what an impact this would have and his past track record of ruining holidays and other occasions makes having him too risky. I add that she can and should tell Father Dan this.

Jimmy responds that he agrees. The eight months is a good point because it shows that he only thinks of himself and if he truly cared he would have waited to make the wedding easier on Grace. He adds, "When things were bad, Mom would always say, 'Just gotta get through the weddings and I'll figure it out after that' and he didn't even have the decency to wait 8 months. And yeah, definitely drive home that things were so bad leading up to when he moved out of the house, and you just can't risk there being an incident on the most important day of your life. It's too important to risk including such a volatile person in your wedding."

Grace responds that they are all good points, and she will adjust it. She states, "My biggest worry is that he'll continue to interrupt me, and I won't be able to get my points across."

Matty says, "Well then you'll really know you're making the right decision."

Jimmy agrees and says, "By interrupting you he'll be turning it into more of an argument, which will prove your point."

Grace wonders how to respond if Nikolai indicates he will show up anyway. Matty suggests the following:

First you couldn't wait 8 months to file for divorce after a 29-year marriage. If nothing else, it shows how selfish you are. You couldn't have the foresight to realize how this whole thing would affect my wedding? It was the first thing out of everyone's mouth when they found out... "Oh my God, you're getting married in less than a year. How's this going to work?" It's clear that thought never even entered your mind. And on top of that, your track record has been horrible with family events. You've exploded at people, ruined holidays, and the like... and that was when things were going "well." This is my day, not anyone else's. I want it to go perfectly and it's already not. But your being there and making it awkward for all my guests and not knowing how you'll act because of how reactive a person you are, makes me know that it's safer for MY day to not have you there. And aside from how your actions affected me and my wedding day directly, you were also horrible towards the rest of my family. You turned your back on everyone, you stole money blah blah blah blah blah ... and that goes back to where I started of how selfish you are. I hope you can respect my decision because if you don't it will really speak loudly of how you feel about me and if you want a relationship with me down the road.

A few days later, Grace has the fateful call with Nikolai. Patrick is with her, and they explain all their reasons. Grace must tell Nikolai that if he interrupts her again, she will terminate the call, and he is respectful after that. Patrick suggests that Nikolai seek help for his mental health. Nikolai scoffs at that.

A few days later, Nikolai texts Grace and Patrick, which she shares with all of us.

Nikolai says that he and I got into an argument on our way back from Maine in the car. He asked me to put the money back into his Fidelity account, but I refused. He says he withdrew money from the account to help both his brothers with their medical bills—Boris fighting lung cancer, Igor fighting bladder cancer and just having kidney surgery—and because his mother isn't doing well. He said he told me about that, and I got angry. Once we got home, he says I left with Matty to go to the Poconos, and upon my return, I asked him to leave the house. This was the second time he was told to leave, if for nothing else but helping his brothers and mother with financial aid. After I told him to leave, he contacted an attorney and filed for divorce. He ends by saying, "That's the truth."

I don't weigh in on this one. I'm so sick of all the lies. He never brought up his sick family to me, but I have no way of proving that. I don't know it at this time, but I believe he dreamt that one up to try and justify the ATM cash withdrawals. Matty immediately responds that "we found the papers dated September 9th, a week before we went to the Poconos."

Grace informs us that Nikolai tried to call her again two minutes before the text was sent after she told him she wouldn't be speaking to him anymore. Jimmy states that Nikolai probably "took some time to think about what other lies he could tell and came up with that. Now it's all about his brothers. He never mentioned that before."

The next day, Nikolai texts Grace and Patrick again, asking them to please reconsider and saying that he will not cause any trouble, he will be gracious at their wedding. He just needs to walk his daughter down the aisle. He tells them they are both great, and he loves them both.

Grace notes that it's all about what Nikolai "needs." It's all self-ish and he acts like a "complete s**t." In the end, she decides not to respond.

Two weeks later, I receive a text from Nikolai, accusing me of convincing Grace not to invite him to her wedding. He adds that it's unbelievable and no one else can believe it either and ends with, "Good job."

I send it to the kids. Jimmy responds with a middle finger. Grace says, "That's funny because I explicitly explained to him that you were not involved in the decision."

"I told you it would be all my fault," I say.

Jimmy responds, "Have a nice life, a**hole."

They all agree I should not respond.

Three weeks later, I receive another text from Nikolai, asking me to tell Grace to invite me to the wedding.

I respond, "Contrary to what you want to believe, I had nothing to do with Grace's decision. I told her I could not be involved because I could not be objective and whatever she decided I would accept and act accordingly. You need to take this up with Grace."

Nikolai replies that I could have told her to do the right thing, which is to include him regardless of my opinion. I do not respond. He then texts Grace asking her to include him. She responds:

> *Patrick's and my decision is final. We don't want you there. Like we said in our phone conversation, you could have waited 8 months to do all of this but didn't, which shows that you don't care for anyone but yourself. Your presence is going to make our wedding day unenjoyable and stressful due to your unpredictable emotional outbursts. In the process of this divorce over the last 8 months, you've done nothing but destroy our family and sabotage our mother. I have nothing else to discuss on this matter. You're not welcome.*

Nikolai replies that I am the one making it hard with the divorce, that he wanted to settle out of court, but I insisted on going to court. He says he is sorry, that he wanted to wait for after the wedding, but I made it unbearable. He doesn't want her to later regret not having him as part of her wedding. He says he was a good father to them, and he is not sure why, in good conscience and as a good Catholic, she is doing this. He wishes he could understand but he can't, nor can others. He says again that he would not be disruptive, but he guesses she is using that to justify her decision.

The kids are sickened that he plays the Catholic card. Two priests left the decision up to Grace. Neither said she must have her father at her wedding. Grace comments that Nikolai's attempt to make her feel guilty reinforces her decision to not have him there. Jimmy comments, "I love how it's Mom's fault he didn't wait the 8 months. Just keep blaming everyone else for your mistakes. He's so predictable."

"Everything is always my fault," I write.

Matty replies, "I mean it's just not, so don't beat yourself up over it. His words don't reflect reality and that's all that matters. Words are just words."

I answer, "I know, but it helps hearing it!"

Jimmy writes, "Mom, I think the four of us here know for a fact that it's all his fault! That's all that matters!"

Nikolai then follows up with Grace, again saying that I told him to leave the house after I came back from the Poconos with Matty in September. He said he knew right then that he had to file for a divorce, that I didn't value him. There are a lot of things you don't know, he adds.

Once again, his lies don't add up, since he filed for divorce before we even left to go to the Poconos. Grace opts not to respond and states, "Anything I say won't matter. He'll still be on his high horse in psychopath land."

CHAPTER 14

A Broken Process

May and June bring some action on the divorce front. After a threatening letter from my attorney, we receive Nikolai's responses to our discovery requests. Discovery is where I made one mistake. My lawyer served discovery on Nikolai at the end of January. A week later, Nikolai's lawyer retaliated with discovery on me. I figured since Nikolai's due date was before mine, why not just wait until we get his response before sending mine. In my legal world, a deadline is etched in stone and a judge can immediately be brought in to enforce it. Not so in this legal world. Perhaps I should have known better since Nikolai submitted his deficient financial papers one month past the due date. And so, I didn't rush to draft responses. When Nikolai's due date came and went, I inquired of my lawyer how we enforce it, and she responded that we can't enforce anything until we first respond to theirs. Seriously? Talk about a broken system. I quickly provided my responses, which only delayed the process by two weeks. At the time, I was disgusted with myself for the two-week delay. Little did I know, I had a long way to go.

Nikolai's discovery response consists of 291 pages of mostly garbage. He does not provide any bank statements, only statements from his stock account showing my transfers. His responses reveal a couple of new things. One, he is claiming he gave his brothers and mother

$63,000 to help with their medical care. This is downright ludicrous. He never gave them anything without his arm being twisted in all the time we were married and now he gives them this large sum of money? Two, he indicates that I have two leaf blowers and that my mother is living with me. How does he know this? I took one of the leaf blowers from the vacation home just before we sold it. I never told anyone. I simply put it in the garage. My mother has spent most of her time with me sleeping on the couch in a room in the back of the house. Three, he provides his lease, which shows that his move-in date was December 11, 2020, four days before I changed the locks. He also had all his mail forwarded effective December 14, 2020, one day before I changed the locks. So much for his lawyer's argument that he couldn't live there until the 18th and a claim for reimbursement of a hotel that he allegedly had to stay in. Of course, no receipts are ever provided for any hotel. He makes some other bogus irrelevant allegations including that he helped pay for my student loans, that he paid for our wedding reception entirely himself, which cost over $20,000, and that he only took his work computer and his clothes when he left the home. He conveniently forgot that he took ten carloads plus a pickup truck full of possessions and that we both paid for the wedding, I made more money than he did at that time, and the wedding only cost $9,000.

I share the responses with the kids, noting that it's a pack of lies, and he can't keep them straight. Matty responds, "I'm more than happy to testify. I lived through at least half of those lies." With respect to Nikolai's claim of giving his family money, Jimmy states, "Hopefully it's just a lie and he didn't give his family 60K because he's too money obsessed, and that money is sitting in one of his secret bank accounts." Matty comments, that if he did give his family money, it must have been withdrawn from one of his accounts and there must be other money. Grace weighs in:

Yea, I would think that the money is either sitting in these accounts or he pulled it out closer to the divorce proceedings and then it's still going to be counted. Unless he bought something huge we don't know about (or is drug dealing—I'm sticking with this one), then there's no place this money would have gone other than in accounts that he doesn't think we know about (possibly the off-shore one?) and then when the subpoena comes, we can see exactly how much and when he's moved the rest of this money and I can pretty much guarantee you that he didn't move it or use it earlier than right before the divorce because he thought he had nothing to worry about and the bank accounts were secret.

Since we didn't get an adequate response to our discovery requests, in mid-May, my attorney sends out subpoenas to all the known bank accounts of Nikolai. So much for a quick and amicable divorce. We receive back the joint appraisal for the house, something for which Nikolai had to be hunted down to pay his fair share. The value comes in at $540,000 as of April 30. It's a little higher than I hoped due to COVID, but I can live with it. It's not so high that I can't afford to buy Nikolai out. Nikolai asks me for the username and password to the business bank account with respect to the vacation rental business. Since the house has been sold and no longer rented, I am in the process of closing out the business. I need to get final tax returns and pay the taxes. Once that is done, I plan to give Nikolai half of what's left. Matty suggests I tell him the username is "youraliar" and the password is "Gotohell." I don't respond to Nikolai and a few days later, I discover that he has gone to the bank, closed out the account and taken all the proceeds. While eventually I will get my fair share, I am so mad I see red.

Matty says, "He's just a lousy piece of s**t. Making things complicated and being an a**hole for zero reason. But I mean that's classic at this point."

Grace writes, "And completely losing his kids. Thinking his decisions don't affect how we feel. Actually ridiculous. Doesn't care at all about us."

We all agree that this makes Nikolai look bad so it should have only a positive effect for me. Nikolai's lawyer spins his actions to put the blame on me. He claims Nikolai was concerned I would dissipate the funds since I transferred money from his stock account four years prior. He makes wild accusations of fraud. It always comes back to that. My lawyer asks me about it, and I explain that Nikolai had given me sole control over the stock accounts (plus his 401K), and I made investments as I chose. The money was transferred into an account in my name and is all accounted for. If Nikolai's lawyer would perform his obligations as a representative of the bar, he would see that the money is all there.

I express my frustrations to the kids. Matty responds:

> *He's a complete a**hole and he can consider himself dead to this family once this is all over but stay strong keep pushing and don't let his horrible character get you down. The evidence should show for itself. Be patient let everything unfold and if you're gonna get upset, get upset at something that's actually real. Not his blatant attempt to try and make you seem like you stooped down to his piece of s**t level which never even happened!*

I thank them for the encouragement and express that sometimes I just need to hear that it's going to be okay. Jimmy replies, "It's definitely going to be okay! I'd say the four of us have a pretty strong bond because of years of this crap! We'll get through it together."

Nikolai's lawyer then issues subpoenas for my bank accounts. It's a ridiculous tactic since I provided all my statements in discovery.

A settlement conference before a panel of two lawyers is scheduled for June 29. I'm confident this will all be concluded in July. I sell all my stock, figuring I will have to give Nikolai some money in the next couple months, and the market will likely go down. Wrong on both counts. I incur substantial capital gains tax as a result.

In mid-June I am at a trial for my work in Washington D.C. for ten days, one week prior to Grace's wedding. I tell the lead attorney the mess I'm going through, and he is very understanding. He even lets me leave a day early to get home for wedding preparations. While I'm in Washington, the responses to the subpoenas to two of Nikolai's bank accounts come in. It's eye-opening. Ultimately, I enter all the bank information on a spreadsheet, and Matty and Jimmy help me make a graph. It shows his total cash withdrawals of $126,000, and it looks like a flattened bell curve. The withdrawals begin in the spring of 2019 and peak from the end of 2019 through the divorce filing at which point they taper off to very little. He clearly had a game plan back in 2019 to hide money prior to suing for divorce. In the peak nine-month period, he withdrew $80,000 and $70,000 of that was withdrawn in the six months leading up to the filing. This clearly shows the withdrawals were in contemplation of hiding assets for his planned divorce or in this legal world, "dissipation of assets." My Googling indicates that judges look very unfavorably on a party who does this.

Meanwhile, Nikolai changes his name again on Facebook and begins to post things of a religious nature. I conclude that it's his way of trying to justify himself that he really isn't a bad person. Jimmy agrees, but Matty says, "Probably just choosing one of his many personas depending on the woman he's seeing."

As I'm leaving to return home from the trial, I receive a Facebook message from Nikolai's cousin asking about Grace's wedding. I'm stunned that Nikolai hasn't told her anything. I inform her about the divorce and that Grace does not want her father at her wedding and so did not feel comfortable inviting any of his family. I apologize to her for her finding out this way. Taken aback, she says she had to read my message over and over to make sure it was real. She kindly offers to talk if I want.

The settlement conference is a waste of time as most things in this process turn out to be. Nikolai's lawyer argues that I am not entitled to any alimony because I banned Nikolai from his daughter's wedding. The panel admonishes his lawyer, stating he should know better that one has nothing to do with the other (and that's assuming it is true).

———— ◆ ————

There are one sad development and two bright spots during this time. The sad development is when Matty tells me he wants to move to Florida to be with Sarah. She is in a four-year program at school there, and he wants to try to get his job transferred down there. He has discussed it with his brother and sister but dreads breaking the news to me. He knows how hard it will be. One glorious May evening, we are eating dinner outside. As we are finishing, he tells me his plans. The tears immediately pour out. I am losing my rock, my lifeline. He assures me he will come visit often. We discuss the logistics, and then through laughing tears, I say, "How will I do the grass without you?" (Matty has been hard at work, determined to give me a good lawn. He took my soil for testing and applied various chemicals and plans to aerate and seed.) He responds that he'll come home one weekend to work on my grass. I wasn't serious about the grass, just devastated at the news. I will now be completely alone starting in October—or so I think.

The bright spots are my birthday and Grace's wedding. I turn sixty at the end of May. Grace tells me she must work but will try to get off early. The other kids agree they will be with me for dinner. Matty offers to take me out to lunch. I clean the house in anticipation of having my whole gang home, which proves to be fortuitous. Matty takes me to a nice brunch place where I eat too much French toast right near a roaring fire. We drive home, and just as I'm going in the door, I realize I need to get my neighbor's mail for them and turn around and run over there. Matty seems a bit perplexed and waits at the door for me. I come back with the mail and enter my home to find around forty of my friends and family yelling, "Surprise!"

I stop dead in my tracks, my chin is practically on my chest, my hand clasped over my open mouth. I can't believe it. I keep saying over and over, "Oh my gosh, I can't believe you pulled this off." The kids decorated the house beautifully, Grace made a two-layer cake, Matty cooked up some great beef and pork dishes, and Jimmy created a collage of pictures out of a huge 6-0. I am so touched. It's a miracle I don't cry. As Olivia says later, "There was a lot of love in the room."

Months later I will think back to this day and all the people who supported me through this time. After the party I hang up the 6-0 in my closet and periodically look over all the pictures. The pictures show me that I had a lot of joy in my life, something I need to remind myself of during these dark days.

Grace's wedding is less than a month later. There are some glitches: three-hundred chair covers to iron for the ceremony in less than a week, transportation that comes forty-five minutes late, and photographers that don't take the requisite family photos. But she's a beautiful bride, and she and Patrick make a lovely couple. There are moments when it's hard for me. I'm on my own without a mate. It's lonely, and it shouldn't be this way. On the bus between the ceremony and the reception I start to feel emotional; fortunately, Patrick's parents suggest I sit with them, and it helps my outlook. I give a speech at the reception, which goes well. The DJ even asks me if I do public speaking for a living which makes me burst with pride. Olivia, my brother, my nephews, Matty, and Jimmy look out for me and make sure I'm on the dance floor. I'm always happiest when I'm dancing. I'm blessed to have such good people in my life.

———◆———

A book lands in my mailbox in July. We people of faith say there are no coincidences in this life. It's called *Life Is Messy*[8] by Matthew Kelly. Kelly, the founder and head of Dynamic Catholic, is an engaging speaker and prolific writer. When Grace was in college, her friend introduced her to Dynamic Catholic. Back then, if you signed up, you would receive a daily quote in your inbox to help you prepare for Lent or Advent. Over time, that changed to a daily quote all during the year and a short daily inspirational video during Lent and Advent. Grace introduced me to it, and I was hooked. I found it to be such a great way to start my day. I grew to like the organization so much that I started to donate regularly to it, something Nikolai was never happy about. I have several charities I donate to, mostly Catholic ones. I always felt that since we were financially well off, we should try to be generous. Considering our income, I thought we should really do more than I did, but Nikolai was not thrilled about any of it. Because of my donations to Dynamic Catholic, I became an "ambassador," which essentially entitles me to a few extras like some videos in my inbox and the latest book that Kelly has written before it's officially released. Talk about the right time and place! Kelly starts *Life is Messy* describing the Japanese art of Kintsugi. In short, a broken vase is not thrown away; rather, it is glued back together with gold dust in the glue to make the cracks appear more obvious. The vase ends up being more beautiful than it was before it was broken. Kelly relates it to the human condition and asks the question, Can someone broken be put back together to be more beautiful than before being broken? The answer is a resounding yes, and the rest of the book discusses different aspects of our messy lives in that regard. This book arrives when I am broken, and I am not certain I can be repaired. I have no idea what the future holds, what kind of person I can be, or what my family will now be like. While I'm comfortable in the fact that I did not engage in verbal abuse, I did not break my marriage vows, I did not hide money, and I did not file for divorce, I can't help but having nagging thoughts in my head as to whether I deserve this life. This book gives me so much hope. Deep down I know that everyone has stuff to deal with, but in reading this book, I know with certainty that I'm not the only one with a mess and there are ways to make it through. I read the entire book very quickly and then reread it, a section at a time each day, and reread it again. It helps me so much to believe that I can get through this darkness, and while life will never be perfect, there is light that will come. The book also equates the gold dust to the people who help us through the difficulties. Kelly encourages us to strive to be gold dust for others. I can say with absolute certainty that an abundance of gold dust has come my way through friends and family.

I feel I have reached a turning point: I have more good days than bad. There are days I feel at peace, like I can or have forgiven Nikolai, but I really am not there yet. I don't want anything to do with him ever again, but on the good days I don't focus on what he's done to me. Do I wish him well? I'm definitely not there yet, which makes me think I have not forgiven him.

But the bad days can still be tough. My heart hurts. This wasn't the dream. I was supposed to live my "golden years" traveling with him, spending time with our grandkids, and just enjoying life. He destroyed that dream. On these days, the mourning for the life I should have had overwhelms me. The simplest thing will bring these feelings on, the smell of coffee that he always drank, feeling like I look good, but no one compliments me. Some days I feel so alone, so bereft of a companion of my generation and mindset. The kids talk among themselves, and sometimes it's like they speak a foreign language— instead of yes, they say "yeash"; someone is not drunk, they are "lit"; and things are not awesome, they are "fire"—and they have their inside jokes. Sometimes, I feel they summarily dismiss me as irrelevant. In those moments, I've never felt more alone—more lonely—than ever in my life, except maybe when I spent a junior-year semester in Washington, DC.

I arrived for my internship at a one-bedroom apartment for three of us. One girl had already gotten there and took one twin bed in the bedroom. I quickly laid claim to the other twin. There was no way I was going to sleep in the living room. The apartment was infested with cockroaches. Each morning, I would turn on the bathroom light with trepidation and watch them all scatter. I had been diagnosed with

Crohn's just before the internship started, so I had bathroom issues, which made me more insecure about the living arrangements. My two roommates immediately bonded, and it quickly became apparent that I was the third wheel who was in the way, an inconvenience for them the entire semester. I had to find friends elsewhere. Instinctively shy, this was a difficult task. Over time, my aloneness turned to loneliness. I spent my free time sightseeing alone. I loved the city, our government, and all things political, and I was determined to see every part of it, every museum, every monument, every branch of government. On the way to tour the Washington Monument one day, I caught myself walking down the street having a conversation with myself out loud. I knew then my loneliness was deep.

The internship itself was a better experience and helped me not feel so alone. I was assigned to the United States Attorney's Office. Washington, DC, is unique in its criminal justice system; every crime is a federal one. If you rob someone in New York, the state of New York— represented by the Assistant District Attorney—will prosecute you. If you use the mail in New York to scam someone (mail fraud), the Federal government—represented by the Assistant United States Attorney—will prosecute you. In Washington, the Assistant United States Attorney prosecutes all crimes. I was assigned to three attorneys. I don't remember the latter two's names as they were useless. They introduced themselves and effectively ignored me for the rest of the semester. J. Alvin Stout III, however, was a Godsend. A tall, Black man with close-cropped hair, a mustache and large horn-rimmed, tortoise-shell glasses, J. Alvin Stout III was impeccably dressed, wearing a three-piece suit every day to work. J. Alvin Stout III brought me into his legal world. He's the reason I know the distinction between state crimes and crimes in Washington, D.C. J. Alvin Stout III shared his case files with me, assigned me research and even had me stay late one night to interview a bunch of witnesses on one of his crazy trespass cases. At the end, J. Alvin Stout III strong-armed the other two attorneys into taking me out to lunch with them, and he wrote me the most amazing recommendation letter for law school.

When I returned to school in the fall, the committee handling law school applicants said it was one of the best letters they had ever read. It wasn't because I did anything out of the ordinary. It was because J. Alvin Stout III was extraordinary. A kind, decent gentleman, he made the internship worthwhile. Midway through the semester, I managed to develop a friendship with another intern from San Diego who was also assigned to work with J. Alvin Stout III. That also helped with my loneliness, but I was happy when the semester ended, and I could return home.

That depth of loneliness hits me now periodically. I can be in a room full of people and feel it. I had hoped to never again feel the way I did on that internship. Hopefully, the loneliness will lessen.

I need to find another dream.

CHAPTER 15

I Poked the Bear!

August-September 2021

Jimmy has been having some health concerns. In the late spring he started complaining of throat discomfort. He went to a doctor who said he had reflux and prescribed medication. It didn't help. In May, he went to an ear, nose and throat specialist who said he had postnasal drip and prescribed nose drops. It didn't help. Then, at the end of June, out of nowhere his lymph node in his neck enlarged to the size of a golf ball. He showed the doctor, and, immediately alarmed, she said he needed to get an ultrasound done at once. He went and got the ultrasound as soon as the radiologist would take him. In early July, he was booked to take the honeymoon in Hawaii that he and Emily hadn't been able to take the year before because of COVID, and they decided to go ahead with their plans. His doctor called him during his trip and told him he needed to arrange for a biopsy as soon as possible, which he did immediately upon his return. I was in constant contact with him, advising him as best I could and supporting him. He said one possibility was Hodgkin's lymphoma. I told him that when I was seventeen, they thought I had Hodgkin's, and it turned out to be an infection of my lymph nodes. I was confident it would be the same with him. On August 4, 2021, I was on a conference call with a judge when Jimmy called me. I quickly texted him back that I couldn't speak then, asking if it was important or could I call him back. He texted back, "I have 'very treatable' lymphoma."

Cancer. The big C. My twenty-six-year-old son. This can't be happening. Life was supposed to get better, not worse.

I am devastated. I am numb. My throat constricts with emotion, but I need to get through this call with the judge. I can't believe I couldn't answer his call this of all times. I call him back, and he doesn't have too much to add. It's a shock for everyone. It's time to research where to go for treatment. All I can do is sob. But I must be strong. He comes over one day, and we talk about it, and I start to cry. He puts his arm around me and tells me it will be all right. How crazy is that. I'm the mother. I'm supposed to ease my baby's pain, not the other way around, not in these circumstances. I am numb most of the time.

———————◆———————

I start to Google as does Emily. I find an article about this special kind of radiation that is targeted so it doesn't damage most of your good cells. I send it to them, and they call the medical center associated with it. It turns out he is not a candidate for this treatment, but the article leads to a doctor who is experienced with lymphoma. Jimmy and Emily meet with the doctor, and they both instantly like him. He is kind and knowledgeable. He tells Jimmy that he likely will not need radiation, just chemotherapy. He wants him to have several tests done, an echocardiogram of his heart, a lung function test, and a PET scan. To get any of them done, he needs a negative COVID test. He arranges to have one at Walgreens only to be told when he gets there that they have no more tests. He can't delay anymore. He's lost so much time since last spring. Emily's parents call their urgent care, and they can take him and administer the test. The doctor comes in, which is odd since it's just a COVID test. He tells Jimmy that his daughter had

Hodgkin's, stage four, and you would never know today that she was sick. It gives him some comfort. He goes for his tests and meets with his oncologist again. The scan shows he has fluid around his heart. He is stage two, but the fluid could make it a stage four. The doctor advises four different chemotherapy drugs every other week for a total of twelve treatments over twenty-four weeks. Jimmy is anxious to get started, and he arranges to have his first treatment on September 3. To start treatment, he needs another COVID test. He tries Walgreens again, only to be disappointed again. He is to start treatment the next day and urgently needs the test. He calls me to share his anxiety. As luck would have it, I had just gone to my allergist two days prior and noticed signs for COVID tests there. I call the office, and they agree to take Jimmy and Emily for tests. They both test negative, and thank goodness treatment can begin.

He gets to the cancer treatment center at 9 a.m. and is there until 3 p.m. It is a long process. Each drug goes individually through an IV in his arm. Some of the drugs are quite irritating to the vein. He endures and arrives home exhausted and nauseous. It takes him several days to feel a semblance of normal. This will be a pattern for the next twenty-four weeks. The week following treatment he will feel weak, tired, and sick with varying symptoms. Sometimes he has excruciating pain in his arm where the IV was, sometimes his mouth has sores all over it, sometimes he gets a pounding headache. It's a rough journey. He has a port implanted, which alleviates the arm pain from the IV but comes with other discomforts. He has mouthwash to help his mouth. He cuts down on the anti-nausea medicine, which alleviates the headaches. And of course, he begins to lose his hair. Why is that last one so hard for me? When he tells me that he wakes up in the morning with hair all over his pillow, I need every ounce of strength in me to not start sobbing. Later, he tells me one day that he lost all his eye lashes overnight. Again, I want to cry. Remarkably, he has a positive attitude and just forges ahead through the pain. I find him inspiring at times. The chemotherapy causes him to lose virtually all his white blood cells. Thus, he is severely immunocompromised, unable to fight even the common cold. He and Emily conclude that he cannot see anyone, and Emily takes extra precautions to not bring any germs home. This is harder than the hair for me. I can't visit my son. I can't hug him. I can't be in his presence.

One day while eating dinner with Matty, I say to him, "I know this sounds crazy, but I wonder if we should tell your father about Jimmy."

Matty says, "It's not crazy; I was thinking the same thing. But we must let Jimmy call the shots on this one."

I agree and try to convince Jimmy that his father needs to be told. Jimmy responds that he can't presently deal with him on top of everything else he's going through, but he will think about it. We do everything we can to help and to keep things as stress-free as possible for both Jimmy and Emily. Matty mows the lawn. I make soup and chicken salad for him and leave it on the front porch. We have all the family members and friends do a video wishing him well. There isn't much we can do, but we all try to be positive when we speak with him and keep as much stress from him as possible. That unfortunately does not include Nikolai.

———— • ————

Matty cancels his plans to move to Florida because Sarah decides to return home. Grace then asks if she and Patrick can move in to save money while he is in school. So, I go from planning on being alone starting in October to having a full house. That is certainly better for me.

On September 9, 2021, Nikolai and I attend our first mediation session. This is done via Zoom. The mediator begins by telling us about himself. He spends twenty minutes talking about his three marriages and his familiarity with the process. I nod and politely smile but inside I am thinking, *I'm paying you $350 an hour and my lawyer $375 an hour to listen to you talk about yourself. I've just spent $242 to hear about your marriage failures.* After more discussion, we break into separate groups and the mediator speaks with Nikolai and his lawyer first. I am with my lawyer for a half hour before the mediator returns. At first, I pepper her with questions and talk strategy. I figure I'm paying for her, I might as well. Then we just end up shooting the breeze. The mediator enters our breakout room and has very little to offer. He discussed the situation with Nikolai, but he can't reveal his confidences. There is no proposal on the table about the assets. In fact, not a single asset is mentioned to start negotiations. The mediator simply suggests to my lawyer that she might want to depose Nikolai about the bank accounts, get an updated appraisal of the house since Nikolai claims it's worth more than the appraiser said in April, and hire a forensic accountant. All I hear in my head is cha-ching, cha-ching, cha-ching. How much of my money does he want to spend? We all get back together on Zoom and the mediator suggests that each party submit to him a "last best offer" in confidence. He will then try to settle the case from there. It is a total waste of my time, like so much of this process, and I've already spent over $30,000 for my lawyer.

I make another mistake, and this one is bad. A few days after the mediation, I poke the bear. After consulting with my lawyer, on Monday, September 13, 2021, I email Nikolai asking if he wants to try and resolve this without the lawyers. I figure what do I have to lose? Little do I know. It's just never worth poking the bear. His first response back, the next morning, is, "I need you to send me a check for $2,300 for the tax refunds. And I will consider your offer. You know my address." Now, this is rich. On June 28, 2021, I met him at my bank so he could sign the refund checks. I then deposited them into my account and wrote him out a check for his half, which he immediately deposited into his account. This was the first and only time I was in his presence in the previous nine months, and he acquired over $2,500 from me. Second, I never made him an offer. But, in an effort to move the process along, I simply respond back with the cancelled check for his share and that I had no idea what he was talking about.

He responds that he forgot and asks why the kids don't talk to him.

"You would have to discuss this with the kids," I reply. "My best guess is they are not happy with your behavior."

He follows up sarcastically asking if it's that easy to cut off their father, and if I had nothing to do with this. He says it's hard to believe and asks why I don't tell them to contact him. He says it is quite amazing, that folks are talking behind my back, that it is very shameful.

The next day, I write back, "Let me know if you want to attempt to negotiate to potentially save thousands of dollars in lawyer's fees." I never hear back. But I poked the bear, and there are consequences for that.

———— ◆ ————

On Thursday, September 16, 2021, the day after my last email exchange with Nikolai, he sends Jimmy a text telling him that Jimmy has until next Friday night to return his car and if he doesn't leave it on his driveway by then, he will report it stolen. He ends by telling Jimmy that he knows where he lives.

We had purchased Jimmy a brand new 2013 Dodge Dart at the end of his freshman year. His college was much cheaper than his siblings, so it seemed fair to give him a new car. For insurance purposes, we put the car in Nikolai's name with the plan to transfer it to Jimmy when he turned twenty-five. Since he was marrying a few months after he turned twenty-five, it seemed logical to wait so he could get car insurance with Emily. Two months after the wedding, Nikolai filed for divorce, so the transfer of the car was never made. But in everyone's mind, the car belonged to Jimmy. It was a gift. Nikolai's text comes through while I am outside on the patio talking to Jimmy about how he is feeling from his first cancer treatment. Jimmy shares the text with me and his siblings. Grace immediately comes outside crying. She cannot believe someone could be so cruel to her twin who is dealing with cancer. Matty and Patrick join us, and everyone is outraged. We strategize how to respond to Nikolai's latest nonsense.

Matty and Patrick jokingly suggest getting Nikolai in a dark alley and beating the s**t out of him. They fantasize about leaving the car for Nikolai without any wheels on it. Ultimately, it is agreed that I will call Nikolai the next day and inform him of Jimmy's diagnosis and demand that he back off with respect to the car.

As Friday morning dawns, I am tied up in knots at the prospect of speaking to Nikolai, but for Jimmy's sake I must be strong. Grace thinks it is a good idea to record the conversation, since I can never trust Nikolai. Standing at the kitchen island, I call with Grace at the ready to record and get his voicemail and leave a message. I go back upstairs to try and work. Thirty minutes later, my phone rings, and I can see it is him. I yell out to Grace and race down to the kitchen. I am out of breath when I finally answer, which makes me sound more nervous than I am. Here's how our conversation goes:

> *Nikolai: "Hey, it's me. What's up, Maria?"*
> *Me: "Hi, um, Jimmy informed me that you threatened to take his car. I think you should know that Jimmy was recently diagnosed with cancer. And he is having his second round of chemo as we speak and —."*
> *Nikolai: "Why didn't you tell me this? Why didn't you tell me all this, Maria?"*
> *Me: "I'm telling you right now."*
> *Nikolai: "Why didn't you tell me before?"*
> *Me: "I don't know—*
> *Nikolai: "Why, why didn't you tell me before if it's his second round of chemo. Why didn't you tell me that initially? I'm his father, for God's sake. What's wrong with you?"*
> *Me: "I was told not to tell you so—"*
> *Nikolai: "I don't care what you were told—"*
> *Me: "All right, I am not going to continue this conversation. I have told you now. He was diagnosed with cancer. He's undergoing chemotherapy. I don't know what you*

think you're trying to accomplish by taking his car away. I—"

Nikolai: "I didn't know. Listen if I knew what was going on I wouldn't be doing this to him. Because they never, never, all three of them haven't contacted me for nine months, right Maria, and you know that. Right, I am very upset about that— Now you're telling me that he has cancer, this poor kid. Why didn't you tell me that before? I can help, right. I can help a lot. What's up with Jimmy?"

Me: "I just told you what's up with him."

Nikolai: "What type of cancer?"

Me: "Hodgkin's Disease, lymphoma."

Nikolai: "Can I see him? Where is he?"

Me: "He's at home. Right now, he's getting his chemo at the hospital."

Nikolai: "Are you there with him?"

Me: "No."

Nikolai: "Who's there?"

Me: "Emily."

Nikolai: "Can I go see him?"

Me: "I don't think so."

Nikolai: "Why not?"

Me: "He is highly immunocompromised at this point so very few people are seeing him. He needs to be extraordinarily careful."

Nikolai: "When was he diagnosed, Maria? I'm sick right now. [Sobbing] I just went to one [I assume he means his mother's funeral.]. When was he diagnosed? My Jimmy [more sobbing]."

Me: "A couple weeks ago."

Nikolai: "[sobbing] Why did you let me know now?"

Me: "As I said, I was told to keep it quiet, so I did what I was asked."

Nikolai: "By whom?"

Me: "I'm just not going to get into this. This is not my story to tell. I'm informing you now. And—"

Nikolai: "Did Jimmy tell you? Please tell me. I'm not, please tell me. Did Jimmy tell you not to tell me?"

Me: "Again, this is not my story to tell. Jimmy is going through a lot. This is a very difficult time for him and for Emily, and um it would be helpful if he were not subjected to any additional stress."

Nikolai: "I didn't know, right? I didn't know."

Me: "Well, personally whether you knew or not, I think your actions are despicable, whether you knew or not. I don't know what you hoped to accomplish, how you think you can improve your relationship with your children by blackmailing him to return the car that was gifted to him years ago. But that's on you."

Nikolai: "Actions speak louder than words. They haven't contacted me for nine months so to me it tells me that they wanted no part of having me as their father, having a relationship. And that's not my behavior. I wasn't a bad father to them. I don't know what the story is, to be quite honest with you, right. And that's how I wanted him to get in touch with me. I would never have taken his car away. All I wanted was for him to call me and call me dad and respect me and not to forsake his father just like a good Christian, right? And that's what I want from them, all my three kids. I don't think I was a bad father. Don't tell me I was despicable in my actions. "

Me: "That's between you and whatever God you believe in. This is the story. I have conveyed the information to you. What you do with it is your call, and I believe you will be hearing from your lawyer later because I don't even think this is an appropriate thing to do under these circumstances. Whether your son had cancer or not, I don't think under the circumstances that we are currently under that you had any right to take the car. That is a piece of property that is subject to negotiation in the divorce proceedings. So, I don't think you can just go take it like you've taken other stuff. But that's neither here nor there."

Nikolai: "You told your attorney about the car?"

Me: "Yes, I did because everyone was extremely upset that you would take Jimmy's car."

Nikolai: "Whatever I do is extremely upsetting to everybody. Whatever you do is okay, right? It's okay to lie and steal all the money from my Fidelity account, that was consensual. It's consensual huh? You told Bonnie [the one Nikolai had the affair with in 2017] not to tell me anything a month before you took out everything, that you had things you needed to do before she told me s**t, right and that's when you proceeded to go out and take all that money, is that correct? That's not despicable right? You go in and take all my money without my consent. That is correct, that's all fine and dandy, right? Everybody agrees with that right? But when I do something it's despicable right? What are you trying to play here?"

Me: "All right. I am done. Jimmy was the topic—"

Nikolai: "Goodbye."

Me: "Goodbye."

Nikolai: "Go f**k yourself."

Immediately, Nikolai texts Jimmy saying he's sorry to hear what he is going through, that he just got off a call with his mother. He wants to see him and Emily as he thinks he can help. He says the car threat was a way to get in touch with him and he is not taking his car. He asks him to contact him.

He then instantly follows up with a voicemail to both Jimmy and Emily saying he knows what treatment Jimmy needs, and he can help. He can get Jimmy the right doctors, etc. This all takes place while Jimmy is undergoing his second treatment.

I send Grace's recording of my conversation with Nikolai to the kids. Jimmy comments, "It's very sad on his part that most of those seven minutes were not about me. Even after hearing the news, he still would rather attack you than ask more questions."

Nikolai then leaves another voicemail for Jimmy saying he knows good doctors at good hospitals, and he "needs to help."

Nikolai then leaves me a voicemail apologizing for being very upset and screaming and asks if we can work this out and work together to get Jimmy well.

Nikolai calls Matty, but he does not answer.

Jimmy then texts Nikolai the following:

> *I don't want to see you, in fact, I can't see you. I am extremely immunocompromised. My white blood cell count is dangerously low. I basically do not leave the house and for the most part only see Emily because getting sick could do me in. I am going through a lot right now and was planning to tell you everything until you threatened to take away my car. I lost a lot of respect for you in that moment. I can't fathom that you would consider doing that to me regardless of your knowledge of my current situation. Emily and I have done plenty of research, and we know what we are up against. We found an amazing doctor, and I am in very good hands and do not need help. Emily and I want to be left alone, and it is not safe for us to be seeing anyone. Please respect my space, if anything, for my health.*

Nikolai responds that he always respects Jimmy's wishes and he never intended to take the car. He felt it was the only way to get Jimmy to respond after many phone calls and texts. He reminds Jimmy that he is his father and will always love him. He asks the name of the hospital and doctor and whether they can talk. He ends by saying, "You WILL get over this. I am certain about that. Love you, Jimmy."

With Jimmy's agreement, I tell my lawyer to stand down with respect to the car as it seems Nikolai has backed off. At least for now.

Matty texts Nikolai the following:

Look, I don't know what, if anything, you can do for Jimmy, but he's already established at a hospital that he's happy and comfortable with and things seem to be going okay. I would not impose on his treatments even with the mere chance that there may be something better out there. What he's doing is working and under the given circumstances, his stress levels (until yesterday) are low. We have all come to accept that he's doing everything he can to beat this. He's also doing a remarkable job. We have all been supportive and are willing and able to help if we're ever needed by him, but what he and Emily deem is best is our duty to support. If they want to be left alone, then that is the role we take because that's what they think is best. I would recommend you try to live by that as well because all other things considered become trivial when put in this perspective.

Nikolai responds to Matty that he agrees completely and never holds grudges. He forgets and forgives very easily and that it is his nature to try to help. He says that he recommended excellent doctors for his brother, and he is still doing well. He adds that Jimmy is a fighter, and he *will* overcome this. He brings up the car and repeats what he told Jimmy, that he was just trying to get his attention and never wanted the car and would never have taken it from him. He is sure that Matty knows that about him. He then justifies his actions by saying that not one of them has contacted him in close to a year and asks Matty to consider how that makes him feel. He ends by asking to be updated with Jimmy, that he is still in disbelief and writes, "Love you always."

Nikolai attempts to call Matty again, but Matty doesn't pick up. Meanwhile, I send Nikolai the following text:

> *I received your calls and voicemail. I was on work calls all afternoon. I don't see the point in discussing his treatment. He's a grown man with his own family, i.e., Emily. They are fully capable of figuring it out. I accept your apology. I was never looking to fight. I sent you the email in an effort to settle but you responded with vitriol. I will tell my lawyer she doesn't need to follow up with respect to the car.*

Nikolai replies that he is sorry again and will want to settle, but it has to be global on all counts. He says that he wanted to settle back in December, but I didn't want to.

In December 2020, Nikolai's lawyer suggested mediation. Because we had no information on Nikolai's hidden bank accounts and because his financial statement was "woefully inadequate," my lawyer responded that mediation was premature at that time.

Throughout the weekend, Nikolai texts me multiple times asking about Jimmy. I answer his questions as long as they don't reveal specifics. Jimmy does not want him to know where or with whom he gets treatment. Jimmy does not want to worry about Nikolai showing up there. Nikolai texts that he's going to "a Catholic and an Orthodox Mass to light candles for Jimmy. Our darling boy."

I want to vomit on several counts. Is he going to a combo? Is there such a thing? Is he going to two of them? This from someone who repeatedly makes fun of my faith or uses it to bully his way to something?

Jimmy says, "It's gross the amount of times he's brought up religion since the divorce. It really doesn't make sense."

Nikolai texts Jimmy offering to mow his lawn or anything else that doesn't involve contact. He ends it with: "I want to help in any way. Love you guy!"

Jimmy comments that he threatens to take away his car and now wants to mow his lawn.

Since Nikolai opened the door about settling, on Monday, September 20, I email him a proposal with respect to the assets in the divorce. I end my email with "P.S. Jimmy is starting to lose his hair today so not a great day."

He responds back with ridiculous claims regarding alimony, the value of the house, and that I have all the stock (his Fidelity statement shows he has almost $300,000 of stock in his own name). He then responds again that he is sorry to hear about Jimmy and questions why no one wants him to be a part of Jimmy's recuperation. He asks me to consider how that makes him feel. He follows up a third time, "You shouldn't be using Jimmy's condition as leverage to a settlement. That is despicable."

I find it almost comical that he uses the word "despicable" since I said that two days ago about his actions with respect to Jimmy's car. This is classic Nikolai. Over the years, I had often heard my words coming out of Nikolai's mouth soon after I said them. I reply. First, I address his various contentions with respect to the assets and indicate settling would be better than waiting six to twelve months to sell the house and get the money from it. I end it with, "Re: the kids, I don't have all the answers. I was trying to be nice and keep you up to date on Jimmy's condition. Since you view that as despicable, I will no longer do so. In any event, I agree, the two things should be kept separate. "

He responds with some specific comments on the assets and states: "I have all the time in the world." He says I have a responsibility to keep him informed on his son and that he has no problems in a deposition under oath, but I may.

I don't see the point in continuing the process. Clearly, the lawyers will have to settle this. He is impossible to deal with.

Later that evening I am out at a church function. Various relics were brought from the Vatican for viewing. People have suggested to me that I bring Jimmy's picture and touch it to the relics. Will touching Jimmy's picture to relics improve his health? I have no idea. It sounds a bit crazy, but I do believe strongly in a spiritual world, and I have no idea how it all works. So, I figure it can't hurt. I mention how I feel about it to Jimmy, which prompts him to tell me that some nuns who Emily's family knows insisted on getting a piece of his hair to bring to Lourdes, France, to dip in the water. Will that work? I don't know, but it can't hurt. While I am touching Jimmy's picture to selected relics like the wood of the cross and relics of Padre Pio, Pope St. John Paul II, St John the Baptist, and other saints, my phone starts dinging incessantly. The bear is roaring and sending texts to the kids, which they are sharing with me.

Nikolai texts Matty and Grace stating that as their father, he is owed an explanation as to why they have completely severed their relationship. He doesn't know what they think he has done or what I have told them, but he wants to clear the air because they don't know the truth or the entire story and they will understand why he left once they do. They never allowed him to explain his side. He says he wants to put this all aside and focus on Jimmy and be part of his care. He has MD contacts at Memorial Sloan Kettering who know best how to proceed. As their father, he believes he deserves to know what's going on.

Matty responds as follows:

1. *I've verbally and through text communicated the things "you have done wrong." If you do not remember the conversation or are too lazy to "scroll up" from our past conversations, I will summarize for you:*
   - *You cheated on my mother for many years. That hurt her— a woman I love—that hurt our family, and that hurt me.*

- *You continued to have affairs even after you were "very sorrowful." I had expressed my knowledge (for the second time) of your antics to Jimmy and Grace in August of 2020, before any of this happened.*
- *You lied about the process of filing for divorce. I saw the papers dated and signed September 9th and 10th—2 weeks before you "told" everyone you did.*
- *You lied to me and my siblings about continuing to have affairs while the beginning of the whole divorce process started. I overheard many calls.*
- *You would go around every night and take things from the house. No, my mother did not tell me you did that. I heard you do it and informed her and then found countless items in boxes. That's very unethical to me.*
- *You called the police on your own house in a frantic panic while my girlfriend (at the time only dating three months) was over. Oh, and it was because we saw all the shady grimy things that were in your office. I guess that does make sense why you would go to all that trouble of dealing with the police to hide those things, especially what was in the vent.*
- *You left me and my mother without internet for days during a pandemic. Truly brought out your outstanding sense of character.*
- *You've been stealing money by withdrawing cash from ATMs for years. I've seen the bank statements.*
- *Any opportunity you get, you talk s**t about my mother to me. She wasn't the one that broke her marriage vows. She wasn't the one that filed for divorce and broke up our family. Have you forgotten who did those things? Or do you just rationalize your immoral behavior with her taking*

control of "your" money that she has willingly stated she's in control of and will give over her fair share in these proceedings?

- *You've made this entire process hell for me, and that is my own independent thought and feeling. The amount of responsibility I've taken up because you decided to just get up and leave has been a lot for me to handle. Although I will say, a 23-year-old in a little over a year ended up doing a far better job.*

- *You're like a child that can't foresee the consequences to his actions. You choose to not see how greatly the choices you have made affected the people you claim to love. It's remarkable how disconnected one's words and behavior can be. But you are a walking example.*

- *I have not said anything to you because all you do is lie. I will not have a relationship with someone who lies. And no matter what, you will not believe the reality of what I have just written out. You are incorrigible. Nothing can or will get through to you and because of that the relationship you have with your three children has suffered to the point of breaking. You completely lack the accountability of your actions to the point where there is no longer any basis for a relationship to be formed.*

2. *Jimmy does not need your help. Stop trying to push doctors and hospitals he doesn't need. You literally agreed with that notion I had written out for you on Friday. Oh, wait and then you go and act differently from the word you utter. Sound familiar?*

3. *Being my father does not entitle you to a relationship. I'm a grown adult with a job. I make my own decisions and think freely.*

Grace also responds to Nikolai:

> *I agree with everything that Matty just said. You don't de-serve anything more from us. I also explained most of my feelings to you during our conversation about why Patrick and I did not want you at our wedding. I have come to all of my conclusions and made all of my decisions on my own accord. I have prayed on this, and this is where I stand. I know that no matter what we say, you won't believe any of it and because of that, there is nothing more to say to you.*

Of course, Nikolai must have the last word. He says they have the wrong impression, are wrong about a lot of events, and have made conclusions with no real basis in fact. He says, yes, he cheated, but no, it was not for years. He says it's obvious they don't love him enough or at all to hear him out and risk that their assumptions might be wrong. He says no one is 100 percent at fault and they are kidding themselves if they don't realize this. He explains that not knowing what Jimmy is experiencing is what is prompting him to try and help in any way. He has given all his time to raising them and all his love. He adds that Matty is wrong about the divorce filing, that he called the divorce lawyer when Matty and I were at the Poconos house while his brother was here and that he told me immediately after we returned. There was no lag time. He says Matty's information is all skewed and they just love to hate him and that some deadbeat dads are more respected by their kids.

Nikolai says that all he wanted that evening was to get his stuff and Matty and I prevented him from getting his work computer, so he had no choice but to call the police. He adds that I am defrauding him out of a lot of money, that if he took an item here and an item there, he was entitled to it as they were his possessions. He asks Matty if going into his drawers and looking at his personal stuff and kicking down the door is okay. He ends by saying that if they want the truth and his side to let him know. If not, they can move forward not knowing the rest of the story. He says he will always love them if they don't want to see him anymore and maybe in the future, with time, the realization might set in, and they will figure it out on their own.

He immediately follows up to "set the record straight" and says that after the affair in late 2017, he had not had any other affairs. If they don't want to believe that, then it's their problem because their investigations are again faulty.

He follows up again later asking Matty what antics he is referring to that he expressed to Jimmy and Grace since they knew he had had the affair. He says that I had my paycheck direct deposited to my own account for two years and only his salary was going into the joint account. All the expenses were coming from him in 2018 and parts of 2019 until he found out and I started re-depositing again at the joint account.

He ends by asking Matty to enlighten him on what shady, grimy things he found in the office.

The next day he follows up again congratulating Matty for stepping up to the plate as I could not have done it by myself. He says that he was helping his parents who didn't speak English by age ten, and he is glad that his kids did not have to go through all the hardships that he and his brothers went through while growing up.

He adds that I started taking money from his one account by drips and drabs of $10,000 at a time before I ever knew about the affair. He ends by asking them to put this all aside for Jimmy's sake and move on. He wants a relationship with them. He loves all of them unconditionally, something they will realize when they have kids of their own. He can't force them to have a relationship with him as their dad, but he wants to try to mend all this and do everything possible from his end to reestablish their relationship. If they don't want to work on this, then he knows he tried everything possible from his end.

The kids don't respond.

CHAPTER 16

More Legal
Wastes of Time

September 23, 2021

It is three days after the text exchange when I was seeing the relics from the Vatican. Nikolai texts me to say he is having an appraiser come to the house, and he will meet him there on Monday at 11 a.m. He does not ask if it's okay or if I'm available. He just dictates. After running it by my lawyer, I respond that I can accommodate the time but that he should not come because he will not be allowed to enter the house. He responds that he is coming and is permitted to enter the house. I inform my lawyer, and she goes to war with Nikolai's lawyer. Although Nikolai's lawyer supposedly knows the law—at least that's what my lawyer told me when I first retained her a year ago—he certainly doesn't act like it. He insists Nikolai is allowed in the house. Even though Nikolai owns half the house with me, since he has established another residence, he is no longer entitled to come and go in what is now solely my residence. Fortunately, the police know the law better than Nikolai's lawyer appears to.

September 27, 2021

My lawyer never reaches a resolution with Nikolai's lawyer and advises me to call the police if Nikolai insists on coming in. I decide it is better if I take preemptive measures and call them and ask if they can send a car. I explain that we are going through a divorce, he can be violent, and I don't want him in the house. The woman answering my call says she can send a car to "keep the peace." Nikolai's appraisers arrive fifteen minutes early. Thank the heavens. Matty and I peek out the window and see them outside in the street facing the house. We debate what to do, and Matty suggests we go out and talk to them. I have the perpetual knots in my stomach. After some initial introductions, I explain the situation, that the police will be coming per my request, that Nikolai is not allowed in the house, and they agree to get started. I bring them into the house at 10:52 a.m. (my cameras record everything, so I know the exact time). They begin by evaluating the living room and dining room. The one appraiser is chatty, and while he is telling a story, it occurs to me that I should lock the front door in case Nikolai tries to come in. I blankly nod at him, anxiously waiting for a break in his conversation so as not to appear rude and finally go over and lock the storm door. As recorded by the camera, Nikolai comes up to the door at 10:56, about a minute after I locked it. That was a close one. He has come with his brother, but his brother stays in the car. Nikolai bangs on the door, and Matty says, "You can't come in."

Nikolai says, "Yes, I can. Open the door."

Matty says, "No, you can't."

Nikolai says, "Yes, I can."

Matty says, "No, you can't."

But for the seriousness of it, it almost sounds like kids on a playground. Nikolai is then seen on the cameras and by Olivia, from across the street, walking around the front and back of the house. Olivia and Jimmy, who can see what my cameras see, text me simultaneously to tell me of Nikolai's whereabouts just as I am walking the appraisers up the stairs. I stop dead in my tracks and say, "Matty, I think I left the kitchen door unlocked!"

He tells me that he locked it earlier. The cameras show Nikolai trying to enter through the kitchen door and the other back doors and looking in the windows. Thank goodness Matty had thought to lock the doors. At 10:58, Nikolai calls the police and tells them that he lives here (a lie) and that his wife locked him out of the house, and we are in a marital dispute. The police show up thirty seconds later (likely because I asked them to come at 11 a.m.). Nikolai thinks they have come for him and are on his side. Nikolai stands at the end of the driveway, arms flailing as he speaks to the officers. He often looks away as he tells the officer something. His brother briefly exits the car and joins Nikolai and the two officers to offer some feigned support but quickly slinks back to the safety of the car. He's had his own encounters with law enforcement and presumably prefers to stay out of the fray. I finish escorting the appraisers through the house and show them out the back while Nikolai rants to the officers. Here are bits of conversation that we could roughly piece together from everyone who heard it:

> *Officer: "You have every right to be here at the residence, but you don't. . ."*
> *Nikolai: "I know I do. Why wouldn't I right? Why wouldn't I? My wife is insane."*
> *Officer: "When was the last time you lived here?"*
> *Nikolai: "December."*
> *Officer: "December."*
> *Nikolai: "'cause I was kicked out. I had to get out, otherwise she would kill me."*
> *Officer: "She doesn't have to allow you in the house. It's not your house anymore. You both own it, but now you lost the right to go into that house."*
> *Nikolai: "I hope you never get a divorce or you either because you guys. . ."*

Officer: "Let's be clear. I had a divorce."

Nikolai: "Not with her."

Officer: "Let's be clear here. I've been in a divorce. I left my house, and I paid for all my house expenses for six months. So, I've been in your situation."

Nikolai: "So you know."

Officer: "I can empathize and sympathize with your frustrations. I know you want to go in the house, and you feel frustrated with that, but I can tell you right now she doesn't have to let you in. What you're losing sight of is she's allowing the appraiser in the house right now."

Nikolai: "She has to."

Officer: "She doesn't."

Nikolai: "She wants to buy me out, put on her own appraiser. and they are low-balling it and I need to get in there to tell the appraiser of anything that they can't see."

Officer: "You're going to have to do that from outside the house because she won't let you in. I know, it's frustrating. It sucks. It's a big game. I know."

Nikolai: "My daughter…"

Officer: "Let me go see if I can talk to her."

Nikolai: "Last June, my darling wife, didn't allow me to go to my daughter's wedding. That tells you her character. Her personality."

Officer: "I understand."

Nikolai: "Please talk to her. Talk some sense into her."

Officer: "I will."

Nikolai: "I don't think you will because she is a f**king b**ch."

Officer: "I just want to let you know from the start if she doesn't want to let you in, she doesn't have to."

Nikolai: "My other son has Hodgkin's lymphoma, cancer. She waited three weeks and just told me now, because he

wasn't responding to me. I recommended the best doc-
tors.... She's using that as leverage."
Officer: "How old is your son?"
Nikolai: "Twenty-six."
Officer: "He's old enough where he can reach out."

The one officer then knocks on the door, and I let him in. He tells me that Nikolai insists he needs to go around with the appraiser to show him things. He adds that I don't have to let Nikolai in, but if the appraiser needs him, it might be better for the process to allow it. He emphasizes I don't have to. He states that it is very good I allowed the appraiser in. I say that I don't believe the appraiser needs him, but the officer can confirm that with the appraiser. Matty sees the appraiser has come around to the front and indicates that to the officer. The officer responds that he will check with the appraiser, and if he's good to go, he will not see me again. I thank him for coming. We watch while eventually they all drive away. Nikolai lingers for a bit, but the police wait for Nikolai, so eventually he leaves after about fifteen minutes.

Olivia comes over shortly after to give me a big bear hug. (She's awesome and I needed it.) She shares video of Nikolai walking around the house that she took and shares that Nikolai saw her taking the video. She spoke to the police and told them about Nikolai's drive-bys. Olivia told the police that his behavior is creepy, especially as she has two small children who don't understand divorce. This is a nice neighborhood, and she shouldn't have to deal with this because of Nikolai. The officer indicates that if anyone can get a picture of him parked, then I would have grounds for a restraining order.

Later that night, Nikolai texts Jimmy, "How are you feeling?"

I'm struck by how erratic his behavior is. He of course was always volatile but somehow this seems different. He spends the day making a scene with the police and calling me vile names and then turns around and nicely asks Jimmy how he is. Maybe it's because I was so stressed having him here, trying to force his way into my home that he has no legal right to enter. I don't know. He goes from that to acting like a loving dad in a nanosecond. I just can't help thinking, *Do I need to worry that he will come and put a bullet through my head?*

Jimmy suggests I get a security system. Matty tells me the next day that as bad as Nikolai is, Matty doesn't believe he would do that, primarily because he cares too much about himself to risk spending the rest of his life in prison. I guess there's some comfort there.

The next day Olivia texts me first thing in the morning that she found a bunch of screws on her driveway behind her cars. She immediately thinks it's Nikolai and remembers the nail in my tire.

Later that day, I log onto my BJ's membership account. I hadn't thought I had an online account but there it is. And lo and behold, a secondary member has been added to my account: Nikolai, at his new place of residence. When Nikolai did this, I have no idea, but apparently, he wants to mooch off me and have me pay for the membership for him to use. Pay your own $55, Nikolai! The next day I go to BJs and cancel the account and open a new one. One more thing to cross off the list. I wonder how many others are left.

A few days later Nikolai texts me asking how Jimmy is. After the appraisal encounter and having listened to the vile things he said to the police officer, I have decided that I will no longer communicate with him. There doesn't seem to be any point other than to have my peace disturbed. I tried to negotiate with him to no avail. He clearly can't be trusted, he twists what I say at any given moment, and he is nice when he wants information and awful when he feels like it. At this point I need peace. A few days after that, he texts me again about Jimmy. I ignore that text as well. About a week before this, I had unfriended him on Facebook. I had not done it sooner because I thought he might post something that could be helpful in the divorce proceedings. Now, I've concluded it's not worth the disruption to my peace. On October 10, 2021, I post pictures with Jimmy, Emily, Grace, and Patrick at Emily's brother's wedding. I am concerned that once again this is a bear-poke, and there will be a reaction if Nikolai sees this.

Patrick suggests I block Nikolai, which will prevent him from seeing any posts. Another gift to my peace. I had previously not posted things because of Nikolai. Now I can post as I wish.

—————— ◆ ——————

I am tired of this whole process. It is clear neither Nikolai nor his attorney will negotiate in good faith. Nothing ever seems to happen. It's truly ridiculous. But my legal bills are outrageous. I've spent $32,000 so far with no end in sight. I email my attorney on October 15, 2021:

> *In early September, I expressed how disheartened I was that this would not end by year end. You told me to be optimistic as there was still plenty of time. It is now mid-October, and nothing has changed since early September. I keep accumulating legal fees, but the case never seems to move forward. It is now 13 months since Nikolai signed the paperwork and 12 months since the complaint was filed. The new appraisal was almost 3 weeks ago, and we've heard nothing. You emailed Nikolai's attorney 3 times in the last two weeks and received no response (to my knowledge).*
>
> *I would like to move this forward and have an end to it ASAP. I would hope at this point you realize that Nikolai will not negotiate in good faith, nor will his attorney. You had told me a year ago that Nikolai's attorney knows the law. If true, he flouts it, arguing that Nikolai has a right to enter the house for the appraisal—even the cops knew that was not true—arguing that I am not entitled to alimony because I banned Nikolai from my daughter's wedding— even if it were true (which it isn't), it's irrelevant.*
>
> *When I attempted to negotiate with Nikolai, he indicated that alimony was worth no more than $65K and that he had all the time in the world. I assume that as*

each month passes that is one month of alimony that I lose? It seems to be his (or his attorney's) plan to drag this out as long as possible.

I see no point in pursuing mediation. As I said previously, it was a total waste of time and money. (We spent half of it just shooting the breeze). I think we need to get this before a judge, and I would like to do it as soon as possible. I know from what the mediator said, the judge is an unknown, but I know we will end up there anyway.

If you have a REALISTIC alternative, I am all ears. Otherwise, what is the next step to get this before a judge and get this resolved? How quickly can we do that?

She replies by sympathizing with my frustration and reminding me that Nikolai's attorney has not responded to any of her and the mediator's emails. She writes that she just cornered him on the phone, and he said that he expects to have the appraisal report by the close of business on Monday. She adds that she agreed with Nikolai's attorney to submit our last, best offers to the mediator by November 5, and she will get a conference scheduled with the mediator for the week after, at which point we will see where we are and schedule an additional mediation session with all of us. So much for court. Another month to waste.

In the meantime, we receive the appraisal. The value is $630,000. I am further disheartened until I study the appraisal in depth. It is riddled with mistakes, mistakes that always go against me. First, the appraiser increases the value of the home by $20,000 for an oversized, heated, in-ground pool. I don't have an in-ground pool. I have a thirty-year-old rusted, standard sized, above-ground pool, which does not add any value in the appraisal world (arguably it subtracts value). In using comparables to place a value on my house, the appraiser must make adjustments for comparables that have basements, since I do not. He values a basement at only $5,000. The previous appraiser that we had both hired jointly valued a finished basement at $25,000 and an unfinished at $15,000. By only valuing it at $5,000, this appraiser further increases the value of my property. I Google to see what's standard and find that basements have become much more desirable during COVID and many appraisers value them at $75,000. There are other mistakes as well. I don't have a fireplace, but the appraiser increases the value of the comparable for a fireplace when he should decrease it. Every error made goes to increase the value of the house. Interestingly, they both use the same comparable, but this appraiser values it $32,000 more than the previous appraiser. It is incredulous to think that the value of my house increased by $90,000 in the five months from the previous appraisal as alleged by this appraiser. Shortly after, a similar property to mine which is four doors down sells for $487,000. It has a basement. My brother Jack strongly urges me to contact whatever governing board there is for appraisers and file a complaint. He believes the appraisal is fraudulent, that Nikolai likely paid the appraiser to come up with a high value.

On November 9, 2021, the lawyers meet with the mediator after presenting the "last best offer" on November 5. I return to my office in New York City after having been away since March 9, 2020. We have not officially returned to the office. Rather, I'm told I must go into the office to pick up my access card, which expired during the COVID lockdown, and to start cleaning out my office for the upcoming renovations. I make the two-hour trek, in the car, on the train and on the subway. Opening my office door for the first time in twenty months, I first see my desk blotter at March 2020. Disaster movies immediately come to mind where everyone returns years later to find things exactly as they left them when they fled. My eyes next move to the family portrait on my credenza facing forward for all visitors to see. Nikolai is in the center with his arms outstretched, spread-eagle, like a protector of his brood. The bile rises in my throat and that frame immediately goes in the garbage with plans to toss out the picture at home.

I hope to retire in two years if the divorce doesn't destroy me financially. I pack with retirement in mind, assuming for the next two years, I will need very little of the thirty plus years of stuff I've accumulated. My lawyer is negotiating a settlement with Nikolai's lawyer at this moment. I have low expectations and fully expect to go to court and try this debacle. Predictably, nothing is accomplished.

On November 23, 2021, I go out to dinner with Bella. Once restaurants reopened from COVID, Bella and I started meeting every two weeks for dinner. She was one of the first people I confided in about my messy life. She has been a wonderful friend, always supportive, ready to give Nikolai a name that makes me laugh and always keeping my confidences. When anyone asks, she simply says, "It's not my story to tell."

It's a great response, and I've come to use it myself. While we are eating, a close friend of hers is eating at a nearby restaurant in my town. I've met her on occasion, think she's a lovely person, and had told Bella it was okay to tell her of my situation. She texts Bella a picture of Nikolai at a nearby table, out on a date with a woman. It is his birthday so presumably she is taking him out to celebrate. Someone suggests warning the poor woman, but of course no one wants to make that kind of a scene. I find it obnoxious that they chose a restaurant in my town. Nikolai lives about thirty minutes away, and there are plenty of restaurants by him.

———— ◆ ————

On November 30, 2021, my lawyer and I meet with the mediator once again. The mediator asked to have the meeting and even suggested we meet the morning of Thanksgiving. I refuse to have any meetings the entire week. I don't need my holidays ruined by this nonsense. I also tell my lawyer that there is no point in meeting if the mediator hasn't yet met with Nikolai. The mediator responds that Nikolai and his lawyer met with him two weeks ago, so I have a flicker of hope that maybe we can resolve this. I should know better at this point.

The mediator opens our meeting with, "Nikolai is very angry. He's very upset that his children won't talk to him."

I'm thinking, *I don't give a s**t. This is irrelevant to settling the assets. And Nikolai should take a long look in the mirror and maybe he'll see why his kids don't want anything to do with him.*

The mediator says what I'm thinking, indicating that he thought perhaps Nikolai should look in the mirror, but he didn't say that to him. Instead, he suggested to Nikolai that there is a reunification program to reconnect kids with estranged parents after a divorce. I stare blankly at him. What is this to me? Why am I wasting my time and money listening to this? The kids are twenty-six, twenty-six, and twenty-three. I've told them multiple times they can do what they want with respect to their father. They are adults and capable of making their own decisions. But I remain silent. The mediator again expresses my thoughts by saying that they often have difficulty getting kids aged fourteen to sixteen to participate, and he acknowledges that my kids are way past that. He then adds that perhaps I can relay the information to the kids. I just stare, partially nod, and say nothing. We then start to discuss the assets, and it quickly becomes clear that Nikolai has not negotiated anything. I don't think he and his lawyer have even looked at the universe of assets. It's ridiculous that fourteen months later, they don't even know fully what we are fighting about. Once again, it's a total waste of my time and money, which I essentially express. My lawyer senses that I am getting angry and says that we are not going to negotiate against ourselves, and she will go to the judge and ask for a trial date. At last. Unfortunately, it will result in more unnecessary legal expenses, all because Nikolai is malicious and manipulative.

On December 1, 2021, my lawyer writes Nikolai's lawyer to state that additional mediation sessions will not be productive, and she will be forwarding a proposed settlement agreement. He will have ten days to review it and respond. She receives no response to her letter. I share with the kids the mediator's statements on the reunification program. Matty suggests, as a strategic move, to tell my lawyer that he will agree to participate if Nikolai signs the settlement agreement. Grace agrees as well. They both figure they can suffer for an hour listening to him if it will make this all go away. I relay the information to my attorney, but she insists on watering it down, saying that they are amenable to the program once the divorce is final. On December 6, 2021, my lawyer sends the settlement agreement to Nikolai's lawyer. They have until the fifteenth to respond. That is an anniversary of sorts—the day I changed the locks and removed Nikolai from my physical presence. On the morning of the fifteenth, Nikolai texts all the kids expressing that he hopes they are doing well and says that he was told that I had spoken to them about seeing him after the divorce is finalized and conveyed that they are good about that. He asks if they want to do this and says he misses them all very much.

I stupidly think this might be a good sign, that Nikolai might actually consider signing the agreement and ask the kids to respond. Matty reluctantly responds:

> We were asked about how we felt about this reunification program. Jimmy wasn't included obviously because of his situation. Grace and I said we're agreeable to something once the divorce is settled and if things don't get worse but don't want to do anything until everything is over and everyone has time to heal.

Naturally, we hear nothing back on the settlement, so my lawyer contacts the judge asking for a conference to set up discovery deadlines and a trial date. The only date the two lawyers can agree on for a conference with the judge is January 27. Five weeks away. More delays. Then it turns out the judge can't make that day, so they must find another day. Meanwhile, the mediator sends his bill. I owe an additional $927 (after paying $350). He also suggests we have another mediation session Christmas week. My lawyer asks me my thoughts. I send her two emails:

I did not realize that I had to pay all this for the mediator. I will not agree to pay any more to him. It is clearly a total waste of my time and money. I'm paying all this money to listen to his war stories and for some vague strategy recommendations. While he may be offering his time for free for the next call, your time is not free, so I see no point. I will let you know when I've made the payment.

In case my prior email was not clear, I do not authorize you to incur legal fees on my behalf to have a conversation with Nikolai's lawyer and the mediator. (The most recent "mediation" fees involved my listening to the mediator tell me how angry Nikolai is.). Clearly, Nikolai has no intention of negotiating. If he did, he would have responded to your latest overture.

On December 20, 2021, five days after the deadline, Nikolai's attorney sends a letter responding to our proposed settlement. His letter states that he agrees with much of it, but there are some items regarding bank accounts and other matters that he questions. Some account information seems to be accurate and other information is not. Additionally, because of the big difference between the appraisals and the continued increase in property market values, Nikolai will not give up his share of the equity in the home. He once again proposes that we return to mediation, that mediation is the most cost-effective. He proposes at least one more mediation session and notes that many cases require five or more separate mediation sessions before a full settlement is reached. He states that we have not substantially engaged in the mediation process and concretely dealt with specific numbers and asks that my lawyer discuss this with me and get back to him.

I agree with one sentence in the letter: we have not substantially engaged in the mediation process and have not concretely dealt with specific numbers. Why? Because Nikolai refuses to negotiate.

My lawyer responds stating that until we receive a detailed response to our proposal, we simply cannot continue negotiations. This is the second time we have made a proposal with no substantive response from Nikolai other than "let's go back to mediation." She requests a detailed description of what Nikolai does and does not agree with, along with a proposed resolution of the issues to which he does not agree. She states we will then determine whether the differences are insurmountable or whether another mediation session may be productive. She also notes that we can continue negotiations after a trial date has been set. She suggests that having an "end" date might encourage Nikolai to negotiate in good faith.

On December 21, 2021, I receive a bill from my attorney for $5,670. They want payment by December 24, 2021. Merry Christmas to me. My legal fees are now just shy of $40,000.

———————— ◆ ————————

Christmas is fast approaching, and this year will be like no other for me. Jimmy and Emily naturally can't participate. Grace is working. Patrick will go to his parents. That leaves Matty and me. I have never in my life had so few people with which to celebrate Christmas. I periodically fight going into a depression. Sarah's family has invited us over for Christmas dinner, which is very kind of them. I hope I don't feel like a fifth wheel. One of the hardest things about loving your children is encouraging them to move on, to find someone who makes them happy, and to start their own life with that person. Where does that leave me now that I am alone? Going forward, where will I spend Christmas Day and Christmas Eve? If I'm lucky, on one of the days we'll all be together. But what of the other day? Will I be alone? Or will I glom onto one of them, intruding into their own family time? Everyone bereft of their partner must go through a similar thought process.

Christmas turns out better than expected. Sarah's family and friends are lovely and very welcoming. Nikolai texts the kids, "Merry Christmas." No one responds. The day after Christmas, we have a Zoom call with Jimmy, and everyone opens their presents. It's not the same, but it is fun, nevertheless. A new year is now in sight. Will this nightmare end in 2022?

CHAPTER 17

End of the Nightmare

2022

I was never a big New Year's Eve person. I couldn't see the point of losing sleep to watch a ball drop down at midnight. Nothing will change from one day to the next. But now I get it more. It's the symbolism. Saying goodbye to the previous year is a good thing to do. If it's a good one, we likely don't want to see it go, but we can celebrate how great it was. If it's a bad one, we can symbolically close that chapter and start a new one. I didn't stay up this year, but I think going forward I will, even if I'm alone in my family room. I'll watch that ball drop with hope and optimism for a better year.

I post my New Year's Day summary on Facebook:

> *Happy New Year, everyone! Like many of you, I am happy to say goodbye to 2021. A year ago, I posted with hope and expectation for a better year than 2020. I was disappointed. But "Life is Messy" (my new favorite book) and we forge on amidst the mess and there is always something to be grateful for:*

1. *2021 started with a fun time in Tampa with Matty and his girlfriend, Sarah.*
2. *2021 brought me a new family member as Patrick married my sweet girl, Grace.*
3. *2021 showed the incredible depth of character of my daughter-in-law Emily, as barely a newlywed, she shifted her entire life to care for my son Jimmy. I could not have asked for a better caregiver.*
4. *2021 brought remission to Jimmy's cancer, and he now only has one more month of treatments.*
5. *2021 brought a girls' night out in my backyard, which we managed to continue indoors.*
6. *2021 brought the love, support, and prayers of all my friends and family.*
    I'm still happy to close the door on 2021, and I look forward to 2022 once again with hope and expectation. I wish all of you a blessed year to come!
    P.S. In 2021 (yesterday) I managed to change a defective light switch and I didn't burn the house down! "I am Woman, hear me roar!!!"

I cried every day at the end of 2020 and into 2021. Then one day I woke up and didn't cry. Then two days. Finally, by the middle of 2021, I was having more good days than bad— until Jimmy's diagnosis. Then the grief washed over me again. But now it's a new year, and I'm hopeful. I miss Jimmy so much sometimes it feels like a physical pain, like my gut has been wrenched out of me. But he's in the home stretch. In a month I may be able to hug him again. I can't wait for that day. I can't wait until we are all back together again.

———— ◆ ————

Nikolai's lawyer actually responds to my lawyer's proposal. He lies numerous times. His counter proposal is way too low, but it's something. Maybe there is hope for a resolution without going to trial. I try not to get my hopes up too much. They are usually crushed in this process. At my insistence, my lawyer has scheduled a conference with the judge for February 10 during which she will ask for a trial date. I hope the pressure will force Nikolai to negotiate. If not, at least the case can move forward in court.

We get another letter from Nikolai's lawyer. This one is not as conciliatory. He threatens to force a sale of the house, refuses to concede that I am entitled to half of Nikolai's ATM cash withdrawals, money that cannot be accounted for, and raises some more bogus issues. Likely not coincidentally, Nikolai texts Matty, "How is Jimmy doing?"

Angry about the threats to force a sale of the house, Matty responds, "You're threatening a forced sale of the home I grew up in and the current place I'm living in, which also happens to be near my girlfriend, and you expect me to be friendly toward you and 'update you on Jimmy?' F**k off."

Nikolai replies that all he did was ask him how Jimmy was and that clearly, I have poisoned him. He writes that it could have been settled amicably a year ago, but I wanted to have the upper hand. He then reminds Matty that I told him to leave the house after we came back from the Poconos, and he then filed for divorce. He advises Matty to consult a therapist to set him straight.

Nikolai seems fixated on the lie about the timing of the divorce. I've concluded at this point that he believes his own lie. I guess he feels it makes him look better. I mention it to Matty, and he says, "Assuming his lie is true, he filed for divorce after you asked him to leave because he was having affairs and that's supposed to make him look better?" I have no argument in response.

Matty replies to Nikolai:

You can blame my mother for everything that has gone poorly in your life all you want. It doesn't reflect reality and it doesn't do anything in the eyes of your children. I speak for me, and my two siblings: please do not reach out to any of us ever again.

Nikolai responds by stating that he is only looking to get fair market value of the house. Matty does not reply. Nikolai then texts Jimmy asking him how he is. Jimmy does not answer. Nikolai subsequently follows up to Matty's text stating that any signed documents showing the timing of the divorce as alleged by Matty must be forged. He includes the usual disparaging remarks about me—stealing his money, etc.—and says that there is nothing that has gone poorly in his life and he has no regrets. Jimmy finds that last comment outrageous.

Nikolai ends his text to Matty suggesting that Matty should re-evaluate his life because he never wanted to have a heart-to-heart talk with him to understand his position and that makes Matty a coward.

Matty does not respond.

Apparently, my case has fallen through the cracks in the system, but at my lawyer's insistence, the judge agrees to hold the conference, which had been scheduled for February 10. It sounds like things go reasonably well for me. The judge orders Nikolai to produce all his bank statements within thirty days and to state whether we will file our tax returns jointly by the end of the day. He orders both parties to try one more mediation session, and he schedules an "intensive settlement conference" for May 4, during which he will be available to give his opinion on how he would likely rule on various issues. For example, he will provide a range of how much alimony he thinks he would grant. Nikolai's lawyer follows up with my lawyer stating that Nikolai will secure the statements and that he wishes to file separately. I am relieved about the tax filing. There is much back and forth between the lawyers, and it appears my lawyer has finally had enough of their nonsense. In one letter she writes that it is laughable to suggest that we should trust Nikolai while he stole more than $125,000 cash from the family. She states we are not amused by Nikolai's game playing and will no longer tolerate it. She adds that he is free to testify in court that the bank allowed him to open multiple bank accounts with no money.

At the end of one email, she writes that I did not manage all of the parties' finances during the marriage and became aware of Nikolai's secret bank accounts because he left a notebook laying around in the home listing the financial institutions, sometimes the account numbers, and referencing that these accounts were secret from me in Russian. She urges Nikolai's attorney to not allow Nikolai to "pull the wool over his eyes" as he is fully aware that he has secreted accounts and hidden money.

———— ◆ ————

On Super Bowl Sunday, February 13, 2022, Jimmy and Emily surprise me with a visit. We remain outside masked, but it is still good to see them. Jimmy has brought his famous Buffalo chicken dip. We've never had a Super Bowl party without it. I am touched by it. I have not been feeling too great emotionally of late. I probably could now be classified as clinically depressed as nothing new has happened to make me feel this way. It's just my overall life. I can't seem to shake it. I've tried taking walks, getting some sunshine, taking my vitamins, but still, I wake up every day and cry. Perhaps, I need to focus more on what's good in my life: my children. On Valentine's Day, I wake up to find a bouquet of flowers and chocolate candy with a card from the six wonderful people in my life: Jimmy and Emily, Grace and Patrick, Matty and Sarah. I am so fortunate to have them.

The funk I am in continues through all of February. I cry every day. I am contemplating calling the doctor. Perhaps, it's physical. I was put on medication for bone density last September, and it can cause depression. It doesn't make sense that I am so much worse than a year ago. I'm not sure what to do.

March 5, 2022

I get to see Jimmy today! I mean really see him, hug him, touch him, laugh with him. Grace must work, but the rest of us all get together. Matty makes his famous ratatouille and some beef to go with it. I wake up in the morning feeling my usual sad self, and I am worried that I won't be able to relish this long-awaited reunion. Jimmy comes to the door, and I hug him and cry. I don't want to let go. We all sit down and have some wine and beer, and the wine seems to lift my mood and loosen my tongue. I mention for the first time about my depression. We all have a great time, talking, laughing, playing games. I hate to see the night end. As we're going upstairs to bed, Matty stops me and hugs me good night. We then start talking. He is concerned about my emotional state. I tell him all that I've been thinking. He's very understanding and supportive. Maybe that's all I needed, just someone to acknowledge my pain and be there to listen to me. Matty has been so busy with work that we haven't been able to talk like we used to. I miss it. Our talk seems to shift my mood. I start to feel better beginning the next day.

Later in the month, Grace and I go to Florida for a little vacation. We spend two days at Disney and two days on Daytona Beach. The weather is great, and the sun is shining. At Magic Kingdom, we stay for the fireworks around the castle; it is spectacular. We attend the show *Frozen* in Hollywood Studios, and I am moved by the song "Let it Go." It first affected me when I watched *Frozen* at Olivia's in the early days of this nightmare. It needs to be my theme. I need to let it all go and move on to a new life, new adventures.

I come across a group on Facebook for like-minded women who want to travel. I decide to post an introduction of myself, explaining that I am going through an unexpected divorce after thirty years of marriage and was depressed in part because we were supposed to travel in retirement, and I felt such a loss over that—until I found this group. Thirty-two women comment on my post. They are warm, encouraging, and positive. A few are from my state and suggest we meet up. I am excited about the idea.

At the end of March, a man rings my doorbell. I groan, thinking he is selling something. He is a tall, Black man, with some gray in his beard. He is with a Hispanic woman. I open the door, and he introduces himself as a candidate for Congress of our district. He is running on the Republican ticket, which is a challenge in our state. I talk to him for a bit and instantly like him. His slogan is, "Not Black, Not White, American." I tell him he has my vote; I hope he wins. He asks if he can take a picture with me and the next thing I know, our picture is on social media. I go on his website and fill out a form to volunteer on his campaign. I am excited about the prospect.

I paint my bedroom. No more drab beige. I paint one wall "icy breeze" and the other walls "white gallery." The icy breeze has a hint of light blue in it. I buy new bedding with a white print comforter and coordinating light blue pillows, medium blue curtains with white sheers and new wall hangings. I reupholster the hope chest from beige floral to a solid medium blue. I change the green rug to a multi blue shag rug. The room is totally transformed. Hopefully, this will prove to be symbolic of my life.

———◆———

On April 14, 2022, we have another mediation session. This session was driven solely by Nikolai and his lawyer. His lawyer asked the judge to order us back to mediation for one more session and the judge did so. Since they are so anxious for the mediation, I have a flicker of hope that we might settle the case. That flicker is quickly extinguished. The mediator breaks us into different chat rooms on zoom. My lawyer and I take the time to formulate a reasonable settlement proposal while the mediator talks to Nikolai and his lawyer. After a time, the mediator enters our room and says, "Nikolai is very bitter about the children, and it's difficult to negotiate with a bitter person."

My lawyer has laid out everything that should not be in dispute. When the mediator presents it to Nikolai and his lawyer, they respond that they will have to review the documents. At this point, it's not surprising but incredible, nonetheless. I can't figure out what their game plan is, unless it's just more of Nikolai's crazy behavior that's driving their intransigence. They forced the mediation session but refuse to come to the negotiating table. They also dream up two more arguments, which we immediately dismiss as absurd. The mediator says that he explained to Nikolai that to repair the relationship with the kids, it will take ninety-five percent of the effort from Nikolai, and he should expect five percent in return. I would guess that at this point, Nikolai has put in no more than five percent. The mediator sees no point in presenting our settlement proposal as he surmises that they will just try to negotiate from it.

This mediation session, which I did not want, cost me approximately $1,200. Time to go to court.

On April 20, 2022, we receive a letter from Nikolai's attorney outlining a purported settlement. Most of the letter is simply a statement of why they reject our various proposals. He does include a couple of new arguments, which are ludicrous. He states that had I not sold the stock back in 2018, that stock would now be worth over $1 million, and I owe Nikolai that money. He also states that Nikolai paid for all the expenses in 2019, and I owe him that as well. He does offer to let me buy Nikolai out of the house and deduct part of the amount of the money he stole and a small amount for alimony. It's not great, but I view it as offering a flicker of hope. My attorney responds on April 26, 2022, ridiculing his new arguments and making a counteroffer. The intensive settlement conference is scheduled with the court for May 4, 2022, but we seem to be getting closer. On May 2, 2022, I test positive for COVID, and we learn the next day that the court is insisting on an in-person conference, so it must be postponed. Everyone agrees on May 12, when a few days later, Nikolai's attorney states that Nikolai is unavailable. As a result, we agree to try another round of mediation. My lawyer believes we are close, and the mediator "can get us across the finish line." Nikolai and his attorney meet with the mediator on May 19 and send us a settlement letter. We meet with the mediator the next day, and after clearing up some ambiguities in their offer, we realize the offer is worse than the previous one.

Not to be deterred, my lawyer writes to Nikolai's lawyer proposing a better settlement (for Nikolai) than our previous one. I am not thrilled about this since it seems we are simply bargaining against ourselves, but I agree to let her do it. She requests a response by May 23. On May 31, Nikolai's lawyer sends a letter with new fabricated arguments. He is now claiming that I wrote out a check to my brother Jimmy, who died almost forty years prior. That he would bring my deceased brother with whom I had a close relationship into this is extremely offensive. Of course, he has no check, no proof whatsoever. There is no proof because it never happened. He makes up a few more bogus arguments and complains that the car insurance is still in Nikolai's name. Grace was recently rear-ended and filed a claim with the insurance company. For some reason, they continue to send Nikolai the status updates, even though he hasn't contributed a dime toward the premium. Upon receiving the notice of the claim, he texts Grace, asking why her car is still insured by him and demands that she change it.

She does not respond, and he follows up a few hours later demanding that she confirm that she will remove his name from insurance or else he will cancel the policy.

She does not respond, and I send a screen shot of the text to my lawyer. The next day Nikolai again texts Grace expressing that he can't imagine why she has so much hatred towards him, that the divorce had nothing to do with her or her brothers, that he thought he could still have a relationship with all of them and be a father. He writes that we all do things we are not proud of, and this also applies to their mom. He adds that he simply could not live with me any more in the marriage, it was detrimental to his health, I am a control freak, and she will get many glimpses of that in the years ahead. He advises her not to tolerate that; it's her life. He says he couldn't tolerate it anymore, and he had made many sacrifices and compromises for so many years. He notes that the marriage took a downturn in early 2016 when I was siphoning money out of his stock account and withdrawing money from our joint bank account behind his back. It never stopped. He says that he loves her and her brothers dearly, that she will understand when she has kids of her own what it means to be a parent. He says that he did his best raising her and if she wants to talk, he's around. He sends his regards to Patrick, and hopes she is okay from the car accident.

It only took a day for him to express concern about her well-being after the accident. Grace shares the text with all of us and Jimmy responds, "He'll never own up to what he did. Sounded like it was going in that direction but then he threw mom right under the bus. And is 'we all do things we're not proud of' referencing the affairs? Because I thought he was justified."

Grace writes, "Yea, Patrick said, 'It was one paragraph about you and then the rest about your mom—it's like he's living in Groundhog Day.'"

Matty weighs in:

> *I think you should respond, "The fact that you can't imagine or understand why your three children don't want anything to do with you is the entire problem." He will 100% respond but then you should never respond after that.*
>
> *Will letting him sit with that one thought do anything? Probably not, but not answering or answering doesn't change anything at this point and as I just told Mom the most important thing is getting her out of this in the best possible shape and ignoring him doesn't do anything. Ignoring arguably just gives more fuel to the 'I have no relationship with my kids, etc.' bogus argument.*

Grace opts not to respond. My lawyer responds to the scurrilous allegations, suggests he sign over title to all the cars now, which will fix the insurance problem, renews the previous settlement offer, and indicates she will ask the judge for a trial date if we don't receive a substantive offer by June 10. I imagine we will be going to trial unless the judge forces the intensive settlement conference on us. It is now twenty-one months since this legal nightmare began.

————— ◆ —————

In one of my low points back in early 2021, Matty suggested I write down every good thing about Nikolai's leaving. Here's what I wrote in my journal (in no particular order):

1. Every holiday, birthday, vacation, etc. will be peaceful and fun. He won't be there to ruin it, and I won't have to walk on eggshells worrying that he might.
2. I no longer must listen to science lectures at the dinner table.
3. I can decorate exactly how I want and no longer have his ugly artwork.
4. I don't need to cringe at something he says when out with others.
5. I might get bushes to grow in the backyard since he won't be here to constantly pull them out.
6. I found out how great some of my friends are.
7. My kids are always there for me.
8. No more sardines and hot sauce on everything.
9. No more stupid outdated boots to look at.
10. No more yellow-stained sheets and pillows from his oily skin.
11. No more smelly breaths and garlic burps at night.
12. Lots of free time.
13. Everything stays organized.

14. No more feeling embarrassed by things he says or knowing he's lying or stretching the truth when he's talking to others.
15. No more random attacks about money.
16. No more jacket on the dining room table.
17. He can no longer throw out my stuff (like my pretty teacups).
18. I'm no longer relying on an unreliable person who promises things and then it's a shot in the dark on whether he delivers.

Now, as June 2022 begins, I miss having a partner. However, except for some fleeting moments, I don't miss him. The list of eighteen things shows how my life is better without him, and why I don't miss him.

When all this mess began, Matty convinced me to try meditation. I have been doing it ever since. In my head I go to the ocean with Jesus. I sit at the shore and watch the waves. The ocean is much like life. The journey is bumpy, and sometimes it's rough. When the waves are rough, often they pull me under the water for a brief period. But I always struggle to resurface and breathe in the air. Sometimes the ocean is calm. It's not as exciting but much more peaceful. Most of us can never predict what the ocean will be like until we get there. But no matter how the waves are, calm or rough, I will ride them because eventually, they lead me to the shore.

May 12, 2022

I am out with Emily and Jimmy and Emily's parents. Emily is receiving an award for her outstanding teaching. It is an enjoyable evening with dinner and vignettes of each teacher getting an award. It is almost over when Jimmy receives a call from his oncologist. He sits outside on a bench to speak with the doctor. The rest of us are inside finishing up but anxious as to what the call will bring. Eventually, we wander outside to see Jimmy finishing up his call. Emily goes over to him. I wait in the distance watching, and he shakes his head from side to side at me. The cancer has returned.

Devastated cannot begin to describe how I feel. Why? Why? Why? Why must the sweetest boy suffer so much? Why must a young couple be saddled with such burdens? There are, of course, no answers. It's the same as asking why is there evil in the world. My philosophy is this: God is good. He does not create or cause evil. But He gives us free will. Often the exercise of that free will results in evil in the world. The accumulation of that evil results in the randomness of its effects on others. Thus, good people encounter evil. I believe that God shares our tears when someone like Jimmy suffers.

After hugging Jimmy and using every ounce of strength to hold it together, I get in my car and drive home. I drive on autopilot, completely unaware of how I get home. I walk in the house, and Matty is there. He casually asks me how the evening went. I burst into tears and squeak out that Jimmy's cancer has returned. Matty immediately comes to me and holds me. I am in shock.

The doctor has a plan. It's intensive, but it has a 90 percent success rate. Jimmy will undergo a stem cell transplant. They will harvest his stem cells, zap him with intensive chemotherapy drugs to completely wipe out both his good and bad cells, and then reintroduce the stem cells they harvested. He will be like a newborn baby with no immunities. He will need to get all his immunizations again. They schedule him for mid-August. I pray every day that God will restore him to full health.

Summer 2022

God really does work in mysterious ways! Jimmy and Emily come over for dinner, and Jimmy presents me with a small gift bag which he says is an additional birthday present. I reach in and pull out a jar of sauce. I'm confused. I look at the jar and it's the brand Prego. I'm still confused. I see a little sticky note on top with the word *We're* above Prego. I'm still confused. Matty immediately lets out a shriek, and I look over at Emily who I now discover is filming me. She says the sauce will go good with the bun in the oven. The light bulb goes off. Emily is pregnant with my first grandchild. I am over the moon happy! When Jimmy finished his treatment on February 4, 2022, the doctor said to wait three months before trying to start a family. At twenty-eight, Emily was anxious to get started. It was unclear how Jimmy's fertility would be after all the chemotherapy. Once the cancer came back on May 16, starting a family was once again delayed. However, in that brief period from May 4 to May 16, Emily got pregnant! Our miracle baby! Finally, some happy news in my life.

July brings even more good news. Emily and Jimmy have a gender-reveal party, and we all discover the baby is a girl! She certainly will be Daddy's little princess. But that's not all. Grace has learned that she also is pregnant! She was not planning on trying to start a family for another six months, but clearly, God has other plans. Two grandbabies! How blessed can I be? Grace is ten weeks behind Emily. My twins must do everything together!

———◆———

My lawyer never receives a response to her letter to Nikolai's lawyer, so she contacts the judge on June 17, asking for a trial date. The judge responds by ordering us to attend an Intensive Settlement Conference on August 17. Two more months to waste. In the meantime, my lawyer suggests to me that this conference will be a waste of time, and she asks me how I would feel about binding arbitration. My first reaction is to be upset and disgusted. The conference will be a waste? Why is she now after almost two years bringing up arbitration? For the first time, my lawyer tells me that the judge will likely order the house sold rather than trying to determine its value. That is shocking and demoralizing to me. I don't want to move. An arbiter will more likely determine a value. Still having a flicker of hope for the conference, I research arbitration and decide I'm all in. Arbitration will take place before someone who is not the judge. The arbiter will take in all the evidence like at a trial and make a decision, which is binding on us. The rules are more relaxed than a trial, and it can be done more quickly. My lawyer reaches out to Nikolai's lawyer who states he will discuss it with Nikolai. My lawyer also asks him to provide his bottom-line settlement offer. Three weeks pass before we hear anything. There is no word on arbitration, but we receive a settlement offer. It's worse than the previous two offers. He has now upped the value of the house another $20,000 from his appraisal value and does not agree to any bank accounts. It's ridiculous. My lawyer responds with a very strong letter stating we will seek counsel fees because he clearly is not negotiating in good faith. She also presents a counteroffer, which I feel mixed about. It seems like we just constantly negotiate against ourselves. It's now 23 months and $50,500 in legal fees, not counting for this past month.

On August 15, my lawyer emails me stating she is unable to attend the intensive settlement conference scheduled for August 17. I am disgusted. She then calls me to explain that she was in a serious car accident. I feel bad but am starting to think this will never be over. The court reschedules it for September 29.

In the midst of the divorce nightmare, Jimmy is admitted to the hospital for the stem cell treatment. I visit him every day until they no longer want me because he is immunocompromised. He is weak and tired, but Emily urges him to walk a few times each day. He loses all his hair but not his eyebrows and eyelashes like last time. Typical of Jimmy, he never completely loses his appetite, which is a blessing. After three weeks in the hospital, he is discharged and remains home to recuperate. I spend the first week with him so Emily can work, but after that he is strong enough to be on his own. I pray every day that this will be the cure for him.

Throughout the end of August and early September, the lawyers exchange various emails about settling. I have concluded at this point that my lawyer is not a great negotiator. She readily concedes things when a counteroffer should be made. They have now offered a pittance for alimony, and Nikolai wants $30,000 for our thirty-year-old furniture. It's truly unbelievable. It is hard for me to quell the feelings of disgust I have toward him.

On September 24, I wake up with an overwhelming sadness. At this point, it looks like the divorce will finally be resolved, and I should be ecstatic. Yet, I am not. Matty comes down for his coffee, and I discuss with him my feelings. I start sobbing. Poor Matty. He has had to deal with so much of my emotions these past few years. He is his usual supportive self. He tells me that it is perfectly normal for me not to feel happy about the end of my marriage. He would think it strange if I did. I confide that I will now be alone, and I need to figure out a new life. He responds that my day-to-day life will be no different than it has been for the past two years, and I have nothing to "figure out." He suggests I just need to get myself out in the world, join different things, meet new people. Some things I won't like, and I should then quit them. Eventually, I will find my passion. That is how people "figure out" what they are meant to do in life. It is good advice, and he has once again pulled me off the proverbial ledge.

September 28, 2022

It's over. Nikolai has signed the marital settlement agreement my lawyer previously sent over. It is not a great deal for me, but I don't care anymore. It is finally over. I get to keep most of my retirement money and the house, including our old furniture and the junk contained in it. I don't get much else. But I am free. And yet, I feel nothing. Not joy or sadness. Various people congratulate me, and I feel strange. My lawyer's email of the news is worded, it is "my great pleasure" to provide you with the attached Judgment of Divorce.

Does that really give her pleasure? In the narcissist Facebook group that I'm in, someone had posted pictures of herself celebrating her divorce with captions, "I do, I did, I'm done" and "End of an Error." I thought it was hilarious when I read it. But I just feel numb when I finally get the news after two long years. It's hard to celebrate the end of a marriage, no matter how abusive.

September 29, 2022

It is the day after the divorce is settled. I wake up and I feel…happy. How strange. I can't put my finger on why I am happy, but it's a nice feeling, so I don't question it. I assume it won't last.

While I'm relishing this somewhat foreign feeling, I receive a text from Nikolai. It simply says, "How is Jimmy?"

In classic fashion, Nikolai now thinks everything is fine, and we can be best buddies. I am annoyed but determined not to let this text impact my feeling of happiness today. Only because we need to meet to sign some papers do I respond.

I write, "Doing OK. Let me know your availability to meet at the bank to sign the titles."

He responds that we can meet and asks to know when. He then asks if Jimmy is receiving treatments and if I can give him an update with the kids.

Once again, I have allowed myself to get sucked in, and it will never end, unless I stop it. I discuss it with the kids and conclude that after the details are finalized, I will block Nikolai. Quite simply, he disturbs my peace, and I need to work on me for a time. Perhaps, at some point in the future, I can resume some limited contact. But not now. I decide not to respond to his last text. I discuss the texts with my lawyer, and she responds, "I hope you didn't answer." I explain why I did, and she states that it's actually a good idea because we both need to sign real estate documents and have them notarized so we can do everything together.

I wake up the following day and again I feel…happy. And the day after that and the day after that. Lily and her daughter treat me to a full make over and dinner. I know their motivation: they want to ensure that I feel good about myself. They even make comments at dinner that this sordid mess is not on me. It's all Nikolai. I am touched by their kindness and generosity. It is another great day for me.

One week out and still…happy. I can get used to this. I also had one week of sleeping well every night. That hasn't happened in years. I feel the long dark night has finally ended. The weight of the divorce process took more of a toll on me than I realized. I can move on. I can start anew. I can be happy. Matty had advised me to keep trying different things to find my passion and so I did. I went back to reading books. A voracious reader when I was young, I gave it up after I met Nikolai. Now I'm back at it. I didn't keep track, but I would guess I read at least thirty books this year. They run the gamut from religious and self-help to crypto currency to trashy romance novels. I can get lost in the last category for hours at a time. I also joined the choir at church. I always loved music, was proficient at the guitar when I was young, dabbled in the piano, and always enjoyed singing but largely gave all that up as well. I sang twice with the choir at church and loved it. They all sound amazing. I started practicing French. I took French in high school and always wanted to be fluent in it. My dream was to stay in France for a month after I retired. I don't know if I'll do that now but it's possible I will and I might as well be prepared.

I wrote this book. I always liked to write and do quite a bit of it with my job, but I never considered writing a book. Matty suggested I write a book, and at first, I thought he was crazy. What would I write about? After pondering it for a couple of weeks, the topic became obvious. This may be my new passion, and I may write more books in the future. Or I'll try other things and see how I feel about them. Matty advised that if it feels 80 percent right, go all in. People waste years of their lives looking for that perfect 100 percent passion.

I know life won't stay happy all the time. I think I used to operate on the assumption that if I accomplished one particular thing, life would then be good. If I could get past the current blow-up by Nikolai, things would go smoothly. I was always looking to the future for life to be better rather than living in the present. My brother Jimmy had given me a poster when we were teenagers that read, "Happiness is Found Along the Way, Not at the End of the Road." I imagine Jimmy knew how I viewed life, how I tried to get to the next thing so I would be happy. I know now that life just doesn't work that way. It is messy. There will be bumps in the road. And darkness will come again. I hope it won't be as dark as the last two years, but it's bound to come in some form. Right now, however, I'm going to cherish the happiness. I'm going to be a grandma twice over! I can't believe how fortunate I am. It is my intention to live in the present moment and drink in every second with my grandchildren.

I would not have made it through the last two years without the support of my children and their partners. They got me through many a dark day, each in his or her own way. I am forever grateful. I would not have made it through without my faith in God. My prayer every day was that He would help me trust in Him to make it through. And He did not fail me. I'm on the other side now. I would not have made it through without the rest of my family, my friends, and others in my circle who showed me such kindness and support.

I am stronger for what I went through. I am blessed for what I have now in my life. The future is bright, and I am ready to embrace it.

Afterward

July 2023

Am I perfect? Of course not. Could I have done things differently? Maybe. I'm not so sure. How do you deal with someone who will fly into a rage with seemingly no provocation? I should have gotten out earlier but when? In the last few years, I wavered between trying to decide whether living with this maniac is better than being alone and breaking up my family, which is seemingly healthy and happy to those on the outside. My only real regret was that I didn't choose Grace's friend, Mia over him in September 2017. But I didn't know he was having affairs then. That knowledge came a few short months later. Even then, I chose not to break things up. I thought if he could get a handle on his temper maybe we could find a way forward. I was quite naive in retrospect. When I first started telling people what was happening (in late 2020), many reacted with, "This is not your fault in any way." I think they were concerned I might start to beat myself up. But I knew deep down it wasn't my fault. Have I second-guessed certain things? Absolutely. And there were times I felt completely broken, like perhaps I deserved what he had dished out. But I never would have broken my marriage vow of fidelity like he did. Sometimes, I think maybe I was meant to be with him to produce these amazing children. And, I think I had enough self-esteem to not allow his behavior to destroy me. I think someone else might have been crushed by him. I'm sure his behavior affected me, perhaps changed me in ways I'll never know, but in the end, it didn't largely make me question my self-worth.

My next-door neighbor's son and close friend to Matty told his mom that I was better off without Nikolai. Those words comforted me on many a dark day. I think ultimately, I will be better in more ways than what is in my list that Matty encouraged me to make. I still have bad days and feelings of profound loss. However, there are less of those days now. I imagine the bad days will continue to lessen but they may never go away. A trauma like this leaves its scars. But now it's time to move forward.

It took two years and twelve days and over $57,000 in legal fees to legally extricate myself from Nikolai. But now the future is at my doorstep. There are endless possibilities. Another mate is not in the cards for me. My faith doesn't allow it, and I've said in response to some of my friends of faith who have suggested otherwise that just because my faith now has gotten hard for me doesn't mean I should abandon it. While I will miss the companionship, I don't need a man to make a good life for myself. I had one that caused me endless torment; now I can live a life of peace, serenity, and tranquility. One day, I hope I will be able to wish the best for him. Now, the best I can do is pray every morning that God helps me to forgive him and converts his heart. Perhaps one day that will happen. I imagine it will not be for a very long time and hopefully by then I will have soared like an eagle into the future.

It was a privilege to share my story with you and I hope you found value in reading it. It was an emotional roller coaster for me to write it. Please consider sharing it with friends or family and leaving a review online (or even just a star rating). Your feedback and support are always appreciated, and I will read any review you post. Please navigate here if you'd like to leave a review now:

https://www.amazon.com/review/create-review/?ie=UTF8& channel=glance-detail&asin=B0CNWY59S2

About the Author

Maria Schmeig is an attorney, mother, and author of her memoir, *Don't Poke the Bear- Recovering From Abuse By A Narcissist*. While successfully navigating her law career and raising three great kids, she masked to the outside world what she endured at home from her abusive husband. After a lifetime of legal writing, she wrote her personal story. She hopes that her book will help others see their situation for what it is and find hope for a better future. Maria recently retired from the legal profession and spends her time blogging about narcissistic abuse, gardening, and enjoying her ever-growing family, especially her grandchildren and their giggles.

For more information about Maria and *Don't Poke the Bear- Recovering From Abuse By A Narcissist*, see her website and her Facebook page:

www.dealingwithnarcissists.com
Facebook: Don't Poke the Bear!

Discussion Guide

1. Did Maria end things at the right time or should she have done so earlier? If earlier, when?
2. There were only a few incidents of physical abuse in the twenty-eight-year marriage. Should that have been enough to make Maria leave?
3. Why didn't Maria see that Nikolai was also physically abusive?
4. Why didn't Maria see the relationship as abusive like her pastor immediately did?
5. Why do you think Maria stayed as long as she did?
6. What impact do you think Nikolai's behavior had on the children?
7. Could Maria have done more to protect her children?
8. Was Maria justified in taking control of Nikolai's money or did that amount to theft as Nikolai accused her of?
9. Maria was fortunate to have a support system of family and friends. How do you think her life would have been if she didn't have that?
10. Was Maria unusually naive? Should she have seen what was coming much sooner?
11. How significant was the role Maria's faith played in her journey? One priest clearly didn't get it while the other saw immediately. Would Maria have proceeded differently if that first priest truly understood what she was going through?

12. Why did Maria keep so much of Nikolai's behavior to herself? Should she have confided more in others? Would that have changed anything?

13. Maria's children all rallied around her after Nikolai filed for divorce and eventually cut off ties with their father. Why do you think they reacted this way? Were they justified? Was it a morally correct thing to do?

14. Could Maria have handled the divorce negotiations better? Could her lawyer? How?

15. Was Maria right in including her children in everything that was going on with the divorce or should she have sheltered them from it? Why or why not?

16. If Maria had not shared everything with her children, would they have more likely kept in contact with their father? Would that have been a good thing or a bad thing?

Acknowledgements

First and foremost, I have to thank God for getting me through the darkness and trauma. I never could have done it without Him. Related to that is the Church and my pastor who counseled me. I am forever grateful for my faith.

A very close second is my children, Grace, Jimmy and Matty. As I said in my dedication, you are my world. You stood by me, advised me, and gave me your shoulders to cry on whenever I needed them. I love you beyond words.

To the members of my growing family, my heartfelt thanks. Emily, Patrick and Sarah, you gave me support, each in your own way and I will always remember that in my heart. My two grandchildren, you give me so much joy, I can't express it. When you laugh or smile, I think my heart will burst.

To my extended family, I will always be grateful. Whether it was a kind word, an offer to get away or the enthusiasm of my nephew's wife over my writing this book, I am so deeply touched. A special shout out to my brother Jack who has done so much for me in other ways.

To "my girls" from our "girls' night." (You know who you are). You have listened to many of my stories, sympathized and gave me hugs. You have also strongly encouraged me to write this book and have been anxious to read it. Thank you for all of that.

To my early readers and "editors," Jimmy, Emily, Matty, Bella and Ava. Your input was invaluable. A special thanks to Emily who did the final proofread for me and to Sarah who gave me a lot of input on the cover design.

To my official editor Caryn Rivadeneira. Your kindness, encouragement and great suggestions helped move me forward.

Finally, to all who are suffering or have suffered through similar relationships. I hope my story can help you in some way, however small. I hope you can find the peace that I have found. I wish you all a happy life.

Endnotes

1   https://flyingmonkeysdenied.com/2015/11/06/
    why-narcissistic-people-love-to-ruin-birthdays-and-holidays/

2   Ibid.

3   Dutton, Mary Ann; Goodman, Lisa A.; Bennett, Lauren, "Court-
    involved battered women's responses to violence: the role of psycho-
    logical, physical, and sexual abuse." 1999, cited in Maiuro, Roland
    D.; O'Leary, K. Daniel, "Psychological abuse in violent domestic
    relations." New York: Springer Publishing Company, 2001, p. 197.

4   https://www.healthline.com/health/mental-health/
    am-i-dating-a-narcissist

5   Ibid.

6   https://www.weinbergerlawgroup.com/blog/
    divorce-family-law/20-signs-youre-married-to-a-narcissist/

7   https://www.amazon.com/Hasbro-7789-Bop-It/dp/B001TH8F1E

8   Kelly, Matthew. (2021). *Life is Messy*. Blue Sparrow.

www.ingramcontent.com/pod-product-compliance
Lightning Source LLC
Chambersburg PA
CBHW022119080426

42734CB00006B/190